Advanced Information and Knowledge Processing

Series editors
Lakhmi C. Jain
Bournemouth University, Poole, UK and
University of South Australia, Adelaide, Australia

Xindong Wu
University of Vermont

Information systems and intelligent knowledge processing are playing an increasing role in business, science and technology. Recently, advanced information systems have evolved to facilitate the co-evolution of human and information networks within communities. These advanced information systems use various paradigms including artificial intelligence, knowledge management, and neural science as well as conventional information processing paradigms. The aim of this series is to publish books on new designs and applications of advanced information and knowledge processing paradigms in areas including but not limited to aviation, business, security, education, engineering, health, management, and science. Books in the series should have a strong focus on information processing—preferably combined with, or extended by, new results from adjacent sciences. Proposals for research monographs, reference books, coherently integrated multi-author edited books, and handbooks will be considered for the series and each proposal will be reviewed by the Series Editors, with additional reviews from the editorial board and independent reviewers where appropriate. Titles published within the Advanced Information and Knowledge Processing series are included in Thomson Reuters' Book Citation Index.

More information about this series at http://www.springer.com/series/4738

Alfons Josef Schuster

Editor

Understanding Information

From the Big Bang to Big Data

Springer

Editor
Dr Alfons Josef Schuster
(Assistant Professor in Information Studies)
School of International Liberal Studies
Waseda University
4F, Building 11
1-6-1 Nishi-Waseda, 169-8050
Shinjuku-ku, Tokyo, Japan

ISSN 1610-3947   ISSN 2197-8441   (electronic)
Advanced Information and Knowledge Processing
ISBN 978-3-319-59089-9   ISBN 978-3-319-59090-5   (eBook)
DOI 10.1007/978-3-319-59090-5

Library of Congress Control Number: 2017946619

Printed on acid-free paper

This Springer imprint is published by Springer Nature
The registered company is Springer International Publishing AG
The registered company address is: Gewerbestrasse 11, 6330 Cham, Switzerland

To all informational agents – existing in all possible worlds.

Preface

There is an agreement across various domains about the impact of "information" on our modern-day life. Terms such as information, revolution or information society express this realization succinctly.

Simplistically, we may say that we are all involved in a kind of transition or race, in which a postindustrial society passes on its baton to information society. Although there is no single definition for concepts such as information society, it is possible to consider information society as a society where the state of well-being and advancement (on an individual as well as on a collective level) seems to depend on the efficient management of the so-called "life cycle" of information.

Essentially, the life cycle of information considers information as a product and involves fundamental information processes such as the acquisition of information and its storage, manipulation, retrieval, dissemination, or usage.

The relationship between information society and these fundamental information processes is extremely rich and versatile. For instance, the question of how information is generated could be divided into dimensions: material, biological, and mental. The material dimension may consider the processes that are responsible for the existence of our universe, while the biological and the mental dimensions may contemplate the production of biological systems and organisms or the processes of human creativity facilitated by a brain.

The motivation of this edited book is to understand the subject of information from a variety of perspectives. In order to generate this understanding, this book includes contributions ranging from cosmology, quantum physics, biology, neuroscience, computer science, and artificial intelligence to the Internet, big data, information society, and philosophy. Although each chapter provides its own domain-specific treatment of information, this edited book aims to synthesize these individual contributions, in order to generate an understanding that goes beyond the intuitive and often too casual conceptions that exist about one of the most important concepts of modern society and frontier science.

Tokyo, Japan
March 2017

Alfons Josef Schuster

Acknowledgements

I would like to take this opportunity to thank everyone who contributed to this edited book. I am grateful beyond words to the various authors for their wonderful and profound contributions. In times, where time sometimes can be a luxury, I am deeply touched and thankful for experiencing their understanding, dedication, and reliability. The same thankfulness needs to be extended to the various reviewers in this project. Their commitment, thoroughness, and positive feedback always led to an improvement of the quality of this edited book. My gratitude also goes out to the publisher Springer, in particular, to Helen Desmond, for her kind support, advice, and guidance throughout this project. Finally, I simply would like to say many thanks to you all again!

Contents

Contributors

Fred Adams Department of Linguistics and Cognitive Science, University of Delaware Newark, Newark, DE, USA

Fiona Browne School of Computing and Mathematics, Ulster University, Newtownabbey, Co. Antrim, UK

Iztok Fister Jr. Faculty of Electrical Engineering and Computer Science, University of Maribor, Maribor, Slovenia

Karin Fister Faculty of Medicine, University of Maribor, Maribor, Slovenia

Valeriia Haberland Tungsten Centre for Intelligent Data Analytics, Goldsmiths, University of London, New Cross, London, UK

Satoshi Inaba Faculty of International Research and Education, School of International Liberal Studies, Waseda University, Shinjuku-ku, Tokyo, Japan

Tibor Koltay Faculty of Pedagogy, Institute of Learning Technologies, Eszterházy Károly University, Jászberény, Hungary

Gaye Lightbody School of Computing and Mathematics, Ulster University, Newtownabbey, Co. Antrim, UK

Jana Murovec Biotechnical Faculty, University of Ljubljana, Ljubljana, Slovenia

Katsuhiko Sano Department of Philosophy, Graduate School of Letters, Hokkaido University, Sapporo, Hokkaido, Japan

Naoyuki Sato School of Systems Information Science, Future University Hakodate, Hakodate, Hokkaido, Japan

Dr Alfons Josef Schuster (Assistant Professor in Information Studies), School of International Liberal Studies, Waseda University, Shinjuku-ku, Tokyo, Japan

Mai Sugimoto Faculty of Sociology, Kansai University, Suita, Osaka, Japan

Jürgen Vogel Engineering and Information Technology Department, Bern University of Applied Sciences, Biel, Bern, Switzerland

Andrew Whitaker School of Mathematics and Physics, Queen's University Belfast, Belfast, Northern Ireland, UK

Ko Yamada Faculty of Political Science and Economics, School of Political Science and Economics, Waseda University, Shinjuku-ku, Tokyo, Japan

Part I
Introduction

Chapter 1
From the Tannhäuser Gate to z8_GND_5296: A Day Trip on the Life-Cycle of Information

Alfons Josef Schuster

Abstract Modern-day computer power is a great servant for today's information hungry society. The increasing pervasiveness of such powerful machinery greatly influences fundamental information processes such as, for instance, the acquisition of information, its storage, manipulation, retrieval, dissemination, or its usage. Information society depends on these fundamental information processes in various ways. This chapter investigates the diverse and dynamic relationship between information society and the fundamental information processes just mentioned from a modern technology perspective.

1.1 Introduction

Information is an exciting and challenging subject. At the end of this introductory chapter, we hope that the reader will understand that to cover the subject of information within the space of a single chapter is impossible. The goal of this text, therefore, is to provide the reader with a general introduction to various aspects and concepts related to the field. One objective is to create a sense of understanding among readers that information is a concept that appears in a wide range of contexts, each with its own specific motivations, observations, interpretations, definitions, methods, technologies, and challenges. Forthcoming chapters in this edited book are going to explore many of these contexts and idiosyncrasies in more detail. In order to get a taste for the diversity of the subject, we begin our journey of information in the domain of entertainment – science fiction.

The replicant Roy Batty (played by Rutger Hauer) is a charismatic character in Sir Ridley Scotts 1982 classic science fiction film *Blade Runner*. Replicants are genetically engineered organic robots. To the naked eye, they are indistinguishable from humans. Manufactured with a predetermined lifespan, their engineered traits

Dr A.J. Schuster (✉)

(Assistant Professor in Information Studies), School of International Liberal Studies, Waseda University, 4F, Building 11, 1-6-1 Nishi-Waseda, 169-8050, Shinjuku-ku, Tokyo, Japan

e-mail: a.schuster@aoni.waseda.jp

© Springer International Publishing AG 2017

A.J. Schuster (eds.), *Understanding Information*, Advanced Information and Knowledge Processing, DOI 10.1007/978-3-319-59090-5_1

allow them to be utilized for various, often dangerous tasks in off-world colonies. By law, the use of replicants on the Earth is prohibited. With this background, the film revolves around a group of replicants who, disobeying this law, have returned to the Earth to find out more about their existence and the possibility of extending their lifespans.

Blade runners are agents whose job is to hunt down and destroy such rogue replicants. As the story unfolds, the blade runner Rick Deckard (played by Harrison Ford) has hunted down and eliminated all but one replicant in the group – he is unable to overcome Roy. In the climax of the film Deckard and Roy engage in a battle of life and death. The battle ends with Deckard ultimately facing his death. However, in one of the key moments of the film, Deckard is saved from certain death by the replicant Roy, the very 'machine' Deckard was assigned to destroy. As Deckard's life is allowed to continue, Roy's life, with its preset lifespan approaching its end, begins to run out. In the terminating moments of his life, Roy produces the famous *Tears in Rain* soliloquy, one of the most moving monologues in cinema history. In this monologue, Roy reminiscences some of the powerful experiences he had in his life. He recounts attack ships on Orion, or C-beams glitter in the dark near a myth enshrouded 'Tannhäuser Gate'. In the moment of his dying, he is utterly sad and devastated that all these memories, all this information, all this knowledge, should be lost in time forever, like 'tears in rain'.

We have chosen the Blade Runner film as a backdrop to this chapter, because the theme of this classic science fiction centers around some of the key terms (e.g., information, intelligence, technology, or computerized societies) around which this chapter revolves. Nevertheless, it is time now to depart from Roy and the fictional location of the Tannhäuser Gate in order to, very briefly, touch upon the notion of information itself.

For a start, it is worthwhile to mention that it is surprising and very often overlooked that most investigations about information very quickly lead to a paradox. On the one hand, everybody seems to have a natural, intuitive, and immediate understanding about information. This understanding makes it relatively easy for any of us to appreciate, for instance, the important role that information holds as a driving-force behind our short-term actions and desires, as well as our more long-term ambitions and goals. On the other hand, there is the simple fact that, as soon as we look at information more closely, it turns out that information is a rather elusive concept and that it is extremely difficult to pin down, exactly, what information 'is'. It is important to understand, first of all, that there simply is no single, universally acknowledged definition of information. It may be helpful, however, to mention that the study of information could be divided into the following sections:

- One larger section deals with the philosophical side of information, and may involve discussions about the fundamental nature of information, how information may be generated, how it may become meaningful, or how information relates to moral issues such as responsibility or privacy (Wacks 2010).
- The content of the second larger section considers the more physical and technical side of information. This may include the study of different information

representation formats (e.g., as a molecular structure in a human genome, or as a string of bits transmitted over a telecommunication network). It may also include various aspects of information management (e.g., the processing of information, its storage, and maintenance), or the definition of a mathematical framework for the quantification of information (e.g., as in the mathematical theory of information introduced by Claude Elwood Shannon, who is often regarded to be the father of information theory (Roch 2010)).

- The third larger section relates to how information affects various types of agents in various types of information environments such as humans in an information society,[1] biological organisms in a biosphere, or artificial agents and biological agents inhabiting virtual reality worlds (e.g., Press and Williams 2010 or Kadushin 2011).

It is important here to understand that there is no reason to feel intimidated by the sheer complexity of these various dimensions of information. After all, it is a characteristic feature of our world that it is largely unknown to the human mind. Actually, throughout the course of history, the journey of mankind appears to be a perpetual quest in which we try to acquire a more complete understanding about this world, attempt to keep this acquired understanding safe, and make an effort to pass this understanding on from one generation to another.

In this chapter, we try to get a handle on information, by analyzing various sides of the information life-cycle at a time where powerful technology generates enormous amounts of data for a society that is equally information hungry as it is information dependent. In order to achieve this goal, Sect. 1.2 continues by generating an image about the restlessness of the human mind in its quest for universal understanding. Section 1.3 reminds us that the current interest in information is largely based on digital information. The section also describes information as a type of product that, from its conception to its usage, passes through the so-called life-cycle of information. Section 1.4 elaborates on the distinction between data, information, and knowledge. Section 1.5 returns to the information life-cycle. Section 1.6 philosophizes on information society, and Sect. 1.7 ends the chapter with a summary.

1.2 From Caveman to Spaceman

The death of Icarus, who came too close to the sun with his wings that his father Daedalus constructed from feathers and wax, has been interpreted across the categories of art in various ways. The mythological narrative in Ovid's

---

[1]There is no general definition for the phenomenon termed 'information society'. This chapter incorporates a view mentioned by Floridi (2010, pp. 3–18), who comments on information society as a society in which human progress and welfare seems to depend on the efficient management of the so-called 'life-cycle' of information. Section 1.3.1 provides further details on this life-cycle.

Metamorphoses (Ovid 2008, pp. 176–178) is one example, while another example could be the beautiful painting *The Lament for Icarus* by the English Classicist painter Herbert James Draper, who captures the tragic ending of the flight of Icarus by showing the dead body of Icarus surrounded by several curiously lamenting nymphs. Actually, even in our modern-day world the famous myth experiences the occasional revival (e.g., as in the 1983 album *Piece of Mind* of the heavy metal band *Iron Maiden*, which includes the song *Flight of Icarus*).

What is interesting in all of these representations is that it is usually the young and reckless figure of Icarus that captivates the reader, viewer, or listener, while the ingenuity and craftsmanship of his father Daedalus is often overlooked in this wondrous work of Greek mythology. There is another interesting point to this story, namely, how willingly we may accept the discrepancy between Icarus wings, true flying, and actually flying to the Sun. One reason for this willingness may come from a deeply rooted confidence in mankind that one has already completed an astonishing journey that took it from relatively primitive beings (in terms of the development and the utilization of technology) to the restless architects of artifacts of astonishing technical knowhow, sophistication, and beauty.

In this section, we would like to stimulate the imagination of the reader by visualizing this astonishing journey via the following three examples:

- A *cave painting* (e.g., the cave paintings in El Castillo Cave, discovered in 1903, in northern Spain (Pike et al. 2012)).
- The *Voyager 1* spacecraft (a space probe launched by NASA on September 5, 1977).[2]
- A so-called *Golden Record* fitted to the frame of Voyager 1.[2]

It is informative to compare these creations of the human mind from the perspectives of time, space, and intent. In terms of time, the distance between these artifacts accounts for a few thousand years. The cave paintings mentioned in Pike et al. (2012) date back[3] approximately 30,000 to 35,000 years ago, whereas the few Golden Records in existence and the Voyager 1 spacecraft have been produced only a few decades ago in the late 1970s. In terms of spacial distance, taking the Earth as a point of origin, the objects just mentioned convey the following information. The cave paintings mentioned in Pike et al. (2012) are in northern Spain, Europe, here on the planet Earth. For the Golden Record, the notion of the planet Earth may only evoke faint memories. One reason for this technological amnesia may

---

[2] Voyager the Interstellar Mission. http://voyager.jpl.nasa.gov/. Accessed: 2016-11-14.

[3] In terms of timing, it is necessary to highlight that accurate dating of cave paintings is a fairly difficult task. Until very recently, the cave paintings in Chauvet Cave in France have been considered to be the oldest examples of cave art in Europe. Recent discoveries in El Castillo Cave in northern Spain, however, suggest that the earliest examples of European cave art date back to as early as 48,000 years ago. From an information perspective such a finding is crucial. It may suggest that painting caves was not only part of the cultural repertoire of the first modern humans in Europe, but that Neanderthals, perhaps, also engaged in early human symbolic behavior (Pike et al. 2012).

be the fact that the record is fitted to the frame of the Voyager 1 spacecraft – the most distant human-made object in space. For example, at the time of this writing, this silent ambassador of mankind is journeying at a distance of more than 20 billion kilometers from the Earth.[2] Actually, on 12 September 2013, NASA announced that Voyager 1 has entered interstellar space (the space between the stars) to become a truly free interstellar space probe (Gurnett et al. 2013). Finally, regarding the issue of intent, it can only be subjective guesswork to figure out what those who left the cave paintings in El Castillo Cave behind had in mind. In the case of the Voyager 1 spacecraft and the Golden Record, all subjective guesswork can be firmly put aside. They are consciously crafted objects. The Golden Record contains sounds and images[2] that have been carefully selected in order to portray the diversity of life and culture on the Earth, while Voyager 1 stands out as our modern-day Icarus. In a forward-looking gaze, their intended audiences include future descendants of the human race, potential intelligent extraterrestrial life forms, or anybody or anything else who cares enough about crossing their path.

Intriguing as Voyager 1 and the Golden Records may be, they may convey different meanings to different minds. A philosopher, for instance, may see in them the deeply rooted desire of humanity to understand itself and the world at large, and to make itself understood to others and to the world at large, while an anthropologist, perhaps, may regard them simply as two more man-made artifacts created in the course of human evolution. By contrast, the minds of more flamboyant agents such as replicants or science fiction writers may be excited for other reasons. They may foresee journeys that may take mankind beyond places such as z8_GND_529, one of the most distant galaxies in our universe today, and a place where 700 million years after the Big Bang stars form more than 100 times faster than our Milky Way does (Finkelstein et al. 2013). Getting there, however, may require the accumulation of more and more data and information. Digital computers are designed to accomplish such a task.

1.3   Digits, Revolutions, and the Information Life-Cycle

The mathematician and philosopher Norbert Wiener (1894–1964) is widely regarded to be the originator of cybernetics. Crudely, cybernetics may be described as the study of feed-back systems. A feed-back system can be envisaged as a system that draws recourses from an environment, does some processing, and generates and feeds back some output into the environment. This output may be responsible for some changes in the environment, and, in doing so, may challenge the environment to some form of response. The system, which takes its input from a possibly changing environment, experiences a similar pressure. It too, needs to act in order to continue its operations. This process of control and communication repeats itself in a cyclic motion.

Control and communication are fundamental concepts in cybernetics. They are also non-trivial affairs. For instance, any feed-back system of sufficient complexity needs to be able to communicate with its environment (e.g., via sensors), but it also needs to be able to perform some kind of self-evaluation or self-assessment, which may require some form of a higher-order processing unit (e.g., a brain, or some other form of intelligent system). In addition, a crucial assumption in cybernetics is its indifference to the type of system. Cybernetics does not distinguish between biological systems (e.g., humans), and artificial systems (e.g., machines or software applications). It assumes that the mechanisms by which these systems operate are fundamentally the same.

Cybernetics also assumes that data, information, and information processing, play a central role in any communication system.[4] It is useful, therefore, to turn our attention to the fundamental processing unit behind modern-day telecommunication systems (and arguably the so-called digital/information revolution) – the binary digit, or simply the 'bit'.

A simple dissection of the term digital revolution reveals two facts. First, that there has been, or still is going on, or maybe is coming towards us, a 'revolution', and second, that there is a 'digital' element involved in this revolution. Even without any concrete examples, we understand the word revolution by meaning that there has been a fundamental structural change (e.g., physical, meta-physical, or behavioral) in a system previously existing in some pre-revolutionary mode of organization or structure. At a closer inspection, the word digital tells us that the digital revolution is not a revolution that is motivated by an ideology (e.g., like the French Revolution of 1789, which was inspired by the ideas of liberty, equality, and fraternity). Rather, the digital revolution is driven by powerful advances in technology. Actually, a more appropriate and encompassing term than technology alone would be the term ICTs, which stands for Information and Communications Technologies.

Please note the difference between the digital revolution and the information revolution. Although the two terms are intertwined, the digital revolution may refer to the rapid progress of computing and communication technology, which began during the late 1950s, while the information revolution involves the impact this development has (and may have) on human society (individually and collectively). In a sense, the digital revolution may be viewed as a facilitator of the information revolution. For instance, computer technology allows the operation of the Internet, while the higher-level services (typically accessible through the World Wide Web [WWW]) the Internet provides constitute various forms (e.g., print, audio, video) of informational content. This content, of course, has the potential to affect, for better or worse, the members of a modern society in various ways (Schuster and Berrar 2011).

---

[4] In addition, Wiener (1961, p. 132) also clearly comments on the unique character of information in his famous quote that: 'Information is information, not matter or energy'. Note that later in this section, we are going to pick up on this property of information again.

On a time-line the progress in computer technology may be divided into three phases. (Please note that this paragraph is based on Schuster (2016).) Although it is possible to mention many more names for each phase, the list of people who have been instrumental in the first phase may include Alan Mathison Turing (1912–1954), John von Neumann (1903–1957), and Claude Elwood Shannon (1916–2001). In simple terms, Turing specified the ultimate digital machine, the so-called 'universal Turing machine'. Surprisingly, the only difference between such a machine and any ordinary PC is that the former has infinite memory. This subtle difference, however, downgrades any modern-day supercomputer to the status of a mere wannabe.[5] The legacy of John von Neumann includes the description of a computer architecture (often referred to as the von Neumann architecture) that remains to this day a fundamental design feature of any modern computer. Shannon's contributions are similarly lasting. They include a mathematical framework for the treatment of information, as well as an investigation into the question whether the reliable transmission of information through 'any' information channel is possible in principle. The second generation of computing pioneers has been largely responsible for the development of powerful (commercial) computer systems and their underlying hardware and software (e.g., William Henry 'Bill' Gates III [born 1955], or the late Steven Paul 'Steve' Jobs [1955–2011]), as well as for the invention of inventions, the Internet and the WWW (e.g., Vinton Gray Cerf [born 1943], and Sir Timothy John Berners-Lee [born 1955]). The third phase of progress includes the founders of companies like *Google, Facebook, YouTube*, or *Twitter*, naming only a few. They all pursue their business under fancy-full names such as 'Web 2.0' or 'social web'. The social web is a very powerful abstraction. Not only does the social web urge information society to redefine traditional values, such as ownership (Heaven 2013), or friendship (Brent 2014), it is also a synonym for the seamless integration, augmentation, and infiltration of computing devices (of various degrees of intelligence) and the services they provide into our information hungry society as a new way of life.[6]

Let us now return to Norbert Wiener again. If, as Wiener[4] suggests, information is information, not matter or energy Wiener (1961, p. 132), then what is it? In order to understand this question better, it is useful to get a better idea about what

---

[5]At the time of this writing, the *Sunway TaihuLight* spearheads the list of the Top 500 Supercomputers at http://www.top500.org/. On this site, the performance of this supercomputer is given as 93 petaflop/s (quadrillions of calculations per second) on the Linpack benchmark.

[6]Quite naturally, this text can only provide a very short introduction to these fascinating topics. A reader with a wider interest in these topics, may find the following resources rewarding. The textbooks by Wright (2007) and Press and Williams (2010) describe the rise of the value of information through the ages, while the philosopher (Floridi 2011), one of the founders of the field of the 'philosophy of information', provides a sound treatment of the topic of information from a meta-physical, physical, and societal point of view. The books by Cohen (1996) or Jones and Jones (2000) may be useful for those readers with an interest in the theory of computing, or the mathematical theory of information, respectively. Our own work also provided various treatments of related concepts such as intelligent computing (Schuster 2007), or artificial intelligence (Schuster and Yamaguchi 2011), for instance.

type of revolution the digital revolution actually is. We already observed that the digital revolution is not ideology-driven, but its dynamic stems from a progress in technology. This observation makes the digital revolution similar to the Industrial Revolution starting in the late eighteenth century. If the steam engine represents the Industrial Revolution then its digital revolutionary twin is the digital computer. And, if the Industrial Revolution was responsible, among other things, for the mass production of goods that were physical, material, and tangible then the digital computer is responsible for the mass production of information, which is often non-physical, non-material, and non-tangible. At this point, some caution is needed. The text already mentioned that there simply is no universally agreed definition of information. If this is the case, how then can we speak of the mass-production of information? Although forthcoming sections are going to elaborate on this point in more detail, for the moment, we may say that the digital revolution mass-produces informational goods such as emails, YouTube videos, or complete virtual reality worlds. Perhaps, from a Platonic point of view, we may say that we are talking about instances of the idea of information, but that we do not really have a complete understanding about the idea of information itself, 'yet'.

For the sake of getting closer to the idea of information, let us put the notion of information aside for the time being, and instead, let us elaborate on the concept of an information life-cycle. We already mentioned that the Industrial Revolution provided an opportunity for the mass-production of tangible, material goods. While this is true, it soon turned out, however, that the production process itself (i.e., the process from product conception to the final product) became the object of careful study and analysis too. A main goal of this study was directed towards the establishment of general guidelines that would help manufacturers to produce any kind of product in an optimized and clearly defined way, taking into account a range of goals and objectives. To put it simply, the subject of 'project management' (including the study of product life-cycles) and its growing importance became widely recognized. As we shall see, the same concerns apply to non-tangible informational goods and the life-cycle of information too.

1.3.1 The Information Life-Cycle

Although the terminology employed differs occasionally, the following list captures the main processes involved in the so-called information life-cycle.

- Creation and production of information.
- Information gathering and collection.
- Organization, recording, and storage of information.
- Processing of information.
- Distribution and dissemination of information.
- Information application and usage.
- Information maintenance and recycling.

It is necessary to understand that the terms in this list are labels for generic, high-level processes that: (i) apply to most information processing projects in general, but (ii) usually, are realized differently in individual projects.

Take the example of an information system for a dental clinic where data about clients needs to be acquired and collected. For instance, an office worker may take the data personally from the client at the client's first visit. At this visit, the client may need to complete a standardized paper-based document. This data may then be filed by the office worker into a folder. An alternative to this process could be a web-based database system that allows a user (client) to register at the clinic and to enter the required data on-line. Actually, with some flexibility of terminology in mind, the (information) life-cycle outlined before applies to the production process of any product. For instance, the on-line scenario just mentioned may involve a commercial database application. Such a database application may be the outcome of a fully-fledged software project. From conception to utilization, software production is usually undertaken within the framework of a so-called 'software' life-cycle, and involves the steps of problem analysis, system requirement analysis and specification, design, implementation, testing, and maintenance (McConnell 2010, Chapter 7). It is relatively easy to map these fundamental software development processes, including the various tasks they involve, against the terms in the aforementioned list.

In addition, it is necessary to understand that the representation of the information life-cycle as a top-to-down list seems to suggest a natural sequence from the creation and production of information down to information maintenance and recycling. In reality, this assumption is often incorrect. Individual information processes often overlap, they may go through several iterations, and they may be non-sequential. For instance, a software system such as the on-line registration system mentioned before may experience changes for several reasons. Some changes may be required in order to increase the user-friendliness of the system, while other modifications may be needed because of changes in the hardware and software environment in which the application operates. All these changes are based on a new understanding about the services the system should provide – they are all based on new information.

1.4 Data, Information, and Knowledge

The motivation in this section is to explain, briefly, the difference and the relationship between three challenging concepts: *data*, *information*, and *knowledge*. The common understanding is that knowledge encapsulates information and that information consists of data. It is meaningful, therefore, to start our exposition with data.

1.4.1 Data

The Stanford Encyclopedia of Philosophy,[7] which relies on Floridi (2010), provides a simple, but extremely powerful definition for data. (Please note that the forthcoming text, including several definitions, in this section relies on these two sources.)

> *The Diaphoric Definition of Data*: A datum is a putative fact regarding some difference or lack of uniformity within some context.

For instance, take the context of a blank sheet of white paper. It is possible, to describe the sheet of paper as uniformly white. Now imagine someone making a stroke on the white sheet using a black pen. Now, the sheet is no longer uniformly white. There exists a difference or contrast. The diaphoric definition of data above tells us that this lack of uniformity actually is what we call data. It is crucial here to understand that the data is not the black stroke only, but that it is the black stroke on a white paper which creates a difference or contrast that makes up the data. From this perspective, data acquires the character of a non-physical 'pattern' that stands above the physicality of the white and black strokes. This feature of non-physicality has led to interpretations maintaining that information does not necessarily require a material embodiment. Although this is an interesting view, it is a point we do not want to further pursue in this section.

Instead, we mention that Floridi (2010) distinguishes three views in terms of lack of uniformity. First, there is a lack of uniformity in the real world. This means that the world we perceive is not empty. Our world is not uniformly made of nothing, because there are objects in our world. Second, there can be a lack of uniformity between the states of a system (e.g., a fully charged battery) or signals (e.g., a dot and a line in Morse code). Third, data can be lacks of uniformity between two symbols (e.g., the difference between the letters 'B' and 'P' in the alphabet). Together, these three views allow the production of information. For instance, suppose you want to write a text on your laptop (object). In case the battery (object) of your laptop is not empty (state) then, initially, the screen on your laptop may show an empty page (uniformity). Whenever you begin typing, characters (symbols) appear on the screen (lack of uniformity, hence data). If we go one step further by assuming that the text produced in this process is 'meaningful' then, according to the definition that follows, information (understood as semantic content) has been produced.

---

[7]Stanford Encyclopedia of Philosophy. The Diaphoric Definition of Data. http://plato.stanford.edu/entries/information-semantic/#1.3. Accessed: 2016-11-14.

1.4.2 Information

> *The General Definition of Information* (GDI): σ is an instance of information, understood
> as semantic content, if and only if:
>
> (i) σ consists of one or more data;
> (ii) the data in σ are well-formed;
> (iii) the well-formed data in σ are meaningful.

In summary, GDI (adopted from Floridi 2010) above means that information is made of data (e.g., the characters on the laptop screen are data). The data have to be well-formed according to some rules or procedures (e.g., the sentence 'Dear Sir or Madam!' on the laptop screen). If, for instance, the sentence just mentioned introduces a formal letter, then the well-formed data are also meaningful.

We need to mention here that the simple and intuitive GDI above should not create the illusion that information can be so easily dealt with. Information is a much richer concept with many more subtleties involved. For instance, it is not clear how GDI relates to the mathematical theory of information outlined by Shannon, or how it can be used to explain biological instances of information such as, for example, the genetic code or neural information. Nevertheless, GDI is a powerful starting point into the wider world of information. It also serves as a comfortable springboard to plunge into knowledge.

1.4.3 Knowledge

The understanding of knowledge requires the consideration of one important feature of information, namely that of its possible purpose. The following, simple definition of information indicates a possible purpose.

> *Simple Definition of Information*: Information is the act of informing – the communication
> of knowledge from a sender to a receiver that informs (literally shapes) the receiver.[8]

Naturally, this definition leads to the question when are we actually informed. Take the sentences 'Tokyo is the capital of Germany', and 'Tokyo is the capital of Japan'. Clearly, the first sentence is not true. In the terminology of philosophy, the fact expressed by this sentence is not 'veridical'. Meaning, that there is no truthful correspondence between this statement and reality. In cases like this, we are simply not informed. We have the same amount of information as we had before – not more and not less. The second sentence, on the other hand, is veridical, because in our world, Tokyo is the capital of Japan. In this case, our information has increased indeed. Floridi (2010) captures this observation in the following definition.

---

[8]The Information Philosopher. http://www.informationphilosopher.com/knowledge/information. html. Accessed: 2016-11-14.

Factual Semantic Information: *p* qualifies as factual semantic information, if and only if *p* is (constituted by) well-formed, meaningful, and veridical (truthful, corresponding with reality or facts) data.

We are very close now to understand one interpretation of knowledge. Getting there requires the help of an assistant – *Sherlock Holmes*. Typically, in an investigation, Holmes excels in extracting and combining data in unconventional, elegant ways. Usually, but not always, the data are well-organized in a natural way. For instance, someone may have noticed '…the footprints of a gigantic hound!' Doyle (2001, p. 21). On the other hand, the data may be well-organized for other reasons too. The data may have been arranged purposefully by someone carrying the intention to deceive Holmes. Whatever the nature may be, in a story, Holmes usually has various pieces of information available to him. The genius of Holmes lies in his ability to connect these individual pieces of information rightfully and meaningfully, which eventually enables him to convict the culprit in a plot.

Please note the crucial difference here. Typically, it is not possible to identify the villain from a single piece of information. It requires the integration of multiple pieces of information to achieve this. Thus, we could say that knowledge requires and originates form the ability to pool and integrate multiple information sources.

It is no surprise that the talents of Sherlock Holmes have been inspirational to the real-world in various ways. Google Knowledge Graph, for instance, is a knowledge-based system add-on to a Google search engine.[9] Search engine results are usually isolated and low in terms of semantic content, hinting that they are knowledge-poor. In practice, Google Knowledge Graph aims to enrich search engine results by connecting (true, veridical) information from a variety of sources (e.g., Freebase, Wikipedia, or the CIA World Factbook) into a dynamic network structure (graph) that is rich in semantic content and so, arguably, knowledgeable.

One question that arises from such projects is how they may affect our information hungry society. This is why the next section returns to the information life-cycle again.

1.5 Fundamental Information Life-Cycle Processes

In his book, *The Story of Philosophy*, Magee (2010, p. 96) presents an interesting aspect of the personality of the German polymath Gottfried Wilhelm von Leibniz (1646–1716) by mentioning, how the great thinker refers to himself in a moment of self-reflection as follows:

… When I have done something, I forget it almost completely in a few moments, and rather than hunting for it among the chaos of sheets that I have never had time to sort out and index, I have to do the work all over again. …

---

[9]Google Knowledge Graph. https://www.youtube.com/watch?v=mmQl6VGvX-c. Accessed: 2016-11-14.

Most likely, we'll never fully understand the processes of reorganization unfolding in the mind of Leibniz in such a moment. In the context of this chapter, however, we may wonder, how much the great thinker may have benefited from a detailed understanding of the information life-cycle. Although, we may never find out, perhaps, at the end of this somewhat longer section, we may have obtained a more private understanding about how an accurate treatment of data and information may be advantageous for modern-day agents like ourselves.

In order to acquire this insight, we embark on a short walk along the information life-cycle mentioned in Sect. 1.3.1. Along this way, this section provides examples from a modern technology perspective in order to understand the challenging relationship between fundamental information processes and information society. Understandably, many of these examples can only be subjectively selected snapshots, taken from a rapidly changing environment where reports about fascinating findings and amusing trivia alike break into our lives at astonishing speeds.

1.5.1 Acquisition and Collection

Before we progress into these two life-cycle processes, we need to provide a bit more information about the nature of data and information. The previous Sect. 1.4 indicated that not only human beings but nature too, is a great producer of information. Just think about the rings in a tree trunk or the DNA of biological organisms. But then, we may ask, what is the difference between these natural examples of information and, for instance, a musical instrument made of wood, maybe a violin, or a DNA strand engineered in a synthetic biology project?

The distinctions we need to understand here, are those of origin and purpose. Of course, notions like origin or purpose very quickly turn into bigger questions, such as the meaning of life, or how this world comes about. From this point of view, this text tries to avoid questions about whether there is a spiritual entity or a larger purpose behind the existence of anything around us.[10] In order to reflect this position, we simply speak of natural information. In the case of humans, however, we should assume a certain kind of motivation (purpose, intent) behind the creation of informational entities. Actually, we can go a bit further, and assume that the production of informational entities by humans is not only purpose-driven, it is also 'organized'. Indeed, the information life-cycle processes of storage and classification in Sect. 1.5.2 explicitly deal with this issue in more detail.

---

[10]Please note that in the time of the digital revolution this does not prevent researchers from using powerful computers, in order to attempt to prove the existence of God, who, according to the beliefs of the mathematician Kurt Gödel, is a being who possesses all positive properties (Benzmüller and Woltzenlogel Paleo 2013).

After clarifying some of the differences in the production of informational entities (nature, humans), it is also necessary to mention that the modern world acquires and collects and uses, both types of informational entities. For example, a project in computer animation may record the natural movements of a sportsman for a computer game project, while smart-watches or similar devices monitor and provide health services for their users.

Conclusively, we may say that this section concerns the purpose-driven, organized acquisition and collection of informational entities. With these basics in place, it is possible now, to look at some of the projects that require the acquisition and collection of huge amounts of data and information.

1.5.2   Storage and Classification

A good starting point for this section is the realization that 'history is recording'. Any event in history reveals itself only through the information that has been recorded about it. The time before events have been recorded in an organized way, therefore, is correctly termed 'prehistory'.[11] For instance, the root problem with the cave painting mentioned in Sect. 1.2 is that people are struggling with its unknown history. There simply is a lack of recorded information. We just do not know when exactly it was painted, or who its creators or what their intentions were. We could say that the current efforts surrounding the cave painting are an attempt to compensate an information deficit, in order to award the paining its unique history and identity.

The problem of information deficit, however, is not only a problem of the past. Think about conditions affecting the memory of individuals (e.g., various forms of amnesia or dementia). In such cases, individuals may lose memories, or be forced to live in a time-warp of their former selves (e.g., in cases where individuals are unable to acquire new memories) (Foster 2008). A fundamental problem in many of these cases is that these conditions alienate individuals from society, by preventing them from functioning normally. Of course, in a society that depends so heavily on efficient communication this is a serious dilemma.

In addition, recording is only one half of storage. The other half is classification and organization (Taylor and Joudrey 2008). For instance, it is possible to write down the telephone-numbers of all your friends on flashcards and to keep (store) these cards rather unconventionally in an empty pralines box. Clearly, retrieving the telephone number of a particular friend from such a data store can be difficult. This is exactly why, today, telephone numbers are held in smartphones, or are accessible

---

[11]Please note that we are again aware of the distinction between naturally produced records (e.g., the distinct layers of sediment or soil that make the Earth's strata) and records produced intentionally by intelligent human beings (e.g., a library, or a photo album). The focus here is on the latter form of production again.

otherwise on-line. (Please note that in terms of the phone numbers, the pralines box and the smartphone contain the same information. The difference between using one over the other is a matter of convenience in terms of information access and organization.)

1.5.3 Analysis and Manipulation

In terms of the analysis and manipulation of data and information, it is not only important what we analyze and manipulate, but also the quantity of data and information that is involved in these processes. The current information revolution is characterized by excessive amounts of data created every day. 'Big data' is the buzzword under which this phenomenon is currently being dealt with LaValle et al. (2011) and Marz and Warren (2015).

An interesting consequence of big data is that in many domains, not only data acquisition and data collection, but also data analysis and the resulting decision-making processes have been handed over from humans to fully auto-mated, computer-based systems. Although there are many interesting issues related to this change in responsibility (and beyond[12]), the underlying move from an 'hypothesis'-driven approach to a 'data'-driven approach, seems to be particularly interesting.

For instance, any approach that has its eyes on acquiring an understanding about a subject area requires data (e.g., obtained from observations). The hypothesis-driven approach is no exception to that. It is possible to say, however, that the hypothesis driven approach requires some primary data in order to produce a hypothesis that can then be verified (or disapproved) through the generation of some secondary data.

In our most recent time, the Higgs boson may stand out as a landmark example for this approach. The Higgs boson is the elementary particle predicted by the so-called Standard Model of particle physics. The weight of the Higgs boson in the Standard Model of particle physics was of such importance (e.g., for its role for explaining why some fundamental particles have mass) that it was crucial to prove its existence in order to validate the correctness of the Standard Model.

In the context of our discussion, we may say that the Higgs boson (the hypothesis) has been predicted by Peter Ware Higgs (one of the recipient of the 2013 Nobel Prize in Physics), and other physicists, in the early 1960s on the basis of some primary data. The hypothesis has been confirmed in a monumental effort in 2012 through the generation of secondary data in the Large Hadron Collider, which,

---

[12]Perhaps, at this stage, it is meaningful to mention the work of the German philosopher Byung-Chul Han, who provides a rich treatment of various aspects (digital communication, social media, transparency, neoliberalism, etc.) of the relationship between the modern-day information environment and (information) society (Han 2015a,b,c).

at the time of this writing, is the world's largest and most powerful (and with a price tag of about $6 billion, perhaps, also the most expensive) particle accelerator in existence. Actually, there is still a debate going on about what has been found in these experiments. The consensus is that what has been found may be indeed the Higgs boson or at least something that is very similar to it (Chalmers 2012). Either way, the point here is not to discuss what has been found, but rather in what way it has been found, and that way is hypothesis driven.

Examples of the data driven approach may include applications such as Google Translator,[13] or Netspeak.[14] Traditional translation tools used to be grounded on rule-based analysis. This approach required developers to teach a tool the 'meanings' of vocabulary, grammars of languages, syntax of languages, and so on. Languages, however, are extremely complex, and it soon became clear that such translation tools cannot capture the large number of exceptions and nuances languages contain. As a result, the quality of such systems was relatively poor.

Google Translator departs from this traditional approach by employing algorithms that are based on statistical analysis rather than traditional rule-based analysis. In a nutshell, the statistical analysis employed generates statistical models from large volumes of data. The statistical models generated in this process, are then used to translate between languages.

The Netspeak web service employs a similar strategy (Riehmann et al. 2012). Netspeak aims to assist authors to overcome problems when writing in a foreign language by resourcing the WWW. The application can be used, for instance, for checking the commonness of phrases by facilitating the retrieval of alternatives via queries that contain wild card characters. For instance, an author quarreling with a phrase involving: 'waiting ... response' may issue the following Netspeak query: 'waiting ? ? response', where the two question marks in the query stand for two missing words. Netspeak may respond to this query with the output: 'waiting *for a* response', plus the information that this particular phrase has been found 42,000 (71.5%) times in the consulted resources. The emphasis is again that Netspeak does not have a deep understanding (i.e., knowledge) about language or grammar. Instead, Netspeak outcomes originate from data driven, statistical analysis procedures. Ultimately, this is the driving idea employed in many large scale (big) data processing projects.

---

[13]Google Translator. https://translate.google.com/. Accessed: 2016-11-14.
[14]Netspeak. http://www.netspeak.org/. Accessed: 2016-11-14.

1.5.4   Retrieval, Dissemination, Usage, and Maintenance

One only needs to recall the quote by Gottfried Wilhelm von Leibniz at the beginning of this section, to be reminded, how important retrieval is for information and data processing.

In a computing context, we may think of 'search engines' (e.g., Google, Bing, Baidu, or Wolfram Alpha), or 'web crawlers', which are all tools that allow people to find information on the WWW. Search engines rely on database technology as back-end data stores (e.g., the popular open source database MySQL[15]). Important search engine features include the size of a database, its up-to-dateness, its speed, the relevance of query results, as well as several other features. Up-to-dateness and speed provide immediate advantages to dissemination and usage. For instance, the modern-day news business relies on the timely dissemination of content to the widest audience possible.

Of course, dissemination and usage of information also has its darker side. These darker elements may range from violating copyrights, to vandalism, hacking, password and identity theft, to a disturbing world where children and other vulnerable groups in our society are exploited and abused. The so-called 'deep web' may be mentioned synonymously for this other side of the WWW (Bartlett 2015). In a way, the deep web is not part of the WWW standard users surf on-line, the so-called 'surface web'. Usually, the sites of the deep web are not reachable (for various reasons) by standard search engines, which is, perhaps, one motivation for many of its users. In addition, because the deep web is considered to be much larger than the surface web, there exists a diversity of interests in various organizations to get access to its information. One of these organizations, the Defense Advanced Research Projects Agency (DARPA),[16] which is an agency of the United States Department of Defense, runs the so-called Memex program to access and catalog this mysterious on-line world.

The final dimension we intend to explore in this section, relates to the actual producers of web content. From a technical point of view, we first need to differentiate between the Internet and the WWW. The Internet is a global network of interconnected computers. The software on which this network operates is referred to as TCP/IP.[17] The WWW is what users typically access with their web browsers on the Internet. The WWW provides access to content that organizations, businesses, or

---

[15]MySQL. https://www.mysql.com/. Accessed: 2016-07-24.

[16]Defense Advanced Research Projects Agency (DARPA). https://www.nasa.gov/jpl/deep-web-search-may-help-scientists/. Accessed: 2016-07-24.

[17]TCP/IP stands for Transmission Control Protocol (TCP) and Internet Protocol (IP). It is possible to envisage TCP/IP as a large software package that is composed of many smaller software programs (protocols). Combined, these individual protocols work together to accomplish the communication in a computer network, for instance, the Internet (Casad 2011, pp. 7–21). The development of TCP/IP is a milestone in the history of computing. Its development is so important that several of the key contributors have been recognized by the 'ACM A.M. Turing Award', the highest distinction the computer science community awards.

ordinary people produce. Section 1.3 already mentioned that the social web, which has evolved from the early WWW, provides a bustling environment where users interact socially. Actually, a main feature of the social web is that its content, flair, and visual shape, is largely generated by its users. For example, the excitement that websites like YouTube, Instagram, or Twitter provide, has its roots in the videos, pictures, or tweets its users (ordinary people, celebrities, and other representatives of popular culture) upload. From this point of view, it is interesting to see that, in a strange way, the social web could be the canvas onto which the German artist and political activist Joseph Beuys (1921–1986) sketched his vision of a society, in which 'jeder Mensch ein Künstler sei' (where everyone was an artist). Besides this famous phrase, Beuys also coined the mystical term 'social sculpture'. Interpretations of this term suggest social sculpture foremost as a process of transformation or shaping of society through the collective creativity of its members. Let us find out, what information society has to say about that.

1.6   Information Society

Der Zauberlehrling (The Sorcerer's Apprentice) is a well-known poem by one of Germany's most eminent literary figures, Johann Wolfgang von Goethe (1749–1832). The poem recounts the adventure of an apprentice who, in the absence of his master, tries out some magic on his own. Things are getting quickly out of hand for the young apprentice, who, in the end, is saved by his returning master.

If, in an analogy, today, the young apprentice are the producers of technology that causes the (digital) information revolution, and, if the mess the apprentice produces equates to the challenges issued on information society, then, the returning master equates to – who? Maybe, at the end of this final section, there is something like an answer to this very difficult question.

1.6.1   Decentralized Information Society

For a start, we briefly return to the previous section, where we mentioned the TCP/IP Internet protocol suite. TCP/IP provides a wide range of services, including hardware support, or making the Internet reliable and resilient. The designers of the Internet, however, had another fundamental design goal in mind. They wanted to make the Internet a 'decentralized' system.

Two design features stand out behind this intent, end-node verification and dynamic routing. End-node verification means that basically all computers (called hosts or nodes) on the Internet act as equals. This means that each node can manage a complete communication session over the Internet. Dynamic routing is a feature that relates to robustness (Schuster 2008). On the Internet, a message that is sent between two nodes, may travel on different paths. From this point of view, the Internet appears similar to the underground system of a somewhat larger city. Anyone who has ever traveled on such a system, understands that there are usually several routes to a particular destination station. This does not mean that a journey to that station takes the same time on all possible routes, rather, it means that in the case of unforeseen events (e.g., a delay by bad weather) there are alternatives that allow travelers to reach their destination. It turns out now that, in terms of centralization and decentralization, there are similarities between the Internet and information society too.

One similarity stems from the unlikely domain of literature. An important idea in literature and culture is the so-called 'literary canon'. Though the concept of a literary canon is somewhat larger, in a literary context, it may describe a body of books that have been traditionally accepted by scholars as the most important and influential in their society or culture. For instance, *Faust*, by Johann Wolfgang von Goethe is a classic in the German literary canon. In relation to a literary canon, researchers investigating large-scale trends in literary style (Hughesa et al. 2012), found that the influence of classic literature (the literary canon) on writers is declining. Their research on a large body of literary works (current and past) revealed several trends including: (i) authors of any given period are similar in style to their contemporaries, (ii) the stylistic influence of the past is decreasing, and (iii) authors writing in the late twentieth century are instead strongly influenced by other contemporary writers. From our point of view, it is possible to look at the literary canon as a central(ized) entity of past literary activity. Presently, this central role is declining. Instead, the current literary scene is decentralized.

This point of view leads to an interesting observation in computing. In computing, the field of 'swarm intelligence' studies the collective behavior of decentralized, self-organized systems (Hassanien and Emary 2015). In such systems, which can be natural or artificial, agents with limited capacities often achieve outcomes that seem to be beyond the ability of an individual agent. Typical examples include the behavior exhibited by a flock of birds, a school of fish, or an ant colony. Let us use one example, a flock of birds. Migrating birds often show an extraordinary flight behavior. In cases where there is no single leader in a flock of birds, the flight pattern of the birds can look erratic and unorganized. From a closer inspection, however, it is 'self-organized'. A bird may start flying in one direction, this may invite other birds to join in, and soon the entire swarm may follow.

Is it possible to map this behavior to the current literary world? We think it is, at least to some degree. First of all, in comparison to the past, the current literary world, which includes on-line publishing, open-access, or blogs, is huge (Bohannon 2013). It is natural therefore, we think, that new styles of organization evolve. We also think that this new style of organization is decentralized and self-organized. Ultimately, in this environment diverse groups of authors and styles will emerge, compete, and, perhaps, survive or perish.

1.6.2   A Voice for Information Society

In the introduction to this section, the allegory of the returning master who tidies up some harmless wrongdoing by his apprentice, led us to the question about who such a master could be for information society. In order to touch upon this question from a more social, political, and philosophical outlook, we refer back to the mentioning of the French Revolution in Sect. 1.3. There, we mentioned that revolutions usually involve (i) some ideology, (ii) a radical element, as well as (iii) a more moderate, long-term element. The long-term element usually leads to some tangible forms of realization such as a way of life, or a new political party, for instance.

In order to understand these elements in information society, we could take the student movement of the late 1960s happening in the former West Germany, as well as in other places around the world, as a backdrop. Without going too deep into the subject, the ideology of the student movement in Germany involved, among other things, a protest against the Germany of World War II, including the hierarchies, institutions, and people responsible at that time. Other contributing elements include the Cold War, the Vietnam War, and a general desire for social change and more democracy. The radical part includes violent confrontations between protesters and the German authorities. Indeed, the student revolution led to an extreme element with its own turbulent history, the militant organization *Rote Armee Fraktion* (Red Army Faction) (Aust 1998). However, in terms of the long-term element mentioned before, it seems to be fair to say that in Germany, *Die Grünen* (the Green Party) are a major, tangible outcome emerging from this struggle.

Does our information society have a similar story to tell, in Germany or elsewhere? We think that is the case. Similar to the Green Party, there is now (since 2006) a political body, the so-called *Piratenpartei Deutschland* (Pirate Party of Germany). This party, which is part of an international movement, portrays itself in its agenda as a steward for the needs of information society in the time of the digital revolution. Let us now turn to the radical element in information society. Perhaps, this element has its representative in the *Anonymous* movement. Anonymous is an internationally organized network of activists and hacktivists that uses the Internet as a platform to push its agenda through various means. Anonymous cannot be linked to a particular country alone. Perhaps, its nature and mode of operation is best described as being similar to that of *Greenpeace*. Depending on the position taken, therefore, some may describe Anonymous as Internet Robin Hoods, while others may be inclined to call them radicals, or even terrorists.

The final point we want to address in this section, relates to the interesting observation that, somehow, many Germans found the agenda of the young Pirate Party similarly difficult to comprehend as that of the early Green Party. What could be the reason for this? Floridi (2010) provides an insightful analysis for this phenomenon. He mentions that in the past, the center of a moral claim was typically a human being. This is not difficult to understand. The Green movement starting in the late 80th told us that the radius for moral agency should be extended to include our natural environment, be it animate (e.g., animals, or other organic lifeforms), or inanimate (e.g., trees, or mountains). According to Floridi, the concept of information extends this radius into the infinite. In an all-embracing gesture, Floridi argues that any informational agent (a human, a dog, a tree, a book, a star, a character in a virtual world, or a bitcoin) is entitled to a moral claim, however minimal this claim may be. The heralding, little understood Pirate Party movement seems to passionately embrace this view. Of course, the journey that lies ahead for this movement is full of uncertainties. However, by their very namesake – Pirates – the party should be historically and ideologically well equipped to master the swift currents of a self-organizing, decentralized information society.

1.7 Summary

From a birds-eye view, this chapter has three dimensions: information, technology, and information society. The goal in this chapter was to create an introductory understanding about these three dimensions. The chapter investigated these topics via the so-called life-cycle of information and its fundamental information processes. In addition, the chapter provides a wide range of examples to explain the manifold relations between these topics. Despite this range of examples, there is an understanding that much more can be said about each single topic.

Perhaps, some of the interesting findings in the chapter include the realization that information society contains a strong element of decentralization and self-organization. These features provide it with a kind of freedom and elasticity that seems to be necessary to cope with the changes originating from the information revolution. The question of where this freedom and elasticity may lead to is not only an open question, it is also an old question. For instance, in his masterpiece, *Les Misérables* (Hugo 1982), the great French writer Victor Hugo (1802–1885) penned down a powerful observation that may apply not only to this open question, but to all phases of transition and change. He mentioned that the future comes to each individual in various disguises. To the weak, it may come in the disguise of an impossibility; the fainthearted may experience it as an unknown entity; while for the valiant it may be – 'ideal'. From the point of view of this chapter, it may look nostalgic to seek comfort in this observation, but then, there can be more terrible things than envisaging an ideal future where people are valiant and everyone can be an artist.

References

Aust S (1998) Der Baader Meinhof Komplex. Wilhelm Goldman Verlag, München
Bartlett J (2015) The dark net. Windmill Books, London
Benzmüller C, Woltzenlogel Paleo B (2013) Formalization, mechanization and automation of Gödel's proof of God's existence. arXiv:1308.4526 [cs.LO]. Available via https://arxiv.org/abs/1308.4526. Accessed 28 July 2016

Bohannon J (2013) Who's afraid of peer review? Science 342(6154):60–65

Brent L (2014) Friendship: friends with many benefits. New Sci 2970:37–39

Casad J (2011) SAMS teach yourself TCP/IP in 24 hours, 5th edn. SAMS, Indianapolis

Chalmers M (2012) The Higgs problem. New Sci 2890:34–37

Cohen DIA (1996) Introduction to computer theory, 2nd edn. Wiley, New York/Chichester

Doyle AC (2001) The hound of the Baskervilles, New edition. Penguin Classics, London, England

Finkelstein SL, Papovich C, Dickinson M, Song M, Tilvi V (16 additional authors not shown) (2013) A galaxy rapidly forming stars 700 million years after the Big Bang at redshift 7.51. Nature 502:524–527

Floridi L (2010) Information: a very short introduction. Oxford University Press, Oxford

Floridi L (2011) The philosophy of information. Oxford University Press, Oxford

Foster JK (2008) Memory: a very short introduction. Oxford University Press, Oxford

Gurnett DA, Kurth WS, Burlaga LF, Ness NF (2013) In situ observations of interstellar plasma with Voyager 1. Science 341(6153):1489–1492

Han BC (2015a) The burnout society, 1st edn. Stanford Briefs, California

Han BC (2015b) Psychopolitik: Neoliberalismus und die neuen Machttechniken, Auflage 2. Fischer Taschenbuch

Han BC (2015c) The transparency society, 1st edn. Stanford Briefs, Stanford

Hassanien AE, Emary E (2015) Swarm intelligence: principles, advances, and applications. CRC Press, Boca Raton

Heaven D (2013) Lost in the cloud: how safe are your online possessions? New Sci 2910:35–37

Hughesa JM, Fotia NJ, Krakauer DC, Rockmore DN (2012) Quantitative patterns of stylistic influence in the evolution of literature. Proc Natl Acad Sci USA 109(20):7682–7686

Hugo V (1982, Reprint edition) Les Miserables. Penguin Classics, London, England

Jones GA, Jones JM (2000) Information and coding theory. Springer, Berlin

Kadushin C (2011) Understanding social networks: theories, concepts, and findings. Oxford University Press, Oxford

LaValle S, Lesser E, Shockley R, Hopkins MS, Kruschwitz N (2011) Big data, analytics and the path from insights to value. MIT Sloan Manag Rev 52(2):20–32

Magee B (2010) The story of philosophy. Dorling Kindersley, London

Marz N, Warren J (2015) Big data: principles and best practices of scalable realtime data systems, 1st edn. Manning Publications, New York

McConnell SC (2010) Rapid development: taming wild software schedules. Microsoft Press, Sebastopol

Ovid (2008) Metamorphoses. Oxford University Press, Oxford. Translation by Melville AD

Pike AWG, Hoffmann DL, García-Diez M, Pettitt PB, Alcolea J (6 additional authors not shown) (2012) U-series dating of paleolithic art in 11 caves in Spain. Science 336(6087):1409–1413

Press AL, Williams BA (2010) The new media environment: an introduction, 1st edn. Wiley-Blackwell, Malden

Riehmann P, Gruendl H, Potthast M, Trenkmann M, Stein B, Froehlich B (2012) WORDGRAPH: keyword-in-context visualization for NETSPEAK's wildcard search. IEEE Trans Vis Comput Graph 18(9):1411–1423

Roch A (2010) Claude E. Shannon: Spielzeug, Leben und die geheime Geschichte seiner Theorie der Information. gegenstalt Verlag, Berlin

Schuster A (2007) Intelligent computing everywhere. In: Schuster A (ed) Intelligent computing everywhere. Springer, London, pp 3–25

Schuster A (2008) Robustness in nature as a design principle for artificial intelligence. In: Schuster A (ed) Robust intelligent systems. Springer, London, pp 165–188

Schuster A (2016) Forms of organizing human society inspired by technological structures. In: Proceedings of 4th International workshop on philosophy and logic of social reality (SOCREAL'16)

Schuster A, Berrar D (2011) The omnipresent computing menace to information society. J Adv Comput Intell Intell Inform 15(7):786–792

Schuster A, Yamaguchi Y (2011) From foundational issues in artificial intelligence to intelligent memristive nano-devices. Int J Mach Learn Cybern 2(2):75–87

Taylor AG, Joudrey DN (2008) The organization of information, 3rd edn. Libraries Unlimited Inc, Westport, Connecticut, USA

Wacks R (2010) Privacy: a very short introduction. Oxford University Press, Oxford

Wiener N (1961) Cybernetics or control and communication in the animal and the machine, revised 2nd edn. MIT Press, Cambridge

Wright A (2007) Glut: mastering information through the ages. Josef Henry Press, Washington, DC

Part II
The World of Large and Small Systems

Chapter 2
Expanding Beyond the Solar System: Current Observation and Theory

Ko Yamada and Satoshi Inaba

Abstract Galaxies, stars, and planets have captivated and inspired human minds for centuries. A relatively young discovery in our universe is so-called extrasolar planets. First discovered in 1995, these planets travel in great distances, far outside of our solar system. A major challenge in extrasolar planet research is that these planets are extremely difficult to detect. Indeed, in many situations, this challenge demands great ingenuity when it comes to data analysis and information processing. The motivation in this chapter is to describe the general environment in which these challenges take place. In the course of this exploration, the reader is going to travel deep into our universe where silent messengers such as the COROT or Kepler space satellites communicate with us silently, reliably, and continuously in order to increase our understanding about the formation of planets, our solar system, and our universe at large.

2.1 Introduction

Fundamentally, the world we all share is a big mystery. There simply are no clearcut answers to questions such as who we are, where we come from, where we are going to, or what this place we call our universe actually is all about. Various grand theories aim to shed light onto these questions. Darwin's theory of evolution by natural selection, for instance, aims to explain biodiversity at every level of biological organization. On the other hand, the currently prevailing cosmological model, the Big Bang theory, provides an account for the origin of our universe and its ongoing development to our present day and beyond. The relatively young field of extrasolar planet research may be placed into the wider frame of these

K. Yamada (✉)
Faculty of Political Science and Economics, School of Political Science and Economics, Waseda University, 1-6-1 Nishi-Waseda, Shinjuku-ku, 169-8050, Tokyo, Japan
e-mail: k-yamada@aoni.waseda.jp

S. Inaba
Faculty of International Research and Education, School of International Liberal Studies, Waseda University, 1-6-1 Nishi-Waseda, Shinjuku-ku, 169-8050, Tokyo, Japan
e-mail: satoshi.inaba@waseda.jp

© Springer International Publishing AG 2017
A.J. Schuster (eds.), *Understanding Information*, Advanced Information and Knowledge Processing, DOI 10.1007/978-3-319-59090-5_2

theories. Extrasolar planets are planets outside of our solar system. Since they were first discovered in 1995, the number of discovered extrasolar planets has been increasing every year reaching more than 3200 in 2016. One of the biggest challenges in extrasolar planet research is that these planets often can only be discovered indirectly. Over the years, various indirect methods to detect signals of extrasolar planets were developed, including a transit method adopted by space satellites such as COROT and Kepler. This does not mean that taking direct images of extrasolar planets is impossible. For instance, direct images of extrasolar planets were taken in situations when they were located far from a host star.

It should be clear without saying that taking images, direct or indirect, from objects that exist in fast distances from our solar system, poses enormous challenges for data and information processing. Nevertheless, the effort put into attacking these challenges, eventually, may be outweighed by various insights and contributions to the general understanding about the world we all live in. For instance, discovered extrasolar planets indicate that planets are common around main sequence stars in the universe. In addition, finding a variety of planetary systems different from our solar system challenges various aspects of traditional planet formation theory that was established to explain the formation of the solar system. This chapter is going to describe these and other findings, and the challenges they pose in some detail. Overall, the chapter aims to provide a reader with a state of the art understanding about the theory and the environment in which extrasolar planet research takes place.

In order to generate this understanding, Sect. 2.2 begins with a gentle introduction to the field of extrasolar planet observation. The section also describes various fundamental data processing approaches for detecting extrasolar planets. Section 2.3 details some of the characteristics of extrasolar planets. The section also reports on various international projects, collaborations, and organizations that are necessary to carry out extrasolar planet research. Section 2.4 provides an introduction to the theory of planet formation. Like any modern discipline, extrasolar planet research involves data processing at various levels. Section 2.5 comments on some of the data acquisition, data management, and data analysis processes behind extrasolar planet research. Section 2.6 ends the chapter with a summary.

2.2 Observation of Extrasolar Planets

In 1968, just 1 year before the first human step on the Moon by Neil Armstrong (Hansen 2012), Van de Kamp (1969a,b) announced the discovery of a planet with 17 Jupiter masses around the so-called Bernard's star. The Bernard's star is a red dwarf star and was recognized by its large proper motion of 10 arcsec per year. Although a number of astronomers tried to confirm this discovery, further supportive results could not be obtained (Gatewood and Eichhorn 1973). Because of this lack of further evidence, it was suggested that the discovery was induced by a setup error during telescope calibration. Ever since this false announcement, astronomers observed planets outside of the solar system much more deliberately.

Gordon Walker carefully studied 21 solar type stars for 12 years and failed to discover even a single planet around any of these stars. He concluded that it would be difficult to discover a planet outside of the solar system and that planets might be rare in the universe (Walker et al. 1995).

Right after Gordon Walker published his paper in February 1995, Mayor and Queloz (1995) announced the discovery of the first extrasolar planet in November 1995. The first discovered extrasolar planet is a gas giant planet with a Jupiter mass and rotates around a main sequence star, 51 Pegasi, in 4 days. Compared to Jupiter's rotation period of 12 years, the newly discovered gas giant planet has a much shorter rotation period. Using the rotation period along with Kepler's 3rd law, the distance between the gas giant planet and 51 Pagasi was estimated to be 0.05 AU (AU is the mean distance between the Sun and the Earth), which is about one hundredth of the distance between Jupiter and the Sun.

Most astronomers were surprised by the close location of the newly discovered gas giant planet to 51 Pegasi, because astronomers including Gordon Walker looked for a gas giant planet in more distant regions from a host star. This is because theoretical models for the formation of planets (Hayashi et al. 1985) successfully explained core masses of gas giant planets in the solar system and predicted that gas giant planets would be formed in a distant region. There, water is frozen into ice, which contributes to form a core of a gas giant planet. Thus, theoretical astrophysicists were challenged to modify their theoretical model of planet formation in order to solve the puzzle of a giant extrasolar planet near a host star.

The discovery of the first extrasolar planet inspired astronomers around the world to develop methods for discovering such planets (e.g., Marcy and Butler 1998). Extrasolar planets were discovered by applying four different methods (Beuzit et al. 2007; Irwin 2008; Rice 2014):

(i) Radial velocity survey.
(ii) Transit search.
(iii) Gravitational microlensing.
(iv) Direct detection.

With the exception of direct detection method, all other methods are indirect methods to detect extrasolar planets through variations of a host star.

Figure 2.1 illustrates the impact these methods have by showing that the discovery of extrasolar planets gradually increases with time. The figure also shows that about 3200 extrasolar planets were discovered so far. Please note that the recent, sudden increase in this number is due to discoveries by the two space missions, COROT and Kepler (Fischer et al. 2014). We now describe, briefly, each of the four methods just mentioned.

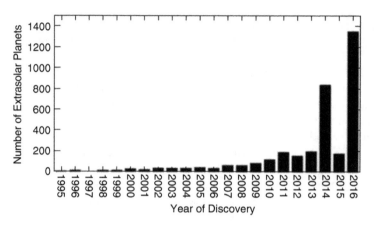

Fig. 2.1 Number of discovered extrasolar planets as a function of year of discovery

2.2.1 Radial Velocity Survey Detection

Radial velocity survey is a method employed to discover the first extrasolar planet around 51 Pegasi and uses the Doppler effect of light emitted by a host star. In a system composed of a star and a planet, both rotate around their center of masses. The wavelength of light from a star becomes shorter and longer when a star moves toward and away from observers on the Earth. An extrasolar planet is discovered by detecting repeated variation of wavelength due to the Doppler effect (Lovis and Fischer 2010). The orbital period of a star is obtained from the period of the repeated pattern of the wavelength changes of a star's light. The orbital period of a star is also written as

$$T = 2\pi \sqrt{\frac{a^3}{G(M_* + M_p)}}, \qquad (2.1)$$

where M_* and M_p are the masses of a star and a planet, respectively, and a is the semi-major axis of a planet. Since a star is much heavier than a planet, Eq. (2.1) is approximately reduced to

$$T \simeq 2\pi \sqrt{\frac{a^3}{GM_*}}. \qquad (2.2)$$

Considering that the mass of a star is estimated by examining the location of a star on the H-R diagram (Clayton 1984), the semi-major axis of a planet is calculated by Eq. (2.2).

The velocity of a star toward and away from an observer on the Earth is obtained from the variation of wavelength of light due to the Doppler effect. We begin with a simple model, in which a star rotates around the center of masses in a circular

Fig. 2.2 Schematic illustration of the relationship between the orbital plane and the line of sight of an observer on the Earth. The x-axis corresponds to the orbital plane of a planet

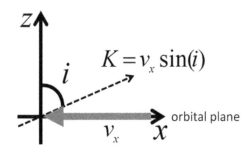

orbit and an observer on the Earth is on the orbital plane of a star and a planet. The velocity toward an observer on the Earth corresponds to the projection of the orbital velocity of a star on the line of sight. The circular orbital velocity of a star around the center of masses can be expressed as

$$v_* = \frac{2\pi r_c}{T} \simeq \frac{M_p}{M_*}\sqrt{\frac{GM_*}{a}}, \qquad (2.3)$$

where r_c is the distance between a star and the center of masses. A massive planet near a host star induces the higher velocity of a star toward an observer and is easily detected by this method.

In general, it is rare that an observer on the Earth is located on an orbital plane of a star. Figure 2.2 shows a general configuration of a star and a planet, in which the line of sight of an observer on the Earth forms an angle of i with the orbital plane of a star and a planet. The orbital velocity of a star projected on the line of sight is calculated by multiplying the orbital velocity of a star with $\sin(i)$ and given by

$$K \simeq -\frac{M_p \sin(i)}{M_*}\sqrt{\frac{GM_*}{a}}\sin(\Omega t), \qquad (2.4)$$

where Ω is the angular velocity of a star. The projected orbital velocity is measured by the radial velocity survey and helps to determine the mass of a planet, M_p, with the uncertainty of $\sin(i)$.

The first discovery of an extrasolar planet faced a number of criticisms because the radial velocity survey is an indirect method (Hearnshaw 2014). It was claimed that the pulsation of a star is also able to generate the Doppler effect of light from the surface of a star (Gray 1997; Gray and Hatzes 1997). The second indirect method, transit search, was applied to confirm the discoveries of extrasolar planets.

2.2.2 Transit Search Detection

When a planet passes on the line of sight toward a star from an observer on the Earth, the brightness of the star decreases because a dark (cool) planet covers a part of the

Fig. 2.3 Schematic
illustration of a transit of a
planet as well as the
brightness of a star as a
function of time. The depth of
the dip in the brightness of a
star is denoted by δ. A large
planet forms a deep dip of the
brightness of a star

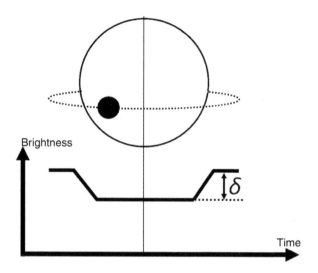

surface of the star during a transit (see Fig. 2.3). For instance, we observe a transit
of the Moon, the solar eclipse, from the Earth when the Moon passes in front of the
Sun and blocks the light from the Sun. The decrease in the brightness is dependent
on the relative size of a planet with respect to that of a host star. The rotation period
of a planet around a star is obtained from periodically repeated transit events and is
confirmed to agree with that obtained by the radial velocity survey.

The transit search is a useful method for determining the radius of a planet.
Brown et al. (2001) measured the decreased brightness of a star, HD209458, with
the Hubble space telescope, and found that the brightness of the star drops by 1.5%.
The radius of the extrasolar planet was estimated to be 1.35 times the radius of
Jupiter. An observer on the Earth needs to be on the orbital plane of a star and a
planet to observe transits of a planet, implying that the inclination of a planet is
nearly 90°. The mass of the extrasolar planet is well determined to be 0.69 times the
Jupiter mass because the uncertainty of planet mass in the radial velocity survey is
removed. The calculated low density of the planet becomes $0.37 \, \mathrm{g/cm^3}$, indicating
that the planet is a gas giant planet mainly composed of hydrogen and helium. More
than 1000 extrasolar planets were discovered with the transit search method (Berta-
Thompson et al. 2015; Sing et al. 2016).

2.2.3 Gravitational Microlensing Detection

The third indirect method for detecting extrasolar planets is the gravitational
microlensing method (Beaulieu et al. 2006). Albert Einstein presented the general
theory of relativity in 1916 and suggested the deflection of light under the
gravitational field (Einstein 1916). When a massive source of gravity (e.g., a galaxy)

is located between an observer on the Earth and a distant galaxy, the light from the distant galaxy is bent by the gravitational field of the massive source of gravity. The massive source of gravity is called a gravitational lens and changes the trajectory of the light. Light from a distant galaxy is bent to form an image of a ring when a massive source of gravity is on the line connecting an observer and a distant galaxy (Zeilik and Gregory 1997). A formed ring is called an Einstein ring (Taylor 2000).

Bending of light from a distant object is caused not only by a galaxy but also by a star. When light emitted by a star passes near the Sun, it is bent by the gravitational field of the Sun. Light from a distant star is weakly bent under the gravitational field of a lens star located between a distant star and an observer. Bent light does not form an Einstein ring, instead increases the brightness of the distant star. A planet acts as a lens even though the lens effect of a planet is much smaller than that of a host star. The brightness of a distant star reaches the local maximum value twice when a star with a planet passes through the line connecting a distant star and an observer (Fischer et al. 2014).

2.2.4   Direct Detection

Finally, the direct detection method (e.g., Marois et al. 2010) is used to detect extrasolar planets. It would be great if we could detect light from an extrasolar planet by this method. The direct images of extrasolar planets confirm the existence of extrasolar planets completely and reveal a lot of information about the planets. However, it is very difficult to separate the light of a dark planet from that of a bright star. A planet far from a host star is the best candidate for the direct method. The Subaru telescope in Hawaii succeeded to detect the direct light from two extrasolar planets rotating around GJ758 (Thalmann et al. 2009). The two planets with 10 and 12 Jupiter masses are located at 29 and 18 AU, respectively (Thalmann et al. 2009; Janson et al. 2011).

2.3   Characteristic of Extrasolar Planets

Statistics of extrasolar planets becomes available as the number of extrasolar planets increases. This enables us to find diversity and similarity among extrasolar planets. The Extrasolar Planets Encyclopedia[1] is a useful database of extrasolar planets discovered by radial velocity survey, transit search, gravitational microlensing, and direct detection. We use the database and present figures to illustrate the relationship between different properties of extrasolar planets. It is important to note that a small

---

[1]Extrasolar Planets Encyclopedia. http://exoplanet.eu/. Accessed: 2016-06-28.

planet and a planet with a long rotation period cannot be discovered by the present methods and are not included in the data. The perturbation induced by a small planet on a host star is too small to be detected by an observer on the Earth. On the other hand, in the case of a long rotation period, it takes too long to observe a single rotation of a planet around a host star when the planet is located far away from a host star.

We could approximate the probability that a main sequence star has gas giant planets after we discovered a number of extrasolar planets around stars. Marcy et al. (2005) found that $1.2 \pm 0.3\%$ of stars have a gas giant planet near the star (<0.1 AU), while 6.6% of stars have giant planets within 5 AU. In the CORALIE planet search program, Udry and Santos (2007) also calculated that 0.8 and 5.6% of stars have a gas giant planet within 0.1 and 5 AU, respectively. Both results agree well with each other.

The masses of extrasolar planets are shown in Fig. 2.4 as a function of orbital period of the planets. Extrasolar planets discovered by the radial velocity survey are shown by squares. A small number of squares are found at the lower right corner of this figure. A less massive extrasolar planet and a distant extrasolar planet from a host star induce small radial velocity amplitude of a host star as shown by the solid lines. The radial velocity method is improved every year and decreases the lowest radial velocity amplitude detected by the method. Squares are filling up the lower right corner of the figure. At present the smallest radial velocity amplitude of a star due to an accompanying extrasolar planet reaches 0.2 m/s (Lovis and Fischer 2010).

Extrasolar planets discovered by the transit search method are denoted by circles in Fig. 2.4. The transit search method prefers to detect an extrasolar planet near a host star and has difficulty to discover a planet with a rotation period longer than

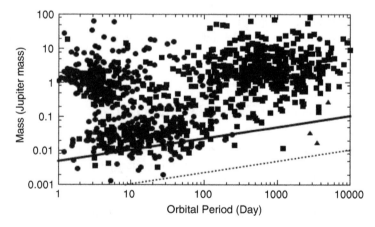

Fig. 2.4 Masses of extrasolar planets as a function of the orbital period. *Squares, circles,* and *triangles* correspond to extrasolar planets detected by radial velocity survey, transit search, and gravitational microlensing, respectively. The *dotted* and *solid lines* are added to show radial velocity amplitudes of $K = 0.1$ and 1 m/s when a star has the solar mass

100 days as shown in the figure. A dark spot formed by the shadow of an extrasolar planet on a host star becomes large when the planet is located close to the star. The transit search method has the advantage to detect a small extrasolar planet, because it measures the total flux of light from a host star, while the radial velocity survey measures the light as a function of wavelength. Space satellites such as COROT and Kepler adopted the transit search to discover extrasolar planets and succeeded to find small planets with even Earth size.

The distribution of planets with the Jupiter mass becomes bimodal having peaks at orbital periods of 3 and 1000 days. A Jupiter-mass planet with a short period is called a 'hot Jupiter' because the surface temperature of the planet is expected to be high. A gap between two peaks is found in Fig. 2.4 and is called a period valley in the distribution (e.g., Jones et al. 2003, or Wittenmyer et al. 2010; Udry et al. 2003). On the other hand, planets with several tens of Earth masses are uniformly distributed and a gap is not clearly visible in this distribution. The distribution of planets are strongly associated with processes of planet formation. In the next section, we will explain a process how a planet moves during the formation. Note that some planets belong to the same host star, forming a planetary system.

All the planets in the solar system except Mercury have small eccentricities (eccentricity is a measure of how an orbit deviates from a circular orbit) and rotate around the Sun in nearly circular orbits. Mercury has the largest eccentricity of $e \simeq 0.2$. In Fig. 2.5, the eccentricity distribution of extrasolar planets is plotted as a function of their semi-major axis. Eccentricities of extrasolar planets are shown to be different from those of the planets in the solar system. Some extrasolar planets have very large eccentricities and are called eccentric planets. Ford and Rasio (2008) proposed that two-body gravitational interactions between extrasolar planets should be responsible for the large eccentricity of an extrasolar planet. The orbit of an extrasolar planet is circularized by tidal force of a host star in 1 Gyr (Cumming 2010) when the planet is located close to the star.

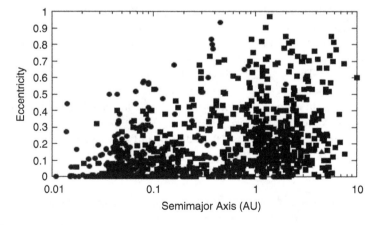

Fig. 2.5 Eccentricities of extrasolar planets as a function of the semi-major axis

The majority of discovered extrasolar planets are gas giant planets because they are easy to be detected due to the large masses and the large radii. The development of technology lowers the minimum size of discovered extrasolar planets, which reaches nearly the Earth size. A planet with the Earth size is too small to keep a heavy envelope, instead it has a small amount of atmosphere on the surface of a solid core. The surface temperature of a planet is mainly determined by the distance from a host star, even though it is also dependent on the atmosphere. A planet close to a host star has water vapor in the atmosphere, while a planet far away from a host star has water ice on the surface. Liquid water is found on the surface of a planet located within a certain range of a distance from a host star. The ring region around a host star is called a habitable zone because liquid water is thought to be essential to support life on a planet.

Two space missions, Kepler and COROT, had a significant role in discovering a number of extrasolar planets with a transit search and revealed the properties of extrasolar planets. In fact, the Kepler mission succeeded in discovering extrasolar planets with the Earth size, one of which is a terrestrial extrasolar planet, the Kepler-452b, located in a habitable zone of a G-type star like the Sun (e.g., Ludwig et al. 2016). The Spitzer Space Telescope uses the infrared between the wavelengths of 3 and 180 μm and provided useful data on the atmospheres of a number of transiting extrasolar planets (Giovanna et al. 2007) and the components of protoplanetary disks. The Atacama Large Millimeter/submillimeter Array (ALMA), which started its operation in 2012, is the largest astronomical interferometer of radio telescopes. The high resolution and sensitivity of the ALMA made it possible to present details of planet-forming protoplanetary disks around nearby stars. Images of protoplanetary disks with gaps and rings taken by ALMA Partnership et al. (2015) suggest that unseen planets may form gaps and rings in a protoplanetary disk.

NASA has a plan to launch the Transiting Exoplanet Survey Satellite (TESS) in 2017 (Fischer et al. 2014) and examine extrasolar planets in the sky wider than that covered by the Kepler. TESS is likely to discover several hundred extrasolar planets with the Earth size, some of which are expected to be located in the habitable zone. ESA also plans to launch the CHaracterising ExOPlanet Satellite (CHEOPS)[2] in 2017 to perform ultra high precision photometry to determine the bulk density of extrasolar planets. CHEOPS will obtain the bulk density of extrasolar planets as a function of the mass and find a critical mass to start a runaway gas accretion of a gas giant planet. The Thirty Meter Telescope (TMT)[3] in Hawaii is an optical/infrared telescope with a large aperture of 30 m and will start observations in 2024 to obtain a direct image of an extrasolar planet with the Earth size. NASA, ESA and CSA are developing the James Webb Space Telescope (JWST)[4] with a 6.5 m primary mirror to study the atmospheres of extrasolar planets by infrared spectroscopy and discover extrasolar planets with atmospheres similar to that of the Earth.

---

[2] CHaracterising ExOPlanet Satellite (CHEOPS). http://sci.esa.int/cheops/. Accessed: 2016-06-28.
[3] Thirty Meter Telescope (TMT). http://tmt.mtk.nao.ac.jp/intro-e.html. Accessed: 2016-06-28.
[4] James Webb Space Telescope (JWST). http://jwst.nasa.gov/index.html. Accessed: 2016-06-28.

2.4 Planet Formation

In the early days of the development of a planet formation theory, the solar system was the only planetary system we could observe. With the exception of the solar system, this lack of evidence made it difficult to probe many aspects of planet formation theory. The discoveries of a number of extrasolar planets reveal similarity and diversity among extrasolar planets. Gas giant planets in the solar system are located far from the star, while some extrasolar planets are found to be close to host stars. We were requested, therefore, to rethink and modify our theory in order for the theory to adequately describe the characteristics of extrasolar planets. This section reviews the canonical planet formation theory.

2.4.1 *Formation of a Protoplanetary Disk*

The temperature of interstellar gas near a massive star such as an O or B star is so high that the gas loses electrons and becomes ionic. An ion and electrons combine to form a molecule when the temperature decreases with the increasing distance from a massive star. A number of molecules are bound by gravity and form a molecular cloud in the interstellar space. The number density of molecules in a molecular cloud is estimated in the range between 10 and 1000 molecules per cubic centimeters. The total mass of a molecular cloud is massive enough to form a number of stars (e.g., Krugel 2002).

Perturbations exerted on a molecular cloud (e.g., interactions with a shock wave generated by a supernova explosion, or collisions with another molecular cloud) might trigger the formation of a star. Some regions in a molecular cloud are expanded by perturbations, while compression of other regions increases pressure and gravity. The compressed region becomes dynamically unstable and contracts when the gravity is larger than the pressure. A star is eventually formed if the gravity is always larger than the pressure during the contraction (Jeans 1902).

Spin motion of a molecular cloud prohibits contraction toward a single point. The centrifugal force acting on a falling gas molecule prevents it from sinking toward the center. The angular velocity of a gas molecule increases during the fall toward the center, leading to the increase in the centrifugal force. Gas molecules accumulate away from the center of a star and form a thin disk, which is called a protoplanetary disk because a planet is considered to be formed in the disk. The Hubble space telescope succeeded to take direct images of protoplanetary disks with radius of a few hundreds AU in 1990s.[5] A protoplanetary disk has a thickness of approximately one tenth of the radius. The mass of a protoplanetary disk is estimated in the range between $10^{-3}M_*$ and $0.1M_*$ where M_* is the mass of a host star.

---

[5]The best of the Hubble space telescope. http://archive.seds.org/hst/OriEODsk.html. Accessed: 2016-06-29.

The Spitzer Space Telescope provides prolific information about the composition of a protoplanetary disk using infrared spectroscopy. Many absorption lines are clearly identified in the spectral distribution, indicating the signature of CO_2, CO, silicate, and water ice (Dunham et al. 2014). Refractory compounds can be found in a hot region of an inner disk near a star (Pontoppidan et al. 2014). The temperature decreases with the increasing distance from a star. Water ice is included as one of the solid components in an outer region of a disk and enhances the surface density of solid. The boundary between an inner region without water ice and an outer region with water ice is called snow line (Hayashi 1981) and plays an important role to examine the formation of gas giant planets.

2.4.2 Formation of Protoplanet

A molecular cloud mainly consists of gas such as hydrogen molecules and helium atoms and contains small amounts of solid particles with the average size of a micrometer. Solid particles occupy only 1% of the total mass of a molecular cloud (e.g., Draine et al. 2007), but are essential components to form planets because terrestrial planets and cores of gas giant planets are made of solid particles. It is crucial to study the growth process of small solid particles in a protoplanetary disk.

Solid particles do not grow significantly during the formation of a protoplanetary disk and are distributed uniformly in a disk. It is sufficient to take into account the gravity of a star due to low disk mass when we consider the motion of a solid particle in a disk. The horizontal component of the gravitational force acting on a solid particle is balanced with the centrifugal force, while the vertical component of the gravity leads to the sedimentation of a solid particle toward the mid-plane of a disk. The gas drag acts on a solid particle and suppresses the falling speed. The falling speed reaches the terminal velocity when the vertical component of the gravity counterbalances with the gas drag of a disk. The terminal velocity is dependent on the size of a solid particle and increases with the increasing size of a particle. A large solid particle catches up a number of small particles and captures them to grow larger. A solid particle grows in size from a few micrometers to a few millimeters during the sedimentation. It is expected to form a thin layer composed of a number of millimeter sized solid particles (Armitage 2013).

A mixture of gas and solid particles rotates around a star at the mid-plane of a disk. A solid particle tends to rotate around a star with a circular Keplerian velocity by balancing the gravity of a star with the centrifugal force. The gas pressure of an inner region of a disk is higher than that of an outer region. The gas rotates around a star with a slightly slower velocity than a solid particle because an additional force due to the pressure gradient acts on the gas. A solid particle feels the drag force from the gas and loses the angular momentum, migrating toward a star. The migration time is much shorter than the typical life time of a disk, 10 million years. A meter sized solid particle migrates toward a protostar in 1000 years (Adachi et al.

1976). This suggests that a growing solid particle might be lost if it cannot grow quickly to a kilometer sized planetesimal.

The density of solid particles in the mid-plane increases by adding solid particles from an upper disk. A thin layer with the enhanced density of solid particles becomes unstable with respect to perturbation. The gravity attracts and collects solid particles in a small region, while both the pressure and the tidal force repel solid particles from the region. A region in a thin layer becomes unstable and contracts when the gravity is larger than the sum of the pressure and the tidal force (Goldreich and Ward 1973). Solid particles in each small region collapse to form a single object called a planetesimal with mass of 10^{18}g at 1 AU through the gravitational instability (Armitage 2013).

The process of the formation of planetesimals seems to be reliable except for the following obstruction that needs to be overcome. A thin layer rich in solid particles is required to be 500 times as thin as a gas disk for the gravitational instability to set in. It was pointed out that the formation of a thin layer with solid particles induces the Kelvin-Helmholtz instability at the upper boundary of the layer (Cuzzietal et al. 1993). A thin layer with solid particles is difficult to be formed because the Kelvin-Helmholtz instability prevents solid particles from falling toward the mid-plane of the disk. Alternative processes to confine solid particles in small regions have been proposed (Inaba and Barge 2006; Johansen et al. 2007).

Planetesimals interact with each other gravitationally and perturb their orbits. A planetesimal might collide with another planetesimal when their orbits cross. At the early stage of the growth, a single planetesimal grows much more rapidly than other planetesimals and becomes dominant in its proximity (Inaba et al. 2001). Once a protoplanet captures all the planetesimals within a feeding zone of 10 Hill radius within which its gravity dominates, it cannot grow further and reaches the isolation mass. The isolation masses are calculated to be Mars mass and several Earth masses at 1 and 5 AU, respectively (Kokubo and Ida 2000). Computer simulations showed that a protoplanet is formed on the order of 10^5 years at 1 AU (Inaba et al. 2001). A protoplanet can gain more mass when it is located beyond the snow line because water ice is also available to form a protoplanet. A protoplanet gravitationally interacts with neighbor protoplanets and collides with each other in the region of the terrestrial planets. It took 100 million years to form the Earth and the Venus by mergers of protoplanets (e.g., Chambers 2010).

2.4.3 Formation of Gas Giant Planets

Gas drag acts on a protoplanet, but the large inertia of a protoplanet prevents it from migrating toward a star in a short timescale. Instead gravitational interactions between a protoplanet and a protoplanetary disk become significant. A protoplanet excites spiral density waves with high density in a protoplanetary disk (Goldreich and Tremaine 1979). Figure 2.6 shows a snapshot of the surface density of a

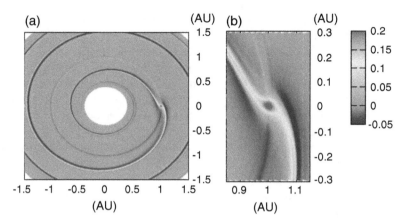

Fig. 2.6 Surface density of a protoplanetary disk when a protoplanet with 3 Earth-masses is located at $x = 1$ AU (the *horizontal axis*) and $y = 0$ AU (the *vertical axis*) and completes 30 rotations around a host star. A protoplanet excites spiral density waves in an inner and outer regions of the disk with respect to the orbit of the protoplanet. The background surface density of the protoplanetary disk is subtracted to show the structure in detail. The *left panel* (**a**) shows an entire disk with a planet. The enlarged region in the vicinity of a planet is illustrated in the *right panel* (**b**)

protoplanetary disk when a protoplanet with 3 Earth masses rotates around a star with a solar mass in a disk. An outer spiral density wave pulls a protoplanet in the opposite direction to the motion of the protoplanet and works to reduce the orbital velocity, while an inner spiral density pulls the protoplanet to accelerate. The net gravitational torque exerted on a protoplanet by the density waves becomes negative, leading to the inward migration of a protoplanet toward a star. The migration process of a protoplanet known as the Type I migration (Ward 1986) is one of the most difficult problems to be solved because a protoplanet migrates inward toward a star in $\sim 10^5$ years much shorter than the lifetime of a protoplanetary disk. Later it was suggested that the gas nearly in the same orbit with the protoplanet exerts positive torque on the protoplanet and leads to even the outward migration of the protoplanet (Paardekooper and Mellema 2006). The direction of motion of a protoplanet depends strongly on thermal structure of a disk. Yamada and Inaba (2012) proposed a protoplanetary disk, in which a protoplanet does not move and remains in the orbit. There would be various migration paths of a planet in a protoplanetary disk. It was suggested that MRI turbulence or plenty of small solid particles in a disk might play an important role in determining the migration of a planet.

A terrestrial planet is composed of a solid core and a small amount of gas as an atmosphere, and is considered to be formed by coalescences of protoplanets. On the other hand, a gas giant planet has a substantial gaseous envelope as well as a small solid core, and requires an additional process to obtain the massive gas (mainly composed of hydrogen and helium) as its envelope (Guillot 1999). The Moon cannot keep the gas as the atmosphere because the escape velocity from the surface of the Moon is 1 km/s and nearly equal to the sound velocity of the gas of a

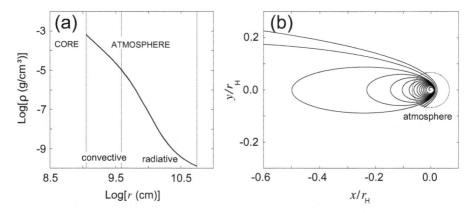

Fig. 2.7 (**a**) The density of the atmosphere as a function of distance from the center of a protoplanet when the core mass, the growth rate of the core ($\dot{M}$), and the grain depletion factor (f) are set to be $1M_\oplus$, 1×10^{-7} $M_\oplus$/year, and 0.01, respectively. The number of grains is expected to decrease compared with that in a molecular cloud due to the formation of planetesimals and protoplanets. The grain depletion factor indicates the ratio of the number of available grains to the initial number of grains in a molecular cloud. (**b**) Trajectories of three planetesimals with different orbits. A planetesimal is shown to be captured in an atmosphere of a protoplanet when it passes through the dense region of the atmosphere by losing the energy and the angular momentum. The radius of an entering planetesimal is 100 m

protoplanetary at 1 AU. Once a protoplanet grows more massive than the Moon, it keeps gas molecules as the atmosphere. Figure 2.7a shows the density distribution of an atmosphere when a protoplanet with an Earth mass is located at 5.2 AU from a star. The density of the atmosphere exponentially decreases outward and approaches that of a protoplanetary disk surrounding the protoplanet.

The atmosphere plays an important role in determining the growth of the protoplanet. A planetesimal enters the atmosphere before it is captured by the protoplanet. An incoming planetesimal supplies solid particles and volatile gas molecules by ablation while it falls toward the solid surface of the protoplanet. A planetesimal does not have to collide directly with the core of the protoplanet to be captured by the protoplanet. The trajectories of three planetesimals entering the atmosphere of the protoplanet are shown in Fig. 2.7b. A planetesimal cannot be captured when it enters far away from the center of the protoplanet even though the planetesimal loses the mass by ablation in the atmosphere. A planetesimal would be captured by the protoplanet when it passes through a dense region of the atmosphere and loses the energy and the angular momentum. Inaba and Ikoma (2003) showed that a planetesimal capture cross section of a protoplanet is significantly enhanced when a protoplanet has an atmosphere.

Inaba et al. (2003) included the enhanced capture cross section of a protoplanet by an atmosphere and calculated the growth of protoplanets located in the outer region of a disk. They showed that a protoplanet with a solid core of about 10 Earth masses is formed at the orbit of Jupiter, 5 AU, by capturing planetesimals near the orbit of the protoplanet within the lifetime of a protoplanetary disk. The mass of an atmosphere increases with an increase in the solid core mass of a protoplanet and becomes nearly equal to the mass of a solid core when the core mass reaches 10 Earth masses. The atmosphere fails to increase the pressure to maintain the stable structure against the gravity of the solid core and collapses toward the solid core (Ikoma et al. 2000). A huge amount of gas starts to flow into the atmosphere from the surrounding gas disk to form a massive envelope around a solid core. This process is called runaway gas accretion and responsible for the formation of a massive envelope of a gas giant planet. Eventually, the flow of gas into an envelope is ceased either by global disk dispersal or by formation of a local gap around a protoplanet.

During the formation, a gas giant planet scatters the surrounding gas disk by the strong gravity and opens a gap near its orbit (Lin and Papaloizou 2011). A gas giant planet is locked inside the gap and cannot move out of the gap. The gas in a disk flows inward toward a star as a whole by transferring the angular momentum outward. A gas giant planet gradually moves inward along with the gas of the disk. This inward migration of a gas giant planet is called the Type II migration (Armitage 2013) and makes it possible for a gas giant planet formed beyond the snow line to approach a host star. The timescale of the Type II migration is on the order of the disk viscous timescale and $\sim 10^5$ years (Lubow and Ida 2010) and seems a favorable mechanism to explain the formation of a hot Jupiter.

2.5 Data Processing for Extrasolar Planet Research

We already mentioned in this text that the number of discovered extrasolar planets increases rapidly over time (see Fig. 2.1). It is critical, therefore, to deal appropriately with the extensive data obtained from a constantly increasing number of observations. This section describes various issues related to data and information processing in extrasolar planet research. These issues include the various types of data (e.g., time variation of the luminosity of a star with an extrasolar planet) that are collected from observations with telescopes on the Earth and in space, or the issue that the generated data is assembled and saved in various formats in a number of databases operated in public or in private. It is important to understand that it is crucial to manage and analyze these data properly in order to extract and develop realistic characteristics and models of extrasolar planets.

2.5.1 Data Acquisition

As soon as the first extrasolar planet around the star 51 Peg was announced to be discovered using the spectrometer build at the Observatoire de Haute Provence (OHP), the Lick Observatory in the USA confirmed the discovery. Discoveries of extrasolar planets were independently validated by several research groups such as the European Southern Observatory (ESO), Keck Observatory, Lick Observatory, or the National Astronomical Observatory of Japan (NAOJ) (Perryman 2011). From the point of data integration, it is necessary here to note that each research group had developed special instruments to detect signals of smaller extrasolar planets.

For instance, the ESO built a high-resolution stabilized échelle spectrometer called the High Accuracy Radial velocity Planet Searcher (HARPS) and attached it to the ESO 3.6-m telescope in La Silla. The HARPS uses the iodine cells with simultaneous Th-Ar calibration and achieves a high accuracy to determine a radial velocity of a star in about 1 m/s (Bozza et al. 2016). The NAOJ constructed the Subaru High Dispersion Spectrograph (HDS) and installed it on the 8.2-m optical-infrared telescope in Hawaii. The HDS is a visible-light spectrograph dividing incoming light into 100,000 different colors and is capable to provide a high spectral resolution. The NAOJ and collaborators further developed the Multi-color Simultaneous Camera for studying the Atmospheres of Transiting exoplanets (MuSCAT) and set it up on the Okayama Astrophysical Observatory 188 cm-telescope. The MuSCAT is able to take three color images in blue, red, and near infrared simultaneously within 0.1% photometric precision in 30 s exposure for stars brighter than 10 mag (Narita et al. 2015).

Two space telescopes, the COROT and the Kepler, have also contributed to the discoveries of extrasolar planets with the transit method. Space telescopes have great advantages to discover extrasolar planets because ground based observations are required to remove or minimize distortions of data due to the Earth's atmosphere. The two space telescopes discovered thousands of extrasolar planets in a wide range of sizes. The COROT possesses a 27-cm diameter afocal telescope with a 4-CCD wide-field camera,[6] while the Kepler equipped with a 95-cm diameter telescope is able to continuously and simultaneously monitor the brightnesses of a large number of stars in the sky.[7]

2.5.2 Data Management

Databases are a dynamic and flexible type of data repository that plays an important role when it comes to the managing and analyzing data of extrasolar planets. Their flexibility and ability to scale up in situations where large amounts of data are generated continuously, are particular useful in extrasolar planets research where the number of discovered planets increases continuously over time. This chapter has already demonstrated some of the benefits databases can provide. For instance, the data for various figures in this text (e.g., in Sects. 2.2 and 2.3) has been retrieved

---

[6]Convection, Rotation and planetary Transits (COROT). http://sci.esa.int/corot/. Accessed: 2016-09-01.

[7]NASA Kepler mission. http://kepler.nasa.gov/Mission/. Accessed: 2016-09-05.

from on-line databases. Clearly, the convenient way to access and to visualize the
data greatly supports the process of interpreting and understanding extrasolar planet
data. Various databases are available at present to retrieve the data (e.g., the mass of
a discovered extrasolar planet) of extrasolar planets.[8] Some of the databases that are
well-known in the extrasolar planet research community include those mentioned in
the remainder of this section.

The Extrasolar Planets Encyclopaedia established in 1995 by the Paris observatory group includes a comprehensive list of extrasolar planets, along with their host
stars in CSV format. The data is constantly updated since 2011 by carefully examining published papers, preprints, and professional web sites such as Anglo-Australian
Planet Search,[9] Kepler candidates,[10] SuperWASP,[11] or Southern Sky extrasolar
Planet search Programme[12] (Schneider et al. 2011). Physical characteristics such
as mass, radius, orbital period, semi-major axis, eccentricity, and inclination of
extrasolar planets are provided as well as the year of discovery and the detection
method. The Exoplanet Data Explorer[13] maintained by Professor Jason T. Wright
at Penn State University is another valuable database and includes the data of
extrasolar planets from peer-reviewed literatures. The Exoplanet Transit Database[14]
is maintained by a project of the Variable Star and Exoplanet Section of the
Czech Astronomical Society since 2008 and includes a list of discovered transiting
exoplanets. The database uses on-line reports of transit observations (TRESCA
project[15]). Photometric curves of stars with extrasolar planets are given for everyone
to confirm the discoveries of extrasolar planets. The database also includes the data
from published scientific papers as well as observations of periodical dimming under
the established rule (Poddaný et al. 2010).

2.5.3   Data Analysis

Computer programs (software) that can process observed data are an important
and essential tool for discovering extrasolar planets. Various computer programs
are proposed to determine orbital parameters of extrasolar planets. The Sys-

---

[8]exoplanets.org. http://exoplanets.org/. Accessed: 2016-08-31.

[9]Anglo-Australian Planet Search. http://newt.phys.unsw.edu.au/~cgt/planet/AAPS_Home.html.
Accessed: 2016-08-31.

[10]Released Kepler Planetary Candidates. https://archive.stsci.edu/kepler/planet_candidates.html.
Accessed: 2016-09-03.

[11]SuperWASP. http://www.superwasp.org. Accessed: 2016-09-03.

[12]Southern Sky extrasolar Planet search Programme. http://obswww.unige.ch/~udry/planet/coralie.
html. Accessed: 2016-08-31.

[13]exoplanets.org: Documentation and methodology. http://exoplanets.org/methodology.html.
Accessed: 2016-09-02.

[14]Exoplanet Transit Database. http://var2.astro.cz/ETD/index.php. Accessed: 2016-09-04.

[15]TRESCA project. http://var2.astro.cz/EN/tresca/. Accessed: 2016-08-31.

temic software, developed by researchers at the University of California at Santa Cruz (Meschiari et al. 2009), is an example of software that is highly appreciated and extremely useful in the field. The software uses radial velocity data to restrict orbital parameters and mass of an extrasolar planet with the reduced chi-square statistic in the narrower range. Removing the contribution of the discovered extrasolar planet from the radial velocity data has the advantage that it might be possible with this software to discover a second extrasolar planet from a residual radial velocity data set.

We mentioned earlier that space telescopes discovered several thousands of extrasolar planets with the transit method. A light curve model is fundamental to determine orbital elements and size of a transiting extrasolar planet. It is difficult to estimate the size of a transiting planet precisely because a central part of a star is brighter than the edge of the star due to the limb darkening. A number of valuable computer programs have been developed considering the limb darkening effect. The PyTransit: Fast and Easy Exoplanet Transit Modeling in Python implements the quadratic limb darkening model and provides a simple light curve in a short computing time (Parviainen 2015). The Transit Analytical Curve maker (TAC-maker) is able to take into account arbitrary limb darkening profiles (Kjurkchieva et al. 2013) and to find a light curve that agrees with that given by observations. There are several other contributions worth mentioning in this section and elsewhere. Because of the limited space that is available in this chapter, we would like to encourage the reader to follow some of the links mentioned in this text. As a result, the reader will recognize that data acquisition, management and analysis are important ongoing activities in the wider, dynamic and exciting adventure of extrasolar planet research.

2.6 Summary

This chapter provided an introduction to the exciting field of extrasolar planet research. The chapter highlights many of the challenges the field holds for (intelligent and sophisticated) data and information management. Obviously, a significant part of these challenges rests in the simple fact that the objects of interest, the extrasolar planets, exist in vast distances away from our Earth. Section 2.2 in this chapter indicated that extrasolar planet researchers addressed this challenge in various ways, for instance, by developing a diversity of (direct and indirect) observation methods. Our chapter also provided information about the larger context of extrasolar planet research. Section 2.3, for example, informed the reader about the more subtle features and characteristics of extrasolar planets, while the aim in Sect. 2.4 was to satisfy the curiosity of those readers with an interest in the processes behind planet formation. In Sect. 2.5, we returned to the issue of data and information management from a more general point of view. The section clearly demonstrated that practitioners in the field of extrasolar planet research have long realized that the field can benefit greatly from a coordinated and organized approach to data and information management. Overall, perhaps, the roots of our chapter on extrasolar planets lead back to those fundamental questions many researchers in the field (and beyond) may carry in their minds: who are we, why are we here in the first place, or where are we going to since everything started in this mysterious event in space and time called the Big Bang? We hope that our chapter contributed to these questions in some way.

Acknowledgements This work was partially supported by JSPS KAKENHI Grant Number 25800250.

References

Adachi I, Hayashi C, Nakazawa K (1976) The gas drag effect on the elliptical motion of a solid body in the primordial solar nebula. Prog Theor Phys 56(6):1756–1771

ALMA Partnership, Brogan CL, Pérez LM, Hunter TR, Dent WRF (80 additional authors not shown) (2015) The 2014 ALMA long baseline campaign: first results from high angular resolution observations toward the HL Tau region. Astrophys J Lett 808(1):L3

Armitage PJ (2013) Astrophysics of planet formation. Cambridge University Press, Cambridge

Beaulieu JP, Bennett DP, Fouque P, Williams A, Dominik M (68 additional authors not shown) (2006) Discovery of a cool planet of 5.5 Earth masses through gravitational microlensing. Nature 439(7075):437–440

Berta-Thompson ZK, Irwin J, Charbonneau D, Newton ER, Dittmann JA (16 additional authors not shown) (2015) A rocky planet transiting a nearby low-mass star. Nature 527(7577):2

Beuzit JL, Mouillet D, Oppenheimer BR, Monnier JD (2007) Direct detection of exoplanets. Protostars and planets V. University of Arizona Press, Tucson

Bozza V, Mancini L, Sozzetti A (2016) Methods of detecting exoplanets: 1st advanced school on exoplanetary science, 1st edn. Springer, Cham

Brown TM, Charbonneau D, Gilliland RL, Noyes RW, Burrows A (2001) Hubble space telescope time-series photometry of the transiting planet of HD 2094581. Astrophys J 522(2):699–709

Chambers J (2010) Terrestrial planet formation. Exoplanets. University of Arizona Press, Tucson

Clayton DD (1984) Principles of stellar evolution and nucleosynthesis. University of Chicago Press, Chicago

Cumming A (2010) Statistical distribution of exoplanets. Exoplanets. University of Arizona Press, Tucson

Cuzzi JN, Dobrovolskis AR, Champney JM (1993) Particle-gas dynamics in the midplane of a protoplanetary nebula. Icarus 106(1):102–134

Draine BT, Dale DA, Bendo GJ, Gordon KD, Smith JD (15 additional authors not shown) (2007) Dust masses, PAH abundances, and starlight intensities in the SINGS galaxy sample. Astrophys J 663(2):866–894

Dunham MM, Stutz AM, Allen LE, Evans NJ, Fischer WJ, Megeath ST, Myers PC, Offner SSR, Poteet CA, Tobin JJ, Vorobyov EI (2014) The evolution of protostars: insights from ten years of infrared surveys with Spitzer and Herschel. Protostars and planets VI. University of Arizona Press, Tucson

Einstein A (1916) Die Grundlage der Allgemeinen Relativitätstheorie. Annalen der Physik 49(1):769–822

Fischer DA, Howard AW, Laughlin GP, Macintosh B, Mahadevan S, Sahlmann J, Yee JC (2014) Exoplanet detection techniques. Protostars and planets VI. University of Arizona Press, Tucson

Ford EB, Rasio FA (2008) Origins of eccentric extrasolar planets: testing the planet-planet scattering model. Astrophys J 686(1):621–636

Gatewood G, Eichhorn H (1973) An unsuccessful search for a planetary companion of Barnard's star BD +4 3561. Astron J 78:769–776

Giovanna T, Vidal-Madjar A, Liang MC, Beaulieu JP, Yung Y (8 additional authors not shown) (2007) Water vapour in the atmosphere of a transiting extrasolar planet. Nature 448(7150):169–171

Goldreich P, Tremaine S (1979) The excitation of density waves at the Lindblad and corotation resonances by an external potential. Astrophys J 233(3):857–871

Goldreich P, Ward WR (1973) The formation of planetesimals. Astrophys J 183:1051–1062

Gray DF (1997) Absence of a planetary signature in the spectra of the star 51 Pegasi. Nature 385(6619):795–796

Gray DF, Hatzes AP (1997) Non-radial oscillation in the solar-temperature star 51 Pegasi. Astrophys J 490(1):412–424

Guillot T (1999) A comparison of the interiors of Jupiter and Saturn. Planet Space Sci 47(10–11):1183–1200

Hansen JR (2012) First man: the life of Neil A. Armstrong, Reissue edition. Simon & Schuster, New York

Hayashi C (1981) Structure of the solar nebula, growth and decay of magnetic fields and effects of magnetic and turbulent viscosities on the nebula. Prog Theor Phys Suppl 70:35–53

Hayashi C, Nakazawa K, Nakagawa Y (1985) Formation of the solar system. Protostars and planets II. University of Arizona Press, Tucson

Hearnshaw JB (2014) The analysis of starlight: two centuries of astronomical spectroscopy, 2nd edn. Cambridge University Press, New York

Ikoma M, Nakazawa K, Emori H (2000) Formation of giant planets: dependencies on core accretion rate and grain opacity. Astrophys J 537(2):1013–1025

Inaba S, Barge P (2006) Dusty vortices in protoplanetary disks. Astrophys J 649(1):415–427

Inaba S, Ikoma M (2003) Enhanced collisional growth of a protoplanet that has an atmosphere. Astron Astrophys 410(2):711–723

Inaba S, Tanaka H, Nakazawa K, Wetherill GW, Kokubo E (2001) High-accuracy statistical simulation of planetary accretion: II comparison with N-body simulation. Icarus 149(1):235–250

Inaba S, Wetherill GW, Ikoma M (2003) Formation of gas giant planets: core accretion models with fragmentation and planetary envelope. Icarus 166(1):46–62

Irwin PGJ (2008) Detection methods and properties of known exoplanets. In: Mason JW (ed) Exoplanets: detection, formation, properties, habitability. Springer praxis books series. Springer, Berlin, pp 1–20

Janson M, Carson JC, Thalmann C, McElwain MW, Goto M (46 additional authors not shown) (2011) Near-infrared multi-band photometry of the substellar companion GJ 758 B. Astrophys J 728(2):85

Jeans JH (1902) The stability of a spherical nebula. Philos Trans R Soc Lond. Ser A Contain Pap Math Phys Character 199(312–320):1–53

Johansen A, Oishi JS, Mac Low MM, Klahr H, Henning T, Youdin A (2007) Rapid planetesimal formation in turbulent circumstellar disks. Nature 448(7157):1022–1025

Jones HRA, Butler PR, Tinney CG, Marcy GW, Penny AJ, McCarthy C, Carter BD (2003) An exoplanet in orbit around τ^1 Gruis. Mon Not R Astron Soc 341(3):948–952

Kjurkchieva D, Dimitrov D, Vladev A, Yotov V (2013) New approach for modelling of transiting exoplanets for arbitrary limb-darkening law. Mon Not R Astron Soc 431(4):3642–3653

Kokubo E, Ida S (2000) Formation of protoplanets from planetesimals in the solar nebula. Icarus 143(1):15–27

Krügel E (2002) The physics of interstellar dust. CRC Press, Hoboken

Lin DNC, Papaloizou JCB (2011) On the tidal interaction between protoplanets and the primordial solar nebula. II – self-consistent nonlinear interaction. Astrophys J 307:395–409

Lovis C, Fischer DA (2010) Radial velocity techniques for exoplanets. Exoplanets. University of Arizona Press, Tucson

Lubow SH, Ida S (2010) Planet migration. Exoplanets. University of Arizona Press, Tucson

Ludwig W, Eggl S, Neubauer D, Leitner JJ, Firneis MG, Hitzenberger R (2016) Effective stellar flux calculations for limits of life-supporting zones of exoplanets. Mon Not R Astron Soc 458(4):3752–3759

Marcy GW, Butler PR (1998) Detection of extrasolar giant planets. Annu Rev Astron Astrophys 36(1):57–97

Marcy GW, Butler PR, Fischer D, Vogt S, Wright JT, Tinney CG, Jones HRA (2005) Observed properties of exoplanets: masses, orbits, and metallicities. Prog Theor Phys Suppl 158:24–42

Marois C, Zuckerman B, Konopacky QM, Macintosh B, Barman T (2010) Images of a fourth planet orbiting HR 8799. Nature 468(7327):1080–1083

Mayor M, Queloz D (1995) A Jupiter-mass companion to a solar-type star. Nature 378(6555):355–359

Meschiari S, Wolf AS, Rivera E, Laughlin G, Vogt S, Butler P (2009) Systemic: a testbed for characterizing the detection of extrasolar planets. I. The systemic console package. Publ Astron Soc Pac 121(883):1016–1027

Narita N, Fukui A, Kusakabe N, Onitsuka M, Ryu T, Yanagisawa K, Izumiura H, Tamura M, Yamamuro T (2015) MuSCAT: a multicolor simultaneous camera for studying atmospheres of transiting exoplanets. J Astron Telesc Instrum Syst 1:4

Paardekooper SJ, Mellema G (2006) Halting Type I planet migration in non-isothermal disks. Astron Astrophys 459(1):L17–L20

Parviainen H (2015) PYTRANSIT: fast and easy exoplanet transit modelling in PYTHON. Mon Not R Astron Soc 450(3):3233–3238

Perryman M (2011) The exoplanet handbook. Cambridge University Press, Cambridge

Poddaný S, Brát L, Pejcha O (2010) Exoplanet transit database. Reduction and processing of the photometric data of exoplanet transits. New Astron 15(3):297–301

Pontoppidan KM, Salyk C, Bergin EA, Brittain S, Marty B, Mousis O, Öberg KI (2014) Volatiles in protoplanetary disks. Protostars and planets VI. University of Arizona Press, Tuscon

Rice K (2014) The detection and characterization of extrasolar planets. Challenges 5:296–323

Schneider J, Dedieu C, Le Sidaner P, Savalle R, Zolotukhin I (2011) Defining and cataloging exoplanets: the exoplanet.eu database. Astron Astrophy 532:A79

Sing DK, Fortney JJ, Nikolov N, Wakeford HR, Kataria T (16 additional authors not shown) (2016) A Continuum from clear to cloudy hot-Jupiter exoplanets without primordial water depletion. Nature 529(7584):59–62

Taylor EF (2000) Exploring black holes introduction to general relativity. Benjamin Cummings, San Francisco

Thalmann C, Carson J, Janson M, Goto M, McElwain M (15 additional authors not shown) (2009) Discovery of the coldest imaged companion of a Sun-like star. Astrophys J 707(2):L123–L127

Udry S, Santos NC (2007) Statistical properties of exoplanets. Annu Rev Astron Astrophys 45(1):397–439

Udry S, Mayor M, Santos NC (2003) Statistical properties of exoplanets. I. The period distribution: constraints for the migration scenario. Astron Astrophys 407:369–376

Van de Kamp P (1969a) Alternate dynamical analysis of Barnard's star. Astron J 74(8):757–759

Van de Kamp P (1969b) Parallax, proper motion, acceleration, and orbital motion of Barnard's Star. Astron J 74(2):238–240

Walker GAH, Walker AR, Irwin AW, Larson AM, Yang SLS, Richardson DC (1995) A search for Jupiter-mass companions to nearby stars. Icarus 116(2):359–375

Ward WR (1986) Density waves in the solar nebula: differential Lindblad torque. Icarus 67(1):164–180

Wittenmyer RA, O'Toole SJ, Jones HRA, Tinney CG, Butler PR, Carter BD, Bailey J (2010) The frequency of low-mass exoplanets. II. The period valley. Astrophys J 722(2):1854–1863

Yamada K, Inaba S (2012) Type I migration in optically thick accretion discs. Mon Not R Astron Soc 424(4):2746

Zeilik M, Gregory SA (1997) Introductory astronomy and astrophysics, 4th edn. Brooks Cole, Boston

Chapter 3
Information in Quantum Theory

Andrew Whitaker

Abstract This chapter outlines the 'engineering' and 'scientific' approaches to the study of information in classical physics, and the fairly minor changes that came with the arrival of quantum theory in the early twentieth century. The main advances came from the mid-1990s when quantum information theory developed enormously, with important work, theoretical and experimental, carried out in quantum computation, quantum cryptography and quantum teleportation. The concept of information as the fundamental building-block of the Universe also became important, and also the idea that the Universe was a quantum computer.

3.1 Introduction

In the fields of science and engineering outside quantum theory, the concept of information appears in two rather different guises, which may even seem to be competitors for the 'true' meaning of the concept (Smith 2000).

What may be called the 'engineering' point of view insists that the meaning of information lies in 'information theory' (Shannon 1948), which is structured in terms of an information system including a coder, transmitter, propagator, receiver and decoder. The system is designed by and for the use of humans. While such systems are constructed for the transmission of information, similarly computers are designed and constructed for its manipulation, and they too are very easily visualised in this 'engineering' point of view.

The other point of view, which may be termed very broadly 'scientific', relinquishes the human-made superstructure and relies on the study and analysis of the system itself. We may consider both human and scientific systems. As a human example, a study of an electoral system showing that 90% of men support one political party, and 90% of women support another one, clearly provides much more valuable information to the parties than if 50% of each gender support each party. Similarly if a chamber is divided by a partition into two regions, each

A. Whitaker (✉)
School of Mathematics and Physics, Queen's University Belfast, University Road,
BT7 1NN, Belfast, Northern Ireland, UK
e-mail: a.whitaker@qub.ac.uk

© Springer International Publishing AG 2017
A.J. Schuster (eds.), *Understanding Information*, Advanced Information
and Knowledge Processing, DOI 10.1007/978-3-319-59090-5_3

containing different gases, useful information is available, which is lost when the partition is removed and the gases mix. It is clear that in this case the decrease in information is directly related to the increase of entropy given by the second law of thermodynamics.

Biologists similarly make use of the concept of information. Developmental biology shows how information in the genome is translated into adult structure, while evolutionary biology explains how the information came to be present at all – as Maynard Smith (2000, p. 123) says – 'Where an engineer sees design, a biologist sees natural selection'.

Our two points of view are in no real sense contradictory. Indeed the idea that computers are necessarily designed by human beings was challenged by the view of quite a few physicists, including Edward Fredkin and Tom Toffoli, in the 1970s, that the Universe was in fact a giant digital computer – a classical or non-quantum computer (Vedral 2010; Whitaker 2012).

Such, as we have said, was the state of affairs before quantum theory or outside its regime. Both points of view have developed considerably with quantum theory, but the 'scientific' viewpoint has developed in a particularly striking way. Under classical theory, information was discussed in a sense parasitically on an underlying and fundamental reality of atoms with definite positions and velocities at all times. In quantum theory this underlying reality is dissolved, and the opportunity is available for quantum information to be heralded as the new ultimate physical reality (Mermin 2002). These topics will be discussed in the remainder of this chapter.

3.2   Quantum Information Theory

With the development of computation in the 1940s and 1950s, it was not immediately obvious that a specific quantum branch was required or even possible for computation, or even for information theory itself. The work of Alan Turing (Hodges 1992) in particular had established a substantial bank of theory and at least the beginnings of practical experience in computation, and it was generally taken for granted that the basic formalism was purely mathematical in nature. While it was recognised that the information itself was represented by physical marks on paper or electronic signals, and computation could be carried out by an adding machine, a computer or firing of neurons in our brains, this was not recognised as significant, so whether the underlying reality was classical or quantum was irrelevant.

It was Rolf Landauer (1991) who was mainly responsible for re-thinking this view. From the 1960s his mantra was 'Information is physical'. He stressed that information was inevitably tied to a particular physical representation: a spin up or down, a hole in a punched card, or many other examples. It did not exist as an abstract entity but only through physical embodiment, and so it is inevitably constrained by laws of physics.

3.3 Quantum Computation

Although Richard Feynman (Feynman et al. 1996; Hey 1999; Whitaker 2012) anticipated many of the concepts of quantum computation in the years before 1995, it was David Deutsch (1985) who recognised the fundamental point, analogous to or even based on Landauer's ideas. Computation, he stressed, is a physical rather than a mathematical process. Thus quantum computation requires a theoretical basis, distinct from that for (what must now be characterised as) classical computation which had been provided by Turing. Deutsch (1997) also pointed out that even to say that classical and quantum computation are just different systems misses the fundamental point. Just as the Universe is actually quantum mechanical, so classical physics is always an approximation to the 'true' theory, though often, of course, an extremely good one, so quantum computation is the 'true' theory of computation, classical computation being just an approximation, again often a very good one.

David Mermin (2007), though, does point out that the term 'quantum computer' may usefully only be used for very special systems in which, in particular and with enormous difficulty, the effect of *decoherence*, the process which transforms quantum superpositions to classical mixtures, is minimised. Decoherence may be caused by virtually any interaction of the computing system with the external environment, or even with other computationally irrelevant aspects of the physical system itself, or by even extremely small exposure to thermal energy.

The fundamental difference between classical and quantum computation theory is that, while in the classical case, the basic unit of information is the *bit*, which takes one of the value 0 or 1, in the quantum case the much more general basic unit is the *qubit*, which is a superposition of the states $|0\rangle$ and $|1\rangle$ and may be written as $c_0|0\rangle + c_1|1\rangle$, where c_0 and c_1 may take any values provided the state is normalised. In general, of course, they will be complex.

For a more complicated system, we may collect a number of qubits in a *register*. For example if we have 4 qubits, there will be 2^4 possible combined values in a register, a typical one being $|1001\rangle$.

At first sight it may appear that this presents enormous advantages for the quantum computer over its classical cousin. For by taking a linear combination or superposition of our 16 combined values, it seems that we should be able to perform essentially 16 calculations simultaneously. Classically we would need to perform 16 distinct calculations, each involving a register containing a single combined value.

Deutsch called this advantage *quantum parallelism*, because it seems that many calculations are being carried out in parallel. It may be noted that, in the study of the foundational aspects of quantum theory, Deutsch is the best-known advocate of the so-called *many worlds* or *many Universes* interpretation of quantum theory, in which, following a measurement, each possible result is obtained in a different world or Universe. It is natural for him to claim that the parallelism of quantum computation results from the fact that each computation is effectively performed in a different world.

However for the moment we must remark that the apparent advantage of parallelism disappears on second sight (although fortunately there will be a third sight). Although, as stated above, many calculations may, at least in a sense, be performed concurrently, and thus many different results may be calculated, as soon as we take any actual measurement of the result, in typical quantum fashion the system collapses down to a single value. (In many worlds terms, though each result may be obtained in a different world, we only have access to the result in our own world.) Thus it is not at all clear that quantum computation actually has any advantage at all over classical computation.

Deutsch was, in fact, able to suggest minor ways in quantum computation could be useful, and later workers were able to go very much further, so we will here explain very briefly a few of the basic ideas. As well as qubit and the register, the most important components of the quantum computer are the logic gates, which are assembled into quantum networks. Quantum computation requires several single-qubit gates but also one double-qubit gate.

The first two of the single-qubit gates needed are the $\pi/8$ gate and the phase gate, both of which change the relative phase of $|0\rangle$ and $|1\rangle$. The $\pi/8$ gate performs the operation:

$$|0\rangle \rightarrow |0\rangle; \qquad |1\rangle \rightarrow \{(1+i)/\sqrt{2}\}|1\rangle,$$

while the phase gate does the following:

$$|0\rangle \rightarrow |0\rangle; \qquad |1\rangle \rightarrow i|1\rangle.$$

The third single-qubit gate is called the Hademard gate and performs the operation:

$$|0\rangle \rightarrow (1/\sqrt{2})\{|0\rangle + |1\rangle\}; \qquad |1\rangle \rightarrow (1/\sqrt{2})\{|0\rangle - |1\rangle\}.$$

It can be seen that this introduces superposition into the computation, essential, of course in any quantum analysis.

The double-qubit gate is the *CNOT* or controlled-*NOT* gate. We can see below that the second qubit swaps between $|0\rangle$ and $|1\rangle$ if, but only if, the first qubit, which is the control qubit, is in state $|1\rangle$. The control qubit itself is unchanged:

$$|00\rangle \rightarrow |00\rangle; \quad |01\rangle \rightarrow |01\rangle; \quad |10\rangle \rightarrow |11\rangle; \quad |11\rangle \rightarrow |10\rangle.$$

In quantum computation the task of the *CNOT* gate is to cause entanglement, also essential in any quantum task. Let us assume, for example, that initially the first qubit is in state $(1/\sqrt{2})\{|0\rangle + |1\rangle\}$, and the second is in state $|0\rangle$. The fact that we are able to express the state of each qubit individually shows that the state of the system is unentangled.

However if we apply the *CNOT* gate to the state we obtain the state $(1/\sqrt{2})\{|00\rangle + |11\rangle\}$, and this is entangled since we cannot express the state of each qubit individually.

In this paper, because practical developments in quantum computation occur so rapidly, we shall discuss them hardly at all, beyond noting that very many implementations have been considered, including trapped ions, nuclear magnetic resonance (NMR), superconductors, cavity quantum electrodynamics with atoms, optical photons, polymers, superconductors, quantum dots and Josephson junctions.

However one centrally important point is that construction of the *CNOT* gate is a crucial task because, with two qubits involved, the difficulties of avoiding decoherence are enormous. It was the ingenious method proposed by Juan Cirac and Peter Zoller (1995) to achieve this for the ion trap implementation of quantum computing in 1995, together with the various algorithms invented at about the same time, to be discussed shortly, that led to renewed confidence that quantum computation might be both possible and useful.

We now turn to the possible applications of quantum computation, and the first was included in the original paper of Deutsch – the so-called Deutsch algorithm, though strangely this may have had the effect of convincing those interested that quantum computation might *not* be worth pursuing from the practical point of view.

The algorithm tackled the problem where input and output may each take one of the values 0 or 1 and the computation requires a long time. We wish to know whether each value gives the same or different values of the output. Classically it would of course take two runs of the program to determine this, while the Deutsch algorithm showed how with a quantum computer a single run would suffice.

From a conceptual point of view this development was massively important because for the first time it showed how the arguments of Turing in the 1930s might be violated by a quantum computer. Yet the problem was of negligible practical interest, and this was accentuated by the fact that the procedure worked only in half the runs. In fact with Richard Jozsa, Deutsch was able to give the solution to a more complicated, though scarcely more important problem (Deutsch and Jozsa 1992), and Artur Ekert and colleagues (1998) were much later able to show how a positive results for the Deutsch algorithm might be obtained for every run.

Before then though, in fact around 1994, two dramatic advances were made in terms of important problems that were shown to be soluble by quantum computation. Together with the work of Cirac and Zoller mentioned above, these discoveries caused interest in quantum computation to increase enormously ever since.

The first, made by Peter Shor in 1994 (Shor 1994; Ekert and Jozsa 1996) related to factorization of large numbers. It is clear that if two moderately large prime numbers are to be multiplied together, the amount of work required is only moderate; if the number of digits in each number is the same and equal to n, the number of operations in fact increases only as a polynomial in n. However given a number which results from this operation, obtaining the original factors is a much lengthier calculation; the number of operations being something like $10^{n/2}$, or in other words increasing exponentially with n. Technically this is crucial because much of today's security industry depends on the difficulty of this procedure, being based on the RSA algorithm of Ronald Rivest, Adi Shamir and Len Adleman.

Shor's great discovery was of a method using quantum computation by which factorisation could be achieved in polynomial time. Speaking rather generally, a problem which might be regarded as in practice totally impregnable in classical computation, factorisation of say a 1024-bit number, might take only a few minutes using Shor's scheme.

The other crucial quantum algorithm was that of Lou Grover in 1996 (Grover 1996), which may be described as searching a telephone directory by number rather than by name. If the directory contains n telephone numbers, a normal search would take about $n/2$ steps, but Grover's algorithm requires only about $\sqrt{n}$, obviously a great saving if n is large. The algorithm has a very wide application; for example it is relevant for any quantum search engine.

As has been said, these two algorithms ushered in an age of an enormous amount of slow but steady practical development in building a quantum computer. One essential aspect of design is *quantum error correction*. As we have seen, left to their own devices, quantum computers will be ultra-sensitive to errors through decoherence. Without steps taken to avoid or compensate for this effect, the possibility of quantum computation would be hopeless.

One conceivable way of coping might seem to be to *clone* a particular quantum state, or in other words to take a number of copies of it. Following an operation it could be that a number of copies might agree with each other and would be adjudged to be correct; others might show a range of differences from these right copies and would be judged wrong. Unfortunately the most basic laws of quantum mechanics tell us that this is impossible; the *no-cloning theorem* tells us that it is impossible to find an operator that clones an arbitrary state that it receives (Dieks 1982; Wooters and Wojciech 1982).

Another difficulty with quantum error correction that does not occur in the classical case is that, as we have seen, we must never perform a measurement on any qubit that contributes directly to the final answer, because we would disturb it. The solution lies in the introduction of extra qubits, called the *ancilla*, after the Latin for maidservant. These qubits take part in the computation process, but do not contribute to the final answer, so there is no restriction on their measurement. The most important early steps in quantum error correction were taken by Shor (1995) and Andrew Steane (1996).

3.4 Quantum Cryptography

We have seen that quantum computation has the potential power to allow the RSA algorithm, which is at the heart of *public-key cryptography* and our present security arrangements, to be broken. It may then perhaps be fitting that quantum information theory also provides a novel means of restoring security. This is the so-called *quantum cryptography*.

An alternative and more meaningful name for quantum cryptography is *quantum key distribution*. This relates to the technique of *private-key cryptography* using the *one-time pad*. In this method Alice and Bob are each in possession of a 'pad' of keys. Alice uses the first key to encrypt her message, and sends it to Bob who is able to decrypt it using the same key. If Eve, the eavesdropper, is able to get hold of the message, she will not, of course, be able to decrypt it as she does not possess the key.

The method is unbreakable, but practical implementation has great difficulties. First there is the matter of length; each key must be the same length as the message being transmitted. Also each key must be used only 'one-time', as using it more than once will enable Eve to obtain some information about it, and hence about the messages themselves. Distributing the necessary amount of keys would be an enormous task, and hence the preference for *public-key cryptography*, at least until the work of Shor on factorisation.

Quantum cryptography provides a means of transmitting keys from Alice to Bob using a quantum channel rather than a physical procedure. The best-known scheme is that of Charles Bennett and Giles Brassard (1984) and is always known as BB84.

In this method, Alice has four photon polarisers available, each of which may polarise photons along a particular direction: horizontal, vertical, or one of two directions bisecting horizontal and vertical, which we may call $+45°$ and $-45°$. On the quantum channel, she sends a stream or photons to Bob, in each case choosing a polariser at random and noting her choice.

Bob detects each photon using one of two analysers chosen at random; one of them distinguishes between photons polarised in horizontal or vertical directions, and the other between photons polarised in $+45°$ and $-45°$ directions.

If Bob makes the 'right' choice of analyser, then the two have generated an element of common knowledge. However if he chooses the 'wrong' analyser, for example if Alice uses the polariser which polarises photons vertically, but Bob uses the analyser that distinguishes between $+45°$ and $-45°$ directions, he will obtain $+45°$ and $-45°$ at random, or in other words his results will be meaningless. Therefore Bob now sends Alice on a public channel a list of the analysers he used, and she replies by sending Bob a list of the occasions when polariser and analyser were compatible. This provides what may be called the *raw quantum transmission* (RQT), the basis of a shared key, but of course one must check for the work of Eve.

Let us now suppose that Eve intercepts the data being transmitted on the quantum channel, and we restrict ourselves to events which entered the RQT. We may assume she investigates each photon with an analyser just like Bob. Of course she will not know which analyser to use, but in 50% of occasions she will choose the 'right' one and her own measurement will not affect Bob's result, However in 50% of occasions she must choose the 'wrong' analyser, and it is easy to see that, while in 50% of *those* cases Bob will obtain the state as it was sent by Alice, in the other 50% he will obtain the wrong value. Note the importance of the no-cloning theorem; in the absence of this, Eve could merely clone a number of copies of the photon she receives from Alice, send one copy on to Bob, and use the others to find its original state easily enough.

So Alice and Bob must now compare a portion of the RQT. From the previous paragraph we may expect that, if Eve has intercepted the photons, roughly one in every four pieces of data will be incorrect. More sophisticated strategies for Eve are available, but, provided the channel itself is noiseless, she will always leave some trace of her actions. Noise does complicate the situation, but, even in the worst possible case, it is always possible to limit the amount of information Eve may obtain.

A different protocol was introduced by Artur Ekert (1991). In this protocol, an EPR or Einstein-Podolsky-Rosen pair of photons is used, one of each pair being sent to Alice and the other to Bob. An EPR pair has maximum *entanglement*, in other words neither photon has an independent state. The state of the EPR pair may be written as $(1/\sqrt{2})\{\chi_1(+)\chi_2(-) - \chi_1(-)\chi_2(+)\}$, where $\chi(+)$ and $\chi(-)$ are states of the individual photon, and 1 and 2 are the two photons. Each of Alice and Bob make a measurement along the x-, y- or z-axes, choice of direction being random. Then, as in the BB84 protocol, they use the public channel to discover those occasions on which their measurements were along the same direction, giving them an RQT.

Checking for the deeds of Eve is performed using the remaining measurement results. If there has been no eavesdropping, Bell's Theorem (Bell 1964; Whitaker 2016) tells us the Bell Inequalities must be violated, as the state will remain a genuine superposition. However, if Eve has been at work, her measurements will have created a measurement result and, effectively, a hidden variable. This means that the Bell Inequalities will be obeyed.

Unlike quantum computation, quantum cryptography is a thriving technique with a variety of practical implementations, some of the major advances having been made by the groups of Nicolas Gisin and Richard Hughes (Muller et al. 1986; Butler et al. 1998).

3.5 Quantum Teleportation

Quantum teleportation is the third of the most important techniques proposed in quantum information theory. In this technique the state of a single particle at one point is created at a distant point without apparently having traversed the space in between.

There are two important points about quantum teleportation arising from fundamental arguments of physics. The first is that the no-cloning theorem tells us that the original version of the particle must be destroyed in the quantum teleportation process. The second, special relativity, says that the process cannot be instantaneous, and we shall see how this requirement is obeyed.

To explain how the technique works, we need to introduce the remaining Bell states, all of which are maximally entangled. We have met one, the EPR state. The others are subtle variations on the same general theme: $(1/\sqrt{2})\{\chi_1(+)\chi_2(-) + \chi_1(-)\chi_2(+)\}$, $(1/\sqrt{2})\{\chi_1(+)\chi_2(+) - \chi_1(-)\chi_2(-)\}$, and $(1/\sqrt{2})\{\chi_1(+)\chi_2(+) + \chi_1(-)\chi_2(-)\}$.

In quantum teleportation, the particle whose state is to be teleported is called particle 1 and is sent to Alice. Particles 2 and 3 are put in to an EPR-state; particle 2 is sent to Alice and particle 3 to Bob. Then Alice makes what may be called a Bell-state measurement on particles 1 and 2. This means that she collapses the combined state of these particles to one of the Bell states, and it is easy to show that the probability of getting each of the Bell states is $^1/_4$.

Her measurement has, of course, also an effect on the state of Bob's particle, and in fact each of Alice's 4 measurement results gives rise to a different state for Bob. If Alice's result corresponds to the EPR state, Bob's particle is left in the original state of particle 1. The other 3 results for Alice are related to that same state but rotated through 180° about the x-, y- and z-axes. For Bob to possess the actual state, Alice must let him know her result over the public channel, so he can apply appropriate rotation. Use of the public channel means, of course, that special relativity is not violated.

The process was invented by Bennett and a group of many of the most famous names in quantum information theory (Bennett et al. 1993). Within a few years, groups of physicists led by Anton Zeilinger, Franceco De Martini and Jeff Kimble carried out rather different types of experiment to demonstrate the effect, while Gisin and his group have led the way in increasing the distance between Alice and Bob, work which may help to extend the scope of quantum cryptography to greater distances.

Quantum teleportation should also be especially important in quantum computation, as it should provide the standard means of moving quantum states from one point in the computer to another.

3.6   Quantum Information

In classical physics we may say that the fundamental reality consists of particles with definite positions and momenta. Information certainly has extremely important properties and uses, but it in itself cannot claim central significance; rather it is always, in a sense, parasitic on the more fundamental classical realism.

In quantum theory, of course, that is all lost. We may say that such realism itself is lost. We may talk of the Heisenberg principle, but more fundamentally the theory just seems to be about the results of measurements rather than what may exist between measurements.

It is not surprising that beginners in quantum theory often jump to the conclusion that all its problems may easily be explained by the concept of information. The general assumption may be that all the classical quantities 'exist', and the wave-function merely tells us what we know. For example, suppose that the wave-function of a system is $\varphi_1 + \varphi_1$, where φ_1 and φ_2 correspond to measurement results O_1 and O_2 respectively. The understanding may be that the physical quantity actually does possess a value at all times, say O_1, but that we do not know it. When we measure it, we find out that it is indeed O_1, and φ_1 becomes the new wave-function. Repeated measurement will, of course, give the same value, and so on.

However it is clear of course that the underlying classical type of substructure on which these ideas about information are parasitic cannot exist, and for 70 years or so after the development of quantum theory in the 1920s, the concept of information was not much in favour.

As an example, when Bell, towards the end of his life, presented his diatribe against the various terms in quantum theory that he felt were ill-defined and confusing (Bell 1990; Whitaker 2016), although 'measurement' was the main offender, he gave a blast to 'information': '*Whose* information? Information about *what*?'

Both seemed good questions! On the first, the use of 'we' in the description of the beginner's approach, may already have aroused suspicion or confusion. On the second, we may indeed add that if the information is about something, why not concentrate on the thing that the information is about rather than the information itself?

One of the answers to Bell's complaints came from the renowned physicist Rudolf Peierls (1991). Peierls remained on very good terms with Bell, though he disagreed with his complaints about the orthodox Copenhagen interpretation of quantum theory of Niels Bohr. Peierls regarded himself as an unequivocal support of Bohr, but surprisingly his reply to Bell put forward an approach seemingly very different to that of Bohr and based on information. His argument was, of course, much more sophisticated than that of the 'beginner' above. (Incidentally, in some of the arguments we discuss, the word 'knowledge' is used instead of 'information'; as others do, we regard these two words as synonymous.)

To 'Information about what?', Peierls replies – the wave-function, or more generally the density-matrix, which represent an ensemble of systems rather than a single system, represent our knowledge of the system we are trying to describe. That may sound a little vague, but at least conforms that if is knowledge of something. This in turn may seem obvious, but we shall meet a contrary suggestion soon.

To the question 'Whose information?', Peierls gives a much more complete answer. He starts by saying that, if the knowledge is complete, in other words the maximum allowed by the Heisenberg principle, we use a wave-function; for less knowledge we use a density-matrix.

An uncontrolled disturbance may reduce our knowledge. Measurement has the power to increase it, but if we start off with complete knowledge in the above sense, and gain some new knowledge by performing a measurement, some of the knowledge already there must be lost. For example, if we know the value of one component of spin and measure a second component, we must lose all knowledge of the first component.

He explains the difference between a physical process and a process in which knowledge is obtained. For example when our knowledge changes, the density-matrix must change, but this is not a physical process and so does not obey the Schrödinger equation. For a measurement the density-matrix changes when the measurement is actually performed, but it reaches its final form, which is the actual result of the experiment, only when the experimenter *knows* the result.

He says that many people may have some information about the state of the system, but the information of different people may differ, and so they may all have different density-matrices. However we must not allow a situation where one person may know, for example, the *x*-component of a certain spin, while another person knows the *y*-component, because quantum theory forbids the simultaneous knowledge of both components. Peierls suggests that the crucial criterion is that the density-matrices of two observers must commute. In other words, if the density-matrices of the two observers are A and B, then AB must equal BA.

Yet at the beginning of the 1990s, the centrality of information in quantum theory was still a minority view. As long as knowledge is 'about something', the most common view might be – we should analyse the 'something' that information is about.

But with the rise of interest in quantum information theory during the 1990s, the opinion of many changed quite dramatically. An interesting example is David Mermin (2002, p. 273). Mermin was present at Bell's lecture, and indeed found it 'close to being the most spell-binding lecture I have ever heard'. At the time he very much agreed with Bell's strictures on information/knowledge – he was 'entirely on Bell's side'. Yet he soon, in his words, 'fell into bad company'. He began 'hanging going out with the quantum information crowd', for many of whom quantum mechanics was 'self-evidently and unproblematically all about information'.

What about Bell's questions? To the first, 'Information about what?', Mermin replies that he now considers this a 'fundamentally metaphysical question that ought not to distract tough-minded physicists'. He believes that there is no way to decide whether the information is about something objective, or is just information about other information. Information itself is the fundamental quantity at the heart of the universe.

Mermin gives the second question, 'Whose information?' a lot more attention. He has studied Peierls's suggestions in detail, and with Chris Fuchs he has been able to come up with situations where these suggestions are clearly incorrect. His comment is that: 'the reasonable thing doesn't work'. However with Todd Brun and Jerry Finkelstein (Brun et al. 2002), he has presented more general though somewhat complicated arguments.

Vedral (2010) has also stressed the centrality of information in the Universe. He argues that information (and not, as he says, matter or energy or love) is the building block on which everything is constructed. He says that it must be the most fundamental, because it can be applied not only to microscopic interactions, where it can explain the behaviour of matter and energy, but also to macroscopic interactions, such as economic and social phenomena. Also it is the only concept we have that can explain its own origin. 'Our reality' he says, 'is ultimately made up of information'.

The connection of information theory via probability and entropy with thermodynamics and statistical mechanics is, of course, well-known. Also well-understood is the fundamental nature of information in biology; genetics developed using the language of preservation and transmission of information, while evolution is merely the inheritance of information with occasional changes in its basic units, the genes.

Vedral also discusses basic economic decision-making in terms of Shannon entropy, and social interaction as sharing information by various interactions such as communication, and hence the individuals becoming correlated. He suggests that the level of development of a society may be linked to its capacity to process information.

To the question – 'Where does information come from?', Vedral answers that: 'Information is created out of no information'. When two people communicate, one generates information for the other. More fundamentally one may think of the evolution of the Universe as starting with all potential realities from which one will emerge. From this initial state, which contains all future possibilities, the first event occurs without any cause, and this provides the first bit of information, from which all later mutual information develops.

In an interesting article, Časlav Brukner and Anton Zeilinger (2005) have also argued that the basic concept of quantum theory is quantum information. Thus quantum theory is only indirectly a science of reality but fundamentally a science of knowledge. They are able to develop some of the main features of quantum theory on this basis, including complementarity and entanglement, and are able to provide a derivation of the quantum evolution of a two-state system.

Both Vedral, and Brukner and Zeilinger claim that they can answer some of the deep conceptual problems raised by the great physicist John Wheeler. One of these is 'Why the quantum?', and the primacy of information tells us that, since information is necessarily quantised, quantisation of fundamental physics follows quite automatically.

Another famous saying of Wheeler is 'Law without law', meaning that it is natural to assume that physical laws can only be explained in terms of more fundamental laws, leading to an infinite regress. Vedral argues that the creation of information from emptiness implies that quantum theory itself does not need to be based on more fundamental physical laws.

Lee Smolin has advocated the use of quantum information in his savage attack on the huge amount of attention paid to string theory as a 'theory of everything'. He suggests that it may be wise to give up the attempt to apply quantum theory to the Universe as a whole, and instead to define sub-systems, and to regard quantum theory as a record of quantum information that one sub-system may have about another. In this way, rather as Vedral has argued, it may be shown how elementary particles emerged from space-time, and our scientific view of the Universe may be fundamentally changed.

3.7 The Universe as a Quantum Computer

We saw earlier that it has been suggested some decades ago that the Universe is essentially a digital computer, but these ideas were naturally expressed in terms of a classical computer. More recently, Seth Lloyd (2006) in particular has suggested that the Universe is actually a quantum computer. He suggests that the history of the Universe is just an ongoing quantum computation. As to the question 'What does it compute?', Lloyd answers: 'It computes its own behaviour'.

At first it produces very simple patterns, but as it processes more and more information, it gives rise to much more complex patterns. On the physical side, these may give rise to stars, planets and galaxies, while on the human side, they will include life, language, human beings, society and culture.

The question may be asked – 'Since the new bits injected into the Universe are random, essentially the result of decoherence, how can complexity emerge?' Lloyd likens this way of thinking to the well-known description of a large number of monkeys typing on typewriters. He remarks that if one replaces the monkeys by every elementary particle in the Universe, and the typing by these particles flipping bits ever since the beginning of the Universe, the longest section of Hamlet, or any other piece of writing, they might have produced, would not be longer than around 12 words.

However the difference between the monkeys typing on typewriters and typing into computers is, Lloyd says, massive. The computers will interpret each string of bits as a program, a set of instructions to perform a particular computation, and Lloyd stresses that there are short, seemingly random programs that tell the computer to do many interesting things. There is, for example, a short program that tells the computer to calculate the digits of π, and indeed an exceptionally short program that tells the computer to compute all possible mathematical theorems and patterns, including every pattern ever generated by the laws of physics! Thus he claims that a computer provided with a random program has a good chance of producing the range of order and complexity that we see in the Universe.

3.8 Summary

Before the coming of quantum theory, the idea of information was extremely important, both technologically in classical information theory, and in thermodynamics and statistical mechanics. Of course it was never considered that information might be the fundamental building block of the Universe.

Perhaps rather strangely, things did not change a great deal for almost a century after Planck, and 70 years after Heisenberg and Schrödinger. It was not until the great advances in quantum information theory in the mid-1990s that the possibilities of quantum computation and quantum cryptography were fully realised.

This in turn led to the intense study of information itself in quantum theory, and the idea that information might be the fundamental quantity at the heart of the Universe and its behaviour, and indeed that the Universe itself might be just a quantum computer.

References

Bell J (1964) On the Einstein-Podolsky-Rosen paradox. Physics 1(3):195–200. [Also in: Bell J (1987) Speakable and unspeakable in quantum mechanics. Cambridge University Press, Cambridge, pp 213–31]

Bell J (1990) Against "measurement". Phys World 3(8):31–40. [Also in: Bell J (1987) Speakable and unspeakable in quantum mechanics. Cambridge University Press, Cambridge, pp 14–21]

Bennett CH, Brassard G (1984) Quantum cryptography: public-key distribution and coin tossing. In: Proceedings of the 1984 IEEE International conference on computers, systems and system processing. IEEE, New York, pp 175–179. Available via http://researcher.watson.ibm.com/researcher/files/us-bennetc/BB84highest.pdf. Accessed 29 July 2016

Bennett CH, Brassard G, Crépeau C, Jozsa R, Peres A, Wootters WK (1993) Teleporting an unknown quantum state via dual classical and Einstein-Podolsky-Rosen channels. Phys Rev Lett 70(13):1895–1899

Brukner Č, Zeilinger A (2005) Quantum physics as a science of information. In: Elitzur AC, Dolev S, Kolenda N (eds) Quantum mechanics. Springer, Berlin, pp 47–61

Brun TA, Finkelstein J, Mermin DN (2002) How much state assignments can differ. Phys Rev A 65(3):032315

Buttler WT, Hughes RJ, Kwiat PG, Lamoreaux SK, Luther GG, Morgan GL, Nordholt JE, Peterson CG, Simmons CM (1998) Practical free-space quantum key distribution over 1 km. Phys Rev Lett 81(15):3823–3826

Cirac JI, Zoller P (1995) Quantum computation with cold trapped ions. Phys Rev Lett 74(20):4091–4094

Cleve R, Ekert A, Macchiavello C, Mosca M (1998) Quantum algorithms revisited. Proc R Soc A 454:339–354

Deutsch D (1985) Quantum theory, the Church-Turing principle and the universal quantum computer. Proc R Soc A 400:97–117

Deutsch D (1997) The fabric of reality. Allen Lane Science, London

Deutsch D, Jozsa R (1992) Rapid solutions of problems by quantum computation. Proc R Soc A 439:553–558

Dieks D (1982) Communication by EPR devices. Phys Lett A 92(6):271–272

Ekert AK (1991) Quantum cryptography based on Bell's theorem. Phys Rev Lett 67(6):661–663

Ekert AK, Jozsa R (1996) Quantum computation and Shor's factoring algorithm. Rev Mod Phys 68(3):733–753

Feynman RP, Hey JG, Allen RW (eds) (1996) Feynman lectures on computation. Addison-Wesley, Reading

Grover LK (1996) A fast quantum mechanical algorithm for database search. In: Proceedings of the 28th annual ACM symposium on the theory of computing (STOC). ACM, New York, pp 212–219. Available via http://arxiv.org/abs/quant-ph/9605043. Accessed 29 July 2016

Hey AJG (ed) (1999) Feynman and computation. Perseus Books, Reading

Hodges A (1992) Alan Turing: the enigma. Random House, London

Landauer RW (1991) Information is physical. Phys Today 44(5):23–29

Lloyd S (2006) Programming the universe: a quantum computer scientist takes on the cosmos. Knopf Publishing Group, New York

Mermin DN (2002) Whose knowledge? In: Bertlmann R, Zeilinger A (eds) Quantum [un]speakables: from bell to quantum information. Springer, Berlin, pp 271–280

Mermin DN (2007) Quantum computer science. Cambridge University Press, Cambridge

Muller A, Zbinden H, Gisin N (1986) Quantum cryptography over 23 km in installed under-lake Telecom wire. Europhys Lett 33(5):335–339

Peierls R (1991) In defence of "measurement". Phys World 4(1):19–20

Shannon CE (1948) A mathematical theory of communication. Bell Syst Tech J 27(3):379–423; 623–656

Shor PW (1994) Algorithms for quantum computation: discrete logarithms and factoring. In: Proceedings of the 35th annual symposium on foundations of computer science, Santa Fe. IEEE, pp 124–134

Shor PW (1995) Scheme for reducing decoherence in quantum computer memory. Phys Rev A 52(4):R2493–R2496

Smith JM (2000) The concept of information in biology. Philos Sci 67(2):177–194. [Also in: Davies P, Gregarsen NH (eds) (2010) Information and the nature of reality: from physics to metaphysics. Cambridge University Press, Cambridge]

Steane AM (1996) Error correcting codes in quantum theory. Phys Rev Lett 77(5):793–797

Vedral V (2010) Decoding reality: the universe as quantum information. Oxford University Press, Oxford

Whitaker A (2012) The new quantum age: from Bell's theorem to quantum computation and teleportation. Oxford University Press, Oxford

Whitaker A (2016) John Stewart Bell and twentieth-century physics. Oxford University Press, Oxford

Wooters W, Wojciech Z (1982) A single quantum cannot be cloned. Nature 299:802–803

Part III
The World of Living Things

Chapter 4
The Potential of Plants and Seeds in DNA-Based Information Storage

Karin Fister, Iztok Fister Jr., and Jana Murovec

Abstract New approaches for data archiving are required due to a constant increase in digital information production and lack of a capacitive, low maintenance storage medium. High-density information encoding and longevity are the two important advantages which have recently made DNA an attractive target for information storage. However, creating new copies of the same encoded information by producing new, artificial DNA sequences is not financially viable. Moreover, a naked DNA molecule can be greatly affected by environmental influences, thus resulting in DNA mutations and changes in the stored information. Our approach demonstrates the great potential of plants and seeds in circumventing these drawbacks. It shows that artificially encoded data can be stored and multiplied within plants.

4.1 Introduction

Data storage is relevant for keeping track of our history and for accomplishing tasks during our day-to-day lives. It has evolved significantly from the first written records of the ancient Sumerian's and Egyptians into our time, where it is embedded in a rapidly expanding data production environment. Stones were replaced by paper, which is being replaced progressively by electronic storage media. Compared to printed data, the latter are characterized by relatively small physical space requirements and by the ease of copying digital data. However, there are some major drawbacks with current storage technologies. The first drawback is their limited capacity. For instance, at the time of this writing, the world's highest capacity

K. Fister (✉)
Faculty of Medicine, University of Maribor, Taborska 8, 2000, Maribor, Slovenia
e-mail: karin.ljubic@student.um.si

I. Fister Jr.
Faculty of Electrical Engineering and Computer Science, University of Maribor,
Smetanova 17, 2000, Maribor, Slovenia
e-mail: iztok.fister1@um.si

J. Murovec
Biotechnical Faculty, University of Ljubljana, Jamnikarjeva 101, 1000, Ljubljana, Slovenia
e-mail: jana.murovec@bf.uni-lj.si

© Springer International Publishing AG 2017
A.J. Schuster (eds.), *Understanding Information*, Advanced Information
and Knowledge Processing, DOI 10.1007/978-3-319-59090-5_4

helium drive can only save up to 10 terabytes (TB) of data. Although the storage capacity of all data storage equipment grew from less than 3 (optimally compressed) exabytes in 1986 to several zettabytes in 2013 and is doubling roughly every 3 years, the International Data Corporation has mentioned that, even in 2007, the total amount of digital data produced on the planet exceeded the amount of available storage (Hilbert and L'opez 2011; Cisco 2016; Gant et al. 2007). The problem of data explosion can also be emphasized in the field of modern biology. Biological data are heterogeneous, they stem from a wide range of experiments. Getting the most from the data requires comparing them to the relevant prior knowledge. That means scientists have to store large data sets and analyse them. The European Bioinformatics Institute (EBI) in UK, one of the largest biology data repositories in the world, currently stores 20 petabytes of data (Marx 2013). Efforts to produce enough storage is resulting in increased production of storage devices and the building of large data centers, all of which increases environmental contamination and raises the costs of their maintenance. Another major disadvantage of electronic storage media is their short lifespan (usually in years), which depends on the frequency of access (Ajwani et al. 2008).

Due to the constant increase of digital data production and the above-mentioned concerns, new approaches for data storage are being sought. DNA has proven to be useful for archival storage, because it offers some major improvements over digital storage media such as: information density, stability when stored under optimal conditions and minuteness. The first message stored in DNA dates back to 1988 (Davis 1996). More recently, in the past 4 years, there have been two major breakthroughs in the field of DNA-based information storage (Church et al. 2012; Goldman et al. 2013). First of all, novel next-generation DNA synthesis and sequencing technologies have expanded the boundaries of previous DNA production approaches, which were able to encode and decode only trivial amounts of information (Davis 1996) and, in addition, lacked the possibility of scaling-up (Clelland et al. 1999). The second advance was achieved with the use of the Huffman code (Brand 2000; MacKay 2003; Ailenberg and Rotstein 2009) as a compression method for large scales of bytes to minor scale DNA bases. Actually, this approach has proven to be the most accurate method and could be scaled beyond the boundaries of current archiving methods (Church et al. 2012; Goldman et al. 2013; Ailenberg and Rotstein 2009). So far, sets of computer files encoded in DNA have been 739 kB (Goldman et al. 2013), 675 kB (Church et al. 2012), and 83 kB (Grass et al. 2015). Encouraged by these achievements, it has been proposed that DNA-based storage might already be economically viable for archives with no extensive access, such as historical and government records or large-scale science projects that generate massive amounts of data (Brand 2000; The Economist 2012).

The stability of DNA is highly dependent on the storage conditions, which should provide constant low temperatures, as in freezers, and protection from atmospheric water, oxygen and ozone. It has been demonstrated that, at room temperature, solid-state DNA degradation through depurination, base deamination, and base or sugar oxidation, is affected greatly by water and oxygen (Bonnet et al. 2010), thus dictating the need for special equipment or preservation procedures. The problem is even more pronounced because laboratory plastic ware is neither moisture nor airtight and storage in refrigerators is not always possible. DNA shells (Colotte et al. 2011; Clermont et al. 2014; Liu et al. 2015) have been presented recently as an alternative to DNA storage at room temperature. Although they provide an alternative approach, the technology assumes an anoxic and anhydrous atmosphere in small glass vials fitted into stainless-steel, laser-sealed mini-capsules, all of which boost storage costs. The same problem is encountered when using dry-state DNA stabilization systems, such as commercial Biomatrica DNA stable plates, trehalose and polyvinyl alcohol (PVA) plates (Ivanova and Kuzmina 2013) or inorganic silica capsules (Grass et al. 2015).

This chapter addresses several of the issues mentioned before. In its essence, the chapter describes a novel approach for DNA-based data storage that does not focus on information quantity but rather on a new storage medium that combines DNA stability and, consequently, information preservation, with low costs for its conservation and multiplication. We chose a living plant, the widely known model plant *Nicotiana benthamiana*, to be the target multi-cellular, eukaryotic organism for digital information hosting. Reasons for choosing this particular plant include the plant's short generation time, its high seed yield and its ease of growing under natural and controlled environments (Goodin et al. 2008). Further, we selected the well-known 'Hello world!' computer program (Langtangen 2006) in a high-level, universally-used programing language, in our work the Python[1] programing language, to be encoded and stored in the plant. In order to provide the reader with a detailed understanding of our work, we organized the remainder of this chapter as follows. Section 4.2 describes the process of storing digital data into plants in detail. We start by describing the coding program that was developed in order to transform the digital information into the DNA sequence. Next, we describe the synthesis of our artificial 'Code DNA' by Integrated DNA Techonolgy and the process of plant transformation by co-cultivation with *Agrobacterium tumefaciens* containing the binary plasmid. We conclude the section with a description of the screening process for detecting the presence of our Code DNA in the plant. Section 4.3 describes the results of our experiment. In Sect. 9.6 we discuss the advantages of storing data into plants and their seeds. Section 7.5 ends the chapter with a summary.

4.2   Materials and Methods

The aim in this section is to provide the reader with a detailed description of our work. The section starts with DNA basics, a description of the basic structure of DNA molecules, as well as the process of transfering information from a mother cell to its two daughter cells. Knowing these basic ideas is crucial for understanding the backbone of our experiment. Next, we describe the coding program. The coding

---

[1]Python. https://www.python.org/. Accessed: 2016-06-30.

program was developed to transform our digital data in the form of bits into the sequence of DNA nucleotides. By using the coding program we transformed a computer program into a sequence of nucleotides. We named this artificial sequence the Code DNA. The section describes the synthesis of this Code DNA in detail. We discuss, briefly, the plant material and focus on the process of plant transformation with *Agrobacterium tumefaciens* containing the binary plasmid. The end of the section focuses on the process of extraction of our Code DNA from the leaf tissue. For a start, Fig. 4.1 presents the key steps of storing data into plants and obtaining data from it.

4.2.1 DNA Basics

A DNA molecule consists of two polynucleotide chains: DNA chains or DNA strands. Each chain consists of four types of nucleotide subunits and each nucleotide is composed of a five-carbon sugar to which are attached one or more phosphate groups and a nitrogen-containing base. In DNA nucleotides, the sugar is deoxyribose attached to a single phosphate group. Therefore, the three basic parts of nucleotides are sugar, phosphate group and base. The base may be either Adenine (A), Cytosine (C), Guanine (G) or Thymine (T). Figure 4.2 presents the structure of

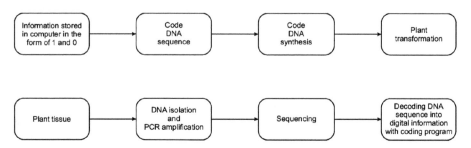

Fig. 4.1 Flow chart, illustrating the key processes involved when storing data into plants (*top*) and obtaining data from it (*bottom*)

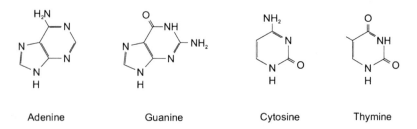

Adenine   Guanine   Cytosine   Thymine

Fig. 4.2 Elementary nitrogenous bases (adenine, guanine, cytosine, thymine) in the nucleic acid of DNA. Usually represented by the letters A–G–C–T

all four nitrogenous bases within DNA nucleotides. The backbone of the DNA chain consists of covalently linked sugars and phosphate groups in alternating fashion. The two chains are held together by hydrogen bonds between the base portion of the nucleotides. The double-helix or the three-dimensional structure of DNA arises from the chemical and structural features of its two chains. The shapes and chemical structure of the bases allow pairing with hydrogen bonds only between A and T and between C and G. This pairing is referred to as Watson-Crick base pair. Because of these base-pairing requirements each strand of the DNA molecule is exactly complementary (called Watson-Crick complementarity) to the nucleotide sequence of its partner strand. Therefore, we can predict the sequence of the second strand by knowing the sequence of the first strand. The sequence of nucleotides of one or another strand carries biological information or, in the case of our experiment, – the artificial information – that must be copied accurately for transmission to the next generation each time a cell divides. At each cell division, the double helix unfolds allowing the pairing with new, complementary bases. Each DNA strand serves as a template for its own duplication. The ability of each strand of a DNA molecule to act as a template for producing a complementary strand enables a cell to copy its genetic information before passing it on to new cells. Therefore, the artificially inserted DNA sequence is copied too, and the digital information, which this artificial sequence presents, is carried to every cell of a plant and to all of its seeds and progenies.

4.2.2   Coding Program

We developed a coding program that first translates text to binary. The whole coding program is available on-line[2] and enables coding text into DNA sequences and decoding DNA sequences into text. The maximum length of inserted characters to be encoded into DNA is limited to 300, while the maximum length of an inserted DNA sequence to be decoded back to text is 1,200 bases. Currently, the program enables coding letters from A to Z and a to z (English alphabet), numbers from 0 to 9 and special characters hashtag (#) and apostroph ('). The program offers two coding options: 'Classic' and 'Compressed1'. The Classic option, which uses 2 bits for coding a base, is as follows: 00 for A, 10 for C, 11 for T and 01 for G. This encoding scheme enables the avoidance of sequences that are: difficult to synthesize, sequences with long repeats and sequences with extreme CG content. The Compressed1 option is upgraded by using the Huffmann compression method. This method reduces the overall number of bits used to encode a string of symbols inserted in the coding window. The Huffmann compression method allows up to 60% higher compression than the Classic option. The percentage depends on the

---

[2] Plant-based data storage project. http://www.storing-data-into-living-plant.net/. Accessed: 2016-07-30.

length of the inserted text. When using the Compressed1 option, users are given a 'Key', which has to be used in order to decode the DNA sequence back to text. This Key links the user to the specific Huffmann tree that was used for compression.

4.2.3   Code DNA Synthesis and Cloning

The 'Hello world!' computer program was structured and written in the form of the syntax #begin print 'Hello world' #end. The syntax was coded using the Classic option of our coding program into the Code DNA. Primer annealing sequences were added upstream and downstream of the Code DNA for subsequent sequencing reactions. The Code DNA was synthesized by Integrated DNA Technology (IDT, Leuven, Belgium) and cloned into the MCS of a linearized plasmid vector pCAMBIA 1302-ZsGreen (Sušič et al. 2014) using a Gibson Assembly Cloning Kit following the manufacturer's instructions (New England Biolabs, Ipswich, MA, USA). The binary plasmid pCAMBIA 1302-ZsGreen-Code contained a hygromycin phosphotransferase (*hptII*) selectable marker gene and the *ZsGreen* reporter gene, both driven by the cauliflower mosaic virus 35S promoter. The binary plasmid was electroporated into ElectroMAX *Agrobacterium tumefaciens* LBA 4404 (Invitrogen).

4.2.4   Plant Material

Here we describe the preparation of plant material for transformation. Seeds of *Nicotiana benthamiana* were surface sterilized and germinated in petri dishes on solid medium containing $2\,g\,L^{-1}$ sucrose (Duchefa Biochemie B. V.) and $8\,g\,L^{-1}$ Daishin agar (Duchefa Biochemie B. V.). Plant seedlings were sub-cultivated every four weeks on fresh medium containing Murashige and Skoog macro- and micro-elements (MS; Duchefa Biochemie B. V.), $2\,mg\,L^{-1}$ thiamine HCl (Sigma), $1\,mg\,L^{-1}$ pyridoxine HCl (Sigma), $1\,mg\,L^{-1}$ nicotinic acid (Sigma), $30\,g\,L^{-1}$ sucrose and $8\,g\,L^{-1}$ Daishin agar. All media were adjusted to pH 5.8 before autoclaving and plant tissue cultures were maintained at $23 \pm 1\,°C$ and a 16-h photoperiod.

4.2.5   Plant Transformation

Containing the binary plasmid pCAMBIA 1302-ZsGreen-Code, *Agrobacterium tumefaciens* was grown overnight at $28\,°C$ by shaking in liquid YEB medium pH 7.0 and prepared for co-cultivation as described in Sušič et al. (2014). Explants were immersed in bacterial suspension for 15 m with periodic shaking. Inoculated

Plant Transformation

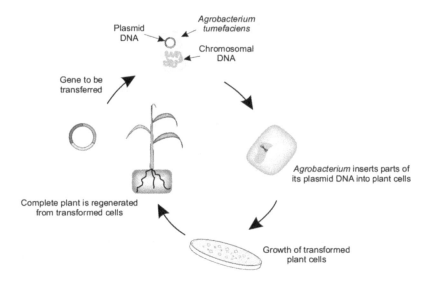

Fig. 4.3 Main steps in the plant transformation process. The starting-point in the process is the gene or synthetic DNA to be transferred. The end-product is a genetically modified plant

explants were blotted on sterile filter paper and transferred to regeneration medium composed of MS macro- and micro-elements, $0.1 \, mg \, L^{-1}$ Fe-Na2-EDTA (Sigma), $0.1 \, g \, L^{-1}$ myo-inositol (Sigma), $0.1 \, mg \, L^{-1}$ thiamine HCl, $1 \, mg \, L^{-1}$ 6-Benzylaminopurine (6-BAP) (Duchefa Biochemie B. V.), $0.1 \, mg \, L^{-1}$ α-naphtalene acetic acid (NAA) (Duchefa Biochemie B. V.), $30 \, g \, L^{-1}$ sucrose, $200 \, \mu M$ acetosyringone (AS), $8 \, g \, L^{-1}$ Daishin agar, pH 5,8. Cultures were incubated in the dark for four days and then washed in $200 \, mg \, L^{-1}$ solution of timentin (Duchefa Biochemie B. V.), blot-dried on filter paper and transferred to petri dishes containing regeneration medium without AS but supplemented with $150 \, mg \, L^{-1}$ of timentin and $10 \, mg \, L^{-1}$ hygromycine (Duchefa Biochemie B. V.). Regenerating shoots were transferred to fresh cultivation medium composed of MS macro- and micro-elements, $2 \, mg \, L^{-1}$ thiamine HCl, $1 \, mg \, L^{-1}$ pyridoxine HCl, $1 \, mg \, L^{-1}$ nicotinic acid, $30 \, g \, L^{-1}$ sucrose, $150 \, mg \, L^{-1}$ of timentin and $8 \, g \, L^{-1}$ Daishin agar, pH 5.8. Figure 4.3 illustrates the main steps of plant transformation.

4.2.6 DNA Isolation and PCR Analysis

Total genomic DNA was extracted from the leaf tissue of plants regenerated on the selective medium by a modified cetyl trimethylammonium bromide (CTAB) method. Sequences of primer pairs used in polymerase chain reactions (PCR) for screening for the presence of the Code DNA and for the presence of selectable

Table 4.1 Sequences of primers used and lengths of amplified fragments (in bp)

Primer name	Primer sequence 5'–3'	Amplified fragment length (bp)
Code-For	GCA AT GAG CGG TAG GAG TG	172
Code-Rev	ACG GTC AGC ATG TGA CAG TC	
HptII-For	ATG ACC GCT GTT ATG CGG CCA TTG	641
HptII-Rev	AAA AAG CCT GAA CTC ACC GCG ACG	
ZsGreen-For	AGA ACT CGT GTC CTG CTG GT	208
ZsGreen-Rev	ATG ATC TTC TCG CAG GAT GG	
β-actin-qPCR-For	CTG GCA TTG CAG ATC GTA TGA	75
β-actin-qPCR-Rev	GCG CCA CCA CCT TGA TCT T	
Code-qPCR-75-For	TCG CAA ATG AGC GGT AGG A	75
Code-qPCR-75-Rev	TTC ACG AGC CGG CGT ACT	

and reporter genes, together with the lengths of amplified fragments, are listed in Table 4.1. PCR reactions were performed according to Susič et al. (2014). The polymerase chain reaction is a technique used to amplify a precisely defined piece of DNA across several orders of magnitude. Therefore, this method generates thousands to millions of copies of a particular DNA sequence and makes its detection and sequencing much easier. qPCR stands for quantitative PCR and is actually a form of PCR method which allows us additionaly to determine the quantity of a target sequence in a sample. Plantlets with positive amplification results were analyzed further by real-time quantitative PCR on an ABI PRISM 7,500 Fast Sequence Detection System and 7,500 Software v2.3 (Applied Biosystems, Foster City, USA). The primers used (see Table 4.1) were designed to amplify a 75-bp section of the Code DNA and a 75-bp section of the tobacco β-actin gene (Faize et al. 2010), which was used as the internal reference gene. Each 10 µl reaction was composed of 5 µl FastStart Universal SYBR Green Master (Rox) (Roche, Basel, Switzerland), 9.5–0.15 ng of DNA and 600 nM of each primer. Amplification was performed under the following thermal cycling conditions: 95 °C 10 m, 40 cycles at 95 °C for 10 s followed by 60 °C for 30 s. Each reaction was run in triplicate (technical replications), and PCR amplification specificity was confirmed by melting-curve analysis and by agarose electrophoresis. The transgene copy number was calculated according to the method developed by Weng et al. (2004).

4.2.7 Sanger Sequencing

Plant DNA was first amplified with primer pair Code-For, Code-Rev using a standard PCR protocol as described in Susič et al. (2014). Unused primers and nucleotides were removed from PCR amplification products with ExoSap-IT and the sequencing reaction was performed separately for each primer with a BigDye®

Terminator v3.1 Cycle Sequencing Kit (Applied Biosystems), both following the manufacturer's instructions. Amplified products were separated by capillary electrophoresis using an ABI PRISM®3100 Genetic Analyzer (Applied Biosystems) and the results analyzed with CodonCode Aligner 4.0.4. The sequence obtained was decoded with the program described above.

4.3   Results

This section provides the results of our work. The main outcome, perhaps, is that inserted Code DNA was obtained successfully from the leaf of a plant.

4.3.1   Coding Program

The complete developed program, which enables coding text into DNA sequences and decoding DNA sequences into text, is available on the Internet.[2] The syntax of the 'Hello world!' program was coded using the Classic option of the program from which the Code DNA was obtained.

4.3.2   Storing Data in N. Benthamiana and Reading Data from the Plant

We obtained several *N. benthamiana* plants and seeds (see Fig. 4.4) with normal phenotypes and growth, which were PCR positive for the Code DNA, selectable marker gene and resistance gene. They were analyzed further by quantitative

Fig. 4.4 *Nicotiana benthamiana* plant, and seeds of *Nicotiana benthamiana* with incorporated Code DNA

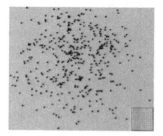

real-time PCR in order to determine the copy number of the inserted Code DNA and only transgenic plants (T0) containing one copy (i.e., hemizygous for the Code DNA) were left for self-pollination.

After germination of their seeds, the T1 progeny were analyzed for the presence of the Code DNA in their genome and a 1:3 segregation of PCR positive results was observed, thus confirming the hemizygosity of their mother plants. Transgene lines (T1) containing two copies of the Code DNA (i.e., homozygous for the Code DNA) were selected and left to self-pollinate for further storage of their seeds. Some of the seeds were germinated and the plants (T2) grew normally. The DNAs of all checked T2 plants contained the Code and was sequenced as described in 2.7 Sanger sequencing. The obtained DNA sequence was decoded, resulting in the syntax of the 'Hello world!' program showing on a display device.

4.4 Discussion

DNA-based storage of data has been proposed as an outperforming replacement for electronic storage devices, due to its durability and low space requirements (Cox 2001; Church et al. 2012; Goldman et al. 2013; Grass et al. 2015). However, since artificial DNA (Grass et al. 2015; Colotte et al. 2011; Clermont et al. 2014; Liu et al. 2015; Ivanova and Kuzmina 2013; Anchordoquy and Molina 2007) and microorganisms (Gibson et al. 2010; Farzadfard and Lu 2014; Ausländer and Fussenegger 2014) require specific pretreatments and equipment for their storage, an alternative approach, i.e., storing data in seeds, is presented here. Seeds are one of the oldest storage media on Earth and they preserve genetic information for thousands of years. Due to their stability and longevity, they are the most often used material for plant genetic resource preservation in the world's over 1,750 genebanks. They are already guardians of our natural and cultural heritage and, with the implementation of our proof-of-concept study presented in this work, their role could be even more pronounced.

Storing data in plant seeds is a simple, safe and economic solution for data storage, since seeds do not need special equipment for storage because they possess a wide range of natural mechanisms of protection and are easy to grow. Seeds have already proved their durability over thousands of years. Examples demonstrating this durability include the 1,600-year-old seeds of *Anagyris foetida*, a relict species endemic to the Mediterranean region, which were germinated successfully (Özgen et al. 2012) or the most ancient viable multicellular plants on Earth – the species *Silene stenophylla* Ledeb. (Caryophyllaceae) – which have been regenerated (Yashina et al. 2012) from approximately 31,800 years old placenta fragments. Seeds of *Nicotiana* spp. are known to preserve their germination ability for up to 10 years under ambient temperatures and/or relative humidity (Agacka et al. 2013), while long-term depositories such as Svalbard Global Seed Vault[3] can protect them even from massive natural or man-made cataclysms. Under a controlled environment with reduced temperature and relative humidity, the need for seed regeneration would be minimal. Taking into account the estimated spontaneous mutation rate for *Arabidopsis thaliana* of 7×10^{-9} base substitutions per site per generation (Ossowski et al. 2010) and the estimated *N. benthamiana* genome size of 3 Gb (Bombarely et al. 2012), there is a negligible chance of a mutation in the encoded DNA. However, by increasing the length of DNA insertions (i.e. amount of stored data) the chances of unwanted mutations also increase. Therefore, before implementation of our proof of concept, the maximum length of heterologous DNA that can be introduced into *N. benthamiana* genome and the mutation rate of such long sequences have to be determined. Data storage in seeds goes beyond plant genome manipulation for biotechnological research and plant breeding or simple embedded 'watermarks' (Liss et al. 2012). It takes advantage of multi-cellular organisms and serves for propagating the encoded information in daughter cells. The host organism is able to grow and multiply with the embedded information and every cell of the organism contains a copy of the encoded information. It avoids the costs of producing multiple copies of the same encoding information synthetically, which has been estimated to be $12,400 per MB (Goldman et al. 2013).

Insertions of short computer programs within plants could also provide a detailed description of given varieties, since a need for such labeling has already been expressed. The incorporation of such information into a plants' own DNA would particularly help consumers in terms of satisfying the ever-growing demand for food quality and origin information. It can also be used as an extremely useful tool for variety protection (Fister et al. 2017).

In relation to manipulating and storing archives, our approach could be leverage for a new look at accessing, browsing and reading information, since hand-held, single-molecule DNA sequencers are becoming available (Pennisi 2012) and upgrading them to being able to obtain an encoded sequence directly from a leaf (Ljubič and Fister 2014) could be the next step.

4.5 Summary

This chapter presented our work on the utilization of a multi-cellular, eukaryotic organism for storing valuable data. Our work describes a free copy-paste method that avoids the costs of synthetic production of multiple copies of the same encoding information, which is currently estimated to be $12,400 per MB for information

---

[3]Global crop diversity trust. https://www.croptrust.org/what-we-do/svalbard-global-seed-vault/. Accessed: 2016-07-26.

storage in naked DNA with negligible additional computational costs. In contrast to a naked DNA molecule, which can be affected by unfavorable environmental conditions, DNA stored in a seed is protected against alterations and degradation over time without the need of any active maintenance. Our approach demonstrates that artificially encoded data can be stored and multiplied in plants without affecting their vigor and fertility. It is inheritable to progeny and authentically reproducible while the reduced metabolism of seeds provides an additional protection for encoded DNA archives.

References

Agacka M, Depta A, Börner M, Doroszewska T, Hay FR, Börner A (2013) Viability of nicotiana spp. seeds stored under ambient temperature. Seed Sci Technol 41(3):474–478

Ailenberg M, Rotstein OD (2009) An improved Huffman coding method for archiving text, images, and music characters in DNA. Biotechniques 47(3):747

Ajwani D, Malinger I, Meyer U, Toledo S (2008) Characterizing the performance of flash memory storage devices and its impact on algorithm design. In: Proceedings of the 7th International conference on experimental algorithms (WEA'08), Provincetown, pp 208–219

Anchordoquy TJ, Molina MC (2007) Preservation of DNA. Cell Preserv Technol 5(4):180–188

Ausländer S, Fussenegger M (2014) Dynamic genome engineering in living cells. Science 346(6211):813–814

Bombarely A, Rosli HG, Vrebalov J, Moffett P, Mueller LA, Martin GB (2012) A draft genome sequence of Michaelicotiana benthamiana to enhance molecular plant-microbe biology research. Mol Plant-Microbe Interact 25(12):1523–1530

Bonnet J, Colotte M, Coudy D, Couallier V, Portier J, Morin B, Tuffet S (2010) Chain and conformation stability of solid-state DNA: implications for room temperature storage. Nucleic Acids Res 38(5):1531–1546

Brand S (2000) Clock of the long now: time and responsibility. Basic Books, New York

Church GM, Gao Y, Kosuri S (2012) Next-generation digital information storage in DNA. Science 337(6102):1628–1628

Cisco (2016) The zettabyte era: trends and analysis. White paper, Cisco Systems, Inc. Available via http://www.cisco.com/c/en/us/solutions/collateral/service-provider/visual-networking-index-vni/vni-hyperconnectivity-wp.html. Accessed 26 Nov 2016

Clelland CT, Risca V, Bancroft C (1999) Hiding messages in DNA microdots. Nature 399(6736):533–534

Clermont D, Santoni S, Saker S, Gomard M, Gardais E, Bizet C (2014) Assessment of DNA encapsulation, a new room-temperature DNA storage method. Biopreserv Biobanking 12(3):176–183

Colotte M, Coudy D, Tuffet S, Bonnet J (2011) Adverse effect of air exposure on the stability of DNA stored at room temperature. Biopreserv Biobanking 9(1):47–50

Cox JPL (2001) Long-term data storage in DNA. Trends Biotechnol 19(7):247–250

Davis J (1996) Microvenus. Art J 55(1):70–74

Faize M, Faize L, Burgos L (2010) Using quantitative real-time PCR to detect chimeras in transgenic tobacco and apricot and to monitor their dissociation. BMC Biotechnol 10(1):53

Farzadfard F, Lu TK (2014) Genomically encoded analog memory with precise in vivo DNA writing in living cell populations. Science 346(6211):1256272

Fister K, Fister I, Murovec J, Bohanec B (2017) DNA labelling of varieties covered by patent protection: a new solution for managing intellectual property rights in the seed industry. Transgenic Res 26(1):87–95

Gant JF, Reinsel D, Chute C, Schlichting W, McArthur J, Minton S, Xheneti I, Toncheva A, Manfrediz A (2007) The expanding digital universe. White paper, International Data Corporation. Available via https://web.archive.org/web/20130310100607/http://www.emc.com/collateral/analyst-reports/expanding-digital-idc-white-paper.pdf. Accessed 26 Nov 2016

Gibson DG, Glass JI, Lartigue C, Noskov VN, Chuang RY, Algire MA, Benders GA, Montague MG, Ma L, Moodie MM (2010) Creation of a bacterial cell controlled by a chemically synthesized genome. Science 329(5987):52–56

Goldman N, Bertone P, Chen S, Dessimoz C, LeProust EM, Sipos B, Birney E (2013) Towards practical, high-capacity, low-maintenance information storage in synthesized DNA. Nature 494(7435):77–80

Goodin MM, Zaitlin D, Naidu RA, Lommel SA (2008) Nicotiana benthamiana: its history and future as a model for plant-pathogen interactions. Mol Plant-Microbe Interact 21(8):1015–1026

Grass RN, Heckel R, Puddu M, Paunescu D, Stark WJ (2015) Robust chemical preservation of digital information on DNA in silica with error-correcting codes. Angew Chem Int Ed 54(8):2552–2555

Hilbert M, López P (2011) The world's technological capacity to store, communicate, and compute information. Science 332(6025):60–65

Ivanova NV, Kuzmina ML (2013) Protocols for dry DNA storage and shipment at room temperature. Mol Ecol Resour 13(5):890–898

Langtangen HP (2006) Python scripting for computational science, 3rd edn. Springer, Berlin

Liss M, Daubert D, Brunner K, Kliche K, Hammes U, Leiherer A, Wagner R (2012) Embedding permanent watermarks in synthetic genes. PLoS One 7(8):e42465

Liu X, Li Q, Wang X, Zhou X, He X, Liao Q, Zhu F, Cheng L, Zhang Y (2015) Evaluation of DNA/RNAshells for room temperature nucleic acids storage. Biopreserv Biobanking 13(1):49–55

Ljubič K, Fister I Jr (2014) How to store Wikipedia into a forest tree: initial idea. In: Proceedings of the first International conference on multimedia, scientific information and visualization for information systems and metrics (MSIVISM'14), pp 45–52

MacKay DJC (2003) Information theory, inference and learning algorithms. Cambridge University Press, New York

Marx V (2013) Biology: the big challenges of big data. Nature 498(7453):255–260

Ossowski S, Schneeberger K, Lucas-Lledó JI, Warthmann N, Clark RM, Shaw RG, Weigel D, Lynch M (2010) The rate and molecular spectrum of spontaneous mutations in arabidopsis thaliana. Science 327(5961):92–94

Özgen M, Özdilek A, Birsin MA, Önde S, Şahin D, Açıkgöz E, Kaya Z (2012) Analysis of ancient DNA from in vitro grown tissues of 1600-year-old seeds revealed the species as Anagyris foetida. Seed Sci Res 22(4):279–286

Pennisi E (2012) Search for pore-fection. Science 336(6081):534–537

Susič N, Bohanec B, Murovec J (2014) Agrobacterium tumefaciens-mediated transformation of bush monkey-flower (Mimulus aurantiacus Curtis) with a new reporter gene ZsGreen. Plant Cell Tissue Organ Cult 116(2):243–251

The Economist (2012) Digital archiving: history flushed. The economist. Available via http://www.economist.com/node/21553410. Accessed 26 July 2016

Weng H, Pan A, Yang L, Zhang C, Liu Z, Zhang D (2004) Estimating number of transgene copies in transgenic rapeseed by real-time PCR assay with HMG I/Y as an endogenous reference gene. Plant Mol Biol Report 22(3):289–300

Yashina S, Gubin S, Maksimovich S, Yashina A, Gakhova E, Gilichinsky D (2012) Regeneration of whole fertile plants from 30,000-year-old fruit tissue buried in Siberian permafrost. Proc Natl Acad Sci USA 109(10):4008–4013

Chapter 5
Memory Processing in the Nervous System

Naoyuki Sato

Abstract The central and peripheral nervous systems manage information processing associated with cognition and behavior and information transmission from/to sensory and effector organs, respectively. Memory, which is the process by which information is encoded, stored, and retrieved, has been extensively studied from the molecular to the whole-organ level. Memory function is managed by multiple parallel neural systems across multiple spatio-temporal scales. Recently, neuroscience data measured by various methods start to be collected to organize big data. New analyses using these data can provide a deeper understanding of information processing in the nervous system. Computational theory is expected to play a dominant role in integrating memory data with knowledge collected from other scientific domains.

5.1 Introduction

Memory refers to the ability to remember things. In biological systems, memory is managed by the central and peripheral nervous systems, which control information processing and information transmission from/to sensory and effector organs, respectively. Importantly, memory enables the production of context-dependent behavior, which provides a significant survival advantage. In humans, memory is an essential component of intelligence and personality as well as of society and culture. Although memory itself remains mysterious, memory processing can be computationally divided into several simple sub-processes, including encoding, storage, and retrieval (Hasselmo et al. 1996; Marr 1971). This property of memory processing facilitates the experimental evaluation of memory, and thus memory has been widely investigated from the molecular to whole-organ level.

N. Sato (✉)
School of Systems Information Science, Future University Hakodate, 116-2 Kamedanakano, Hakodate, 041-8655, Hokkaido, Japan
e-mail: satonao@fun.ac.jp

© Springer International Publishing AG 2017
A.J. Schuster (eds.), *Understanding Information*, Advanced Information and Knowledge Processing, DOI 10.1007/978-3-319-59090-5_5

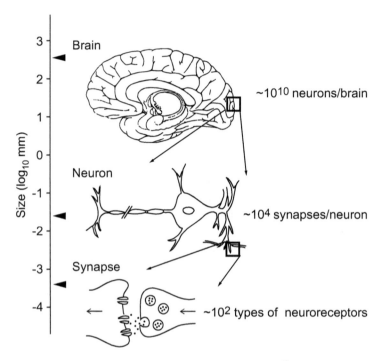

Fig. 5.1 Size of the central nervous system. The brain includes 10^{10} neurons, and each neuron receives input currents from 10^4 synapses from other neurons. Each neuron possesses different types of neuroreceptors, some of which contribute to memory processing

Information processing in the nervous system is different from that of personal computers (PCs). First, whereas PC processing is managed by a central processing unit (CPU) at $\sim 10^9$ Hz, which synchronizes all components in the PC, information processing in the nervous system is implemented in parallel by $\sim 10^{10}$ neurons at $\sim 10^3$ Hz in an asynchronous manner (Fig. 5.1).

Second, memory in the nervous system is stored mainly in $\sim 10^{14}$ connection weights between neurons called synapses, whereas series of data are stored in PCs in $\sim 10^{14}$ bits. Third, values processed by the PC are binary, whereas values processed by the nervous system are analogue. Finally, information processing in the nervous system is implemented autonomously, whereas information processing in the PC is programmed a priori. Furthermore, the nervous system autonomously determines which experiences should be stored or discarded by their own rules, a point that is hypothesized to be key for understanding memory processing. These differences between PCs and the nervous system raise several questions: (1) How is our experience stored in the nervous system? (2) How does memory influence behavior and consciousness? And (3) Is memory an exact copy of our experience or the merger of several experiences?

In this chapter, memory processing in the nervous system, mainly in humans, is reviewed. The next section summarizes the physiological mechanisms underlying memory. Section 5.3 reviews the classification of memory in a parallel-organized central nervous system. Section 5.4 describes the current status of big data in neuroscience, which may lead to qualitative changes in data analysis and computational modeling. The last section summarizes this chapter.

5.2 Physiological Basis of Memory

This section summarizes the physiological bases of memory. Neurons are the main units for information processing. Synapses play a dominant role in memory storage. For further information, see the book edited by Shepherd (2003).

5.2.1 Neuron: The Unit of Information Coding and Processing

The neuron is the major unit for information coding and processing in the nervous system. Unlike other cells, the number of neurons do not increase after birth, and the same neurons are used throughout life. One exception is neurons in the hippocampus, in which $\sim 10^6$ neurons are postnatally generated throughout life (Spalding et al. 2013). A neuron consists of the axon, cell body, and dendrites (Fig. 5.2). The dendrites receive input from the synaptic currents of other neurons.

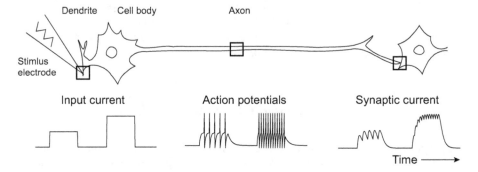

Fig. 5.2 Information transmission in a neuron. Dendrites receive input currents. Normally, this input current is generated from other neurons, but here the input current is depicted by a stimulus electrode. The cell body integrates the input and produces action potentials, the frequency of which depends on the intensity of the input. Action potentials are transmitted via axons and reach synapses on dendrites of other neurons. The action potentials induce synaptic current to the postsynaptic neuron, where the currents are shown to be temporally integrated

The cell body integrates these synaptic currents and generates an output signal. The axon transmits this output signal to other neurons. The size of the cell body is $\sim 10^{-6}$ m and the length of the axon can be as long as ~ 1 m.

Neurons can be regarded as electronic devices. At rest, a constant electrical potential (~ -65 mV) exists between the intracellular and extracellular fluid of a neuron. This electrical potential rapidly changes when the dendrites receive synaptic current input. A large enough spatial and temporal accumulation of synaptic current causes a 'firing' or 'spike' action potential, generating a rapid increase and decrease of membrane potential at the cell body over a duration of several milliseconds. Most action potentials appear as bursts rather than as a single spike. The frequency of burst firing often codes the intensity of the signal to be represented by the neuron. For example, the burst frequency of skin sensory neurons is known to increase in proportion to the intensity of skin pressure. This neural representation is called 'rate coding'.

Neurons are found on the surface of the cerebral cortex, with their axons projecting inward. The cerebral cortex has a well-organized laminar structure. The surface of the cerebral cortex is anatomically divided into several dozen cortical 'areas' that are also known to correspond with particular functions, such as vision, audition, and motor function. Neurons in each area are known to be selectively activated for a specific stimulus or events related to cognition and behavior. For example, some neurons in the primary visual cortex respond to a line segment with specific orientation at a specific location in the retinal coordinate system. This property is termed 'neural selectivity', and suggests that complicated events or behavior will be coded by a population activity of neurons with various selectivities. In population coding, different features constituting one item are represented in a distributed neural network, which raises the following question: How can the distributed features be represented as an integrated item? This question represents the 'binding problem'. One possible solution to the binding problem is neural synchronization (Gray et al. 1989), by which a group of neurons associated with features from one item is represented. This type of coding, which relies on the timing of neural firing, is termed 'temporal coding'.

5.2.2 Synapse: The Principal Component of Memory

The synapse is a structure at the contact site between the axon terminal of the presynaptic neuron and the dendrite of the postsynaptic neuron. Synapses manage information transmission from presynaptic to postsynaptic neurons. At the axon terminal, neurotransmitter, which is chemical material used in signal transmission between neurons, is stored in small vesicles. When action potentials arrive at the axon terminal, neurotransmitter is immediately released into the synaptic cleft. There are many types of neurotransmitters, and their functional roles are common across species. Importantly, each neuron uses just one kind of

(a) Non-associative potentiation

1. Baseline

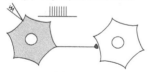

2. Strong presynaptic activation

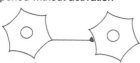

3. A period without activation

4. Long-term potentiation

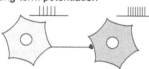

(b) Associative potentiation

1. Baseline

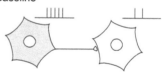

2. Simultaneous activation

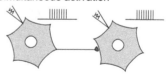

3. A period without activation

4. Long-term potentiation

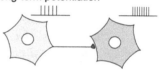

Fig. 5.3 Mechanisms of long-term potentiation. (**a**) Non-associative potentiation. After strong presynaptic activation, synaptic connectivity increases and may persist for a long period. (**b**) Associative potentiation. After strong simultaneous activation of presynaptic and postsynaptic neurons, synaptic connectivity is persistently increased. This principle is named Hebb's rule and is the basis of memory storage for spatial patterns of neural activation

neurotransmitter, which therefore fixes the role of the neuron. For example, glutamate and γ-aminobutyric acid (GABA) are used to excite and inhibit postsynaptic neurons, respectively. Various types of neuroreceptors are located at the postsynaptic site. These neuroreceptors receive the neurotransmitter, which produces synaptic currents for some types of receptors and modulates subsequent cellular responses for other types of receptors. The timescale of signal transmission of neurotransmitters ranges from several milliseconds to several hours or days.

The efficacy of synaptic interaction can be changed by presynaptic activation that appears persistently over a short period. This change is termed synaptic plasticity. As an example, a pair of neurons connected by a single synapse is considered (Fig. 5.3a). At baseline, presynaptic firing evokes a weak postsynaptic activation. When the presynaptic neuron is strongly activated, synaptic connectivity is increased and maintained without additional presynaptic activation, after which presynaptic activation induces strong postsynaptic activation. This effect, which can

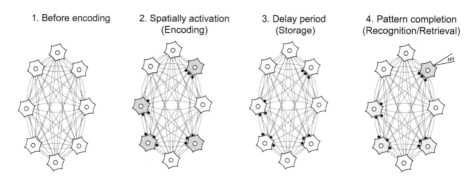

1. Before encoding   2. Spatially activation   3. Delay period   4. Pattern completion
                         (Encoding)   (Storage)   (Recognition/Retrieval)

Fig. 5.4 Auto-associative network. Partial activation of the network induces the facilitation of synaptic connectivity among the activated neurons according to Hebb's rule. The facilitated synaptic connection leads to completion of subsequent activation from partial activation of the neurons

persist for a long period, is termed long-term potentiation (LTP). LTP is thought to be the basis of memory encoding and storage. This long-term effect also can appear in inhibitory synapses, and is termed long-term depression.

The type of LTP described above depends only on presynaptic activation. There is another type of LTP, however, that is induced by simultaneous activation of presynaptic and postsynaptic neurons (Fig. 5.3b). In this type of LTP, a group of reciprocally connected neurons is considered (Fig. 5.4). When a part of the network is strongly activated, synaptic connectivity between simultaneously activated neurons are facilitated according to Hebb's rule ('encoding'), which is a theory describing how neural activation stores spatial patterns. The network structure represented by synaptic connectivity can be retained without additional neural activations ('storage'). When some of the previously activated neurons are reactivated, the activity strongly propagates to the previously activated neurons via the facilitated synapses, which results in completion of the whole pattern ('recognition'). This type of memory network is called an auto-associative network.

5.2.3 Neural Oscillations: Dynamics for Cooperation Among Neural Populations

In contrast to PCs, the nervous system has no explicit 'clock'. The dynamics of neural oscillations, however, are thought to play important roles in synchronizing widely distributed networks (Varela et al. 2001) by which synaptic plasticity can be effectively induced via Hebb's rule. Neural oscillation refers to an oscillatory field potential of the neuronal population appearing at a spectral range of 0.1–500 Hz. Interestingly, there are multiple physiological mechanisms that can generate a particular frequency of neural oscillation, and these mechanisms are known to be associated with specific information processing. The >40 Hz oscillation is known as the gamma-band oscillation, which is generated in the local neural network and is thought to contribute to the segmentation of patterned activations. The ~15 Hz oscillation is known as the beta-band oscillation and is related to attention processes. The ~10 Hz oscillation is known as the alpha-band oscillation, which is thought to be generated by the interplay between neurons in the thalamus and cerebral cortex, and is known to increase during the task-free resting-state. The 4–8 Hz oscillation is known as the theta-band oscillation and is associated with memory processing. The 1–4 Hz oscillation is known as the delta-band oscillation, and along with <1 Hz oscillations, is generated by drives from the thalamus that are known to increase during sleep. These oscillations usually appear transiently in parallel in a distributed network.

Neural oscillations lead to neural activation that appears at a particular phase of the oscillation. When two neural oscillations in two neural populations are synchronized (Fig. 5.5a), the possibility of synchronous firing between neurons in each population is significantly increased, which can facilitate efficient synaptic

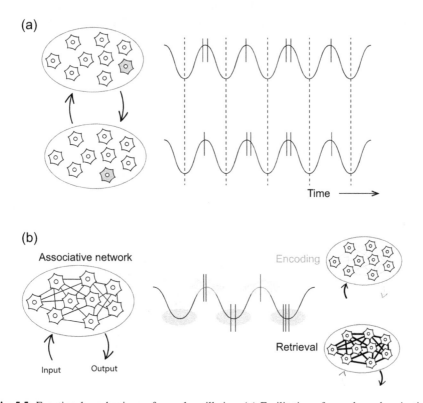

Fig. 5.5 Functional mechanisms of neural oscillation. (**a**) Facilitation of neural synchronization between distantly located neurons in two neural populations with synchronous neural oscillations (Fries 2005). (**b**) A time-sharing mechanism producing alternative encoding and retrieval in an associative network (Hasselmo et al. 2002), where synaptic efficacy is assumed to be rapidly modulated by neurotransmitter changing with the neural oscillation

transmission (Fries 2005). It also has been proposed that the oscillatory phase in an auto-associative network should be a time-sharing process (Fig. 5.5b) (Hasselmo et al. 2002). Synaptic efficacy is rapidly modulated by neurotransmitter release, which alters the neural oscillation and influences the input pattern. Such recurrent interaction can be alternatively changed to produce a change in the network state between encoding and retrieval. This process is thought to contribute to the implementation of cognitive tasks that require memory to be managed based on a given context.

5.3   Memory Classification

There are several types of memory, which are differentiated by several characteristics, including content, encoding and storage timescales, and presence of consciousness. These characteristics are known to be managed in parallel by particular brain regions (Fig. 5.6). This section outlines the different types of memory. For further information, see the book edited by Tulving and Craik (2000).

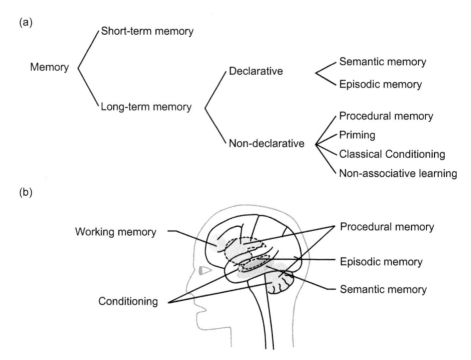

Fig. 5.6 Memory in the nervous system. (**a**) Classification of memory modified from Squire (1992). (**b**) Dominant brain regions in the implementation of each memory category

5.3.1   Development: Shaping the Basic Structure of the Nervous System

Before describing the different types of memory, the process that shapes the nervous system from embryogenesis to adulthood is briefly described here. In neuroscience, such a process is termed 'development', which is not included in memory processing. Development, however, includes the process by which neural selectivity forms via synaptic plasticity, which defines coding in neural populations and produces the basis of memory function.

Before birth, the basic structure of the nervous system is genetically organized, including topographic mappings between cortical areas. Some parts of the projections, such as projections from the retina, are organized by synaptic plasticity based on spontaneous activities of locally connected neurons. Coordination of motor output begins to be learned at this period in cooperation with sensory input from the skin. After birth, input from the environment becomes extremely rich in comparison to that prior to birth. The nervous system is rapidly organized to properly respond to the environment, and is most sensitive during the 'critical period' of several months immediately after birth. After this critical period, synaptic plasticity gradually decreases. In adulthood, neural selectivity is well-established, and the neural network becomes more difficult to reorganize. Computationally, the network of the cerebral cortex has been modeled by a hierarchically organized convolutional network (Cadieu et al. 2007; Fukushima 2007), where each neuron learns to represent particular features.

5.3.2   Short-Term and Working Memory

Memory is categorized into short-term and long-term memory. This section describes short-term memory. Short-term memory refers to the ability to briefly store substantial details and to recall those details immediately. The capacity of short-term memory is limited. Items stored in short-term memory can be retained by rehearsal, but are easily erased by shifting attention to other things. One example of an item that is stored in short-term memory is a telephone number (of approximately 8 digits) learned during a conversation with another person.

Working memory is a type of short-term memory that emphasizes task-dependent memories transiently required to achieve specific tasks. One example of working memory is the ability to remember and carry digits during mental arithmetic. The number that is carried is quickly remembered, can be retrieved immediately for use, and then rapidly released after use. Working memory is modeled as a system consisting of a central executive, a visuo-spatial sketchpad, a phonological loop, and an episodic buffer (Baddeley 2000). The prefrontal cortex is considered to play an essential role in implementing working memory.

5.3.3 Long-Term Memory

Long-term memory is subdivided into declarative and non-declarative memory (Squire 1992). In contrast to non-declarative memory, declarative memory refers to facts and events that can be consciously recalled. Declarative memory is known to be dominantly managed by the medial temporal lobe, whereas non-declarative memory includes various subcategories that are maintained by distributed brain regions.

5.3.3.1 Declarative Memory

Declarative memory is further subdivided into semantic and episodic memory. Semantic memory refers to the memory of facts. For example, knowing that the capital of the U.S. is Washington D.C. is a semantic memory. Episodic memory refers to the memory of events, including personal experiences. For example, remembering that I ate blueberry pancakes this morning is an episodic memory. Both memory types are maintained by the medial temporal lobe, but episodic memory also depends more specifically on the hippocampus. The role of the hippocampus in memory was clearly demonstrated by evidence collected from the amnesic patient H. M., who exhibited impaired memory function after bilateral hippocampal damage. Although H. M. was unable to remember recent experiences and behaviors, he retained memories of experiences that occurred prior to hippocampal damage. In addition, language, short-term memory, and motor skill learning ability remained intact in H. M. These findings clearly demonstrate that the hippocampus transiently stores experiences that are gradually transferred to the cerebral cortex, where long-term mnemonic storage occurs. This process is termed memory consolidation.

Hippocampal memory has been computationally modeled as an auto-associative network, which is consistent with biological evidence (see also a review article by Sato 2017). By assuming fast synaptic plasticity in the hippocampus and slow synaptic plasticity in the cerebral cortex, memory consolidation can be explained as follows (Alvarez and Squire 1994): During encoding, the hippocampus receives cortical activation and rapidly forms an associative memory within the hippocampus, providing an index for cortical activation (Teyler and DiScenna 1986). At this stage, the encoded cortical activation pattern can be retrieved by the hippocampus. When the same cortical activation pattern occurs repeatedly, the cortical associative network gradually learns to store the encoded pattern. Once the encoded pattern has been stored, it can be retrieved without the hippocampus; this process simulates memory consolidation.

5.3.3.2 Non-declarative Memory

Non-declarative memory includes procedural memory, priming, classical conditioning, and non-associative memory (Squire 1992). Each memory is processed without consciousness and automatically expressed for its use. This section describes each non-declarative subcategory.

Procedural memory is memory for motor and cognitive skills. For example, how to ride a bicycle and how to solve the Tower of Hanoi puzzle are examples of procedural memory. Procedural memory requires repeated learning in order for the memory to be formed. After learning, the learned skill autonomously appears, even if the subject has no confidence in the ability to perform the skill. Procedural memory is known to be managed primarily by the basal ganglia and cerebellum. Individuals with damage to either the basal ganglia or cerebellum exhibit great difficulty in learning skills, which is sometimes tested by asking the individual to complete a mirror-image drawing. The basal ganglia is also known to be associated with reward-related behaviors; therefore, its neural mechanism is of interest in terms of autonomous memory processing. Computationally, based on physiological evidence (Schultz 2016), the basal ganglia has been modeled by a network implementing reinforcement learning, which learns actions in an environment to maximize its performance or cumulative reward. The cerebellum has traditionally been modeled by a perceptron, an algorithm for supervised learning.

The remaining subcategories of non-procedural memory are briefly mentioned here. Priming is an effect in which exposure to one perceptual pattern influences the response to another stimulus. Priming is thought to depend on the cerebral cortex. Classical conditioning refers to learning in which a previously neutral stimulus is conditioned to evoke a specific response by repeated pairing with another non-neutral stimulus. Classical conditioning is largely associated with the cerebellum and amygdala. Non-associative learning includes sensitization and habituation phenomena in which the response to a specific stimulus increases and decreases, respectively, by repeat administration of the same stimulus. Its neural mechanism is known to be non-associative synaptic potentiation or depression, respectively, in the reflex pathway.

5.4 The Arrival of Big Data to Neuroscience

Neuroscience data have not been collected in the same manner as data from the area of molecular biology (Sejnowski et al. 2014). Neuroscience data exist across an astonishing range of scales in space and time, ranging from 10^{-4}–10^{3} mm in

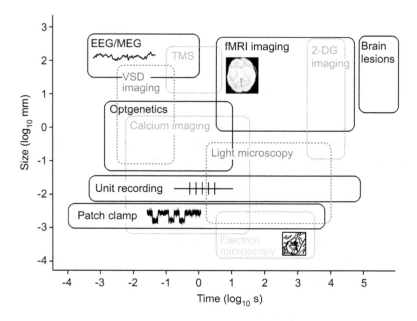

Fig. 5.7 Spatio-temporal domain of neuroscience and the main methods, partially modified from Sejnowski et al. (2014). EEG, electroencephalography; MEG, magneto-encephalography; TMS, trans-magnetic stimulation; VSD, voltage-sensitive dye; 2-DG, 2-deoxyglucose

space and 10^{-4}–10^5 s in time (Fig. 5.7). These data are difficult to standardize across spatial and temporal scales. This complexity is compounded by the existence of data across several species, from worms to mice to humans. Moreover, the integration of data has been accomplished mainly via the collaboration of individual labs, and most data have not been openly available. However, neuroscience data have the potential for further development in terms of big data that could lead to qualitative changes in neuroscience. Recently, there have been a number of challenges to integrate such diverse types of data (Ascoli and Polavaram 2015). This chapter reviews such integration efforts in neuroscience.

5.4.1 Brain Structure Data

Global network structure has been traditionally evaluated by tracer dye injection in animals, which reveals important detailed structures of axon projections from a target location. A milestone study integrating tracer data was presented by Felleman and Van Essen (1991), in which the network structure among monkey cortical areas was summarized. Recently, such data have been systematically collected and shared via the CoCoMac database (Stephan et al. 2001; Bakker et al. 2012), where several hundred tract-tracing studies in monkey brains are freely accessible.

A recent brain imaging method, diffusion tensor imaging (DTI), has been developed to measure anisotropy of the axon tracts in the white matter over the whole brain. DTI is non-invasive and can be applied in humans. The spatial resolution of DTI ($\sim$1) mm is worse than that of tracer injection, but the main advantage is that DTI allows simultaneous measurement of the entire network structure. Moreover, the standardization of data is not a major issue with DTI, because human brain coordinates have already been standardized by functional MRI studies (e.g., Talairach and Tournoux 1998 and MNI [Montreal Neurological Institute] coordinates Evans et al. 1993). One famous project is the Human Connectome Project (Van Essen et al. 2013), which aims to construct a complete map of the network structure of the brain in vivo within and across individuals. Connectome is a term indicating the complete description of the structural connectivity of an organism's nervous system (Sporns 2010). The structural database is expected to organize data for use across interdisciplinary fields, including physiology, psychiatry, and informatics (Sporns et al. 2015).

5.4.2 Database for Task-Related Brain Activation

Brain activity data collected during the performance of cognitive tasks are important for understanding information processing in the nervous system. Compared with structural data, task-related data are difficult to standardize, because cognitive tasks are designed generally to evaluate a unique aspect of cognition. Recently, several projects have been proposed to collect rich meta-data on different experimental tasks under different functional brain imaging methods (Poldrack and Gorgolewski 2014). One famous project is the OpenfMRI project (Poldrack et al. 2013), which collects and shares raw fMRI data measured from >1,800 participants during the performance of cognitive tasks. Meta-analysis studies have demonstrated that new predictions regarding psychological states can be produced by integrating evidence across several studies (Wager et al. 2007). Thus, task-related fMRI databases are expected to drive qualitative changes in imaging analysis for understanding cognition.

5.4.3 Database of Computational Models

Computational modeling is a fundamental approach for understanding information processing in the nervous system. Such models incorporate experimental data to summarize and integrate implicit relationships across multiple data scales, from the molecular to whole-brain level. Unfortunately, there are no standard approaches for computational modeling. Moreover, models sometimes focus on describing one particular set of experimental data. However, with the arrival of big data in neuroscience, the role of computational modeling is expected to change, with a greater focus on the principles and theory of information processing in the nervous system.

Descriptions of neuroscience models vary based on the modality under study, and may include representations such as synaptic dynamics, neural mass dynamics, or binary neurons. Moreover, there are a number of proposals regarding specific neural networks in each region of the brain. These models have not been standardized. However, standardization will be important to obtain an integrated perspective on information processing. In the case of biologically plausible spiking models, there already exist several popular platforms, such as NEURON Software[1] (Hines and Carnevale 1997) and GENESIS Software[2] (Bower and Beeman 2012). No popular platforms exist for other levels of neural description. However, there are projects underway to collect neural models and their codes, such as Hines et al. (2004), which provides an accessible location for storing and retrieving models and currently includes >1,000 models.

5.5 Conclusion

Memory is implemented by the nervous system across multiple scales in space and time. The central nervous system includes $\sim 10^{10}$ neurons. Each neuron manages particular features in cognition and behavior, as calculated by the interaction among $\sim 10^4$ synapses. The synapse, which is a specific structure at the contact site between neurons, produces the bases of memory in the nervous system. In contrast to PCs, memory is autonomously learned in the brain through experiences. There are multiple methods by which experience is learned, including Hebb's rule and reinforcement learning. The memory system is organized to include subcategories associated with various functional demands within the environment, such as short-term versus long-term memory and declarative versus non-declarative memory. Recently, several projects have been launched to collect large volumes of neuroscience data. These data, which have been obtained by various methods, are difficult to standardize but are starting to be organized. In line with the availability of these neuroscience databases, computational modeling should focus on describing the principles and theory behind these data. Theoretical studies converging accumulative knowledge in other areas of science are thought to be key for a deeper understanding of information processing in the nervous system.

References

Alvarez P, Squire LR (1994) Memory consolidation and the medial temporal lobe: a simple network model. Proc Natl Acad Sci USA 91(15):7041–7045. Available via http://www.ncbi.nlm.nih.gov/pubmed/8041742

Ascoli G, Polavaram S (2015) Neuroinformatics. Scholarpedia 10(11):1312

---

[1] NEURON Software. Available via https://www.neuron.yale.edu/neuron/
[2] GENESIS Software. Available via http://genesis-sim.org/

Baddeley A (2000) The episodic buffer: a new component of working memory? Trends Cogn Sci 4(11):417–423. Available via http://www.ncbi.nlm.nih.gov/pubmed/11058819

Bakker R, Wachtler T, Diesmann M (2012) CoCoMac 2.0 and the future of tract-tracing databases. Front Neuroinform 6(30). Available via http://www.ncbi.nlm.nih.gov/pubmed/23293600

Bower JM, Beeman D (2012) The book of GENESIS: exploring realistic neural models with the general neural simulation system, 2nd edn. Springer, New York

Cadieu C, Kouh M, Pasupathy A, Connor CE, Riesenhuber M, Poggio M (2007) A model of V4 shape selectivity and invariance. J Neurophysiol 98(3):1733–1750

Evans AC, Collins DL, Mills SR, Brown ED, Kelly RL, Peters TM (1993) 3D statistical neuroanatomical models from 305 MRI volumes. In: 1993 IEEE conference record nuclear science symposium and medical imaging conference, vol 3, pp 1813–1817

Felleman DJ, Van Essen DC (1991) Distributed hierarchical processing in the primate cerebral cortex. Cereb Cortex 1(1):1–47. Available via http://www.ncbi.nlm.nih.gov/pubmed/1822724

Fries P (2005) A mechanism for cognitive dynamics: neuronal communication through neuronal coherence. Trends Cogn Sci 9(10):474–80. Available via http://www.ncbi.nlm.nih.gov/pubmed/16150631

Fukushima K (2007) Neocognitron. Scholarpedia 2(1):1717. Available via http://www.scholarpedia.org/article/Neocognitron

Gray CM, König P, Engel AK, Singer W (1989) Oscillatory responses in cat visual cortex exhibit inter-columnar synchronization which reflects global stimulus properties. Nature 338(6213):334–337. Available via http://www.ncbi.nlm.nih.gov/pubmed/2922061

Hasselmo ME, Wyble BP, Wallenstein GV (1996) Encoding and retrieval of episodic memories: role of cholinergic and GABAergic modulation in the hippocampus. Hippocampus 6(6):693–708. Available via http://www.ncbi.nlm.nih.gov/pubmed/9034856

Hasselmo ME, Bódel C, Wyble BP (2002) A proposed function for hippocampal theta rhythm: separate phases of encoding and retrieval enhance reversal of prior learning. Neural Comput 14(4):793–817. Available via http://www.ncbi.nlm.nih.gov/pubmed/11936962

Hines ML, Carnevale NT (1997) The NEURON simulation environment. Neural Comput 9(6):1179–1209

Hines ML, Morse T, Migliore M, Carnevale NT, Shepherd GM (2004) ModelDB: a database to support computational neuroscience. J Comput Neurosci 17(1):7–11. Available via http://www.ncbi.nlm.nih.gov/pubmed/15218350

Marr D (1971) Simple memory: a theory for archicortex. Philos Trans R Soc B 262(841):23–81. Available via http://www.ncbi.nlm.nih.gov/pubmed/4399412

Poldrack RA, Gorgolewski KJ (2014) Making big data open: data sharing in neuroimaging. Nat Neurosci 17(11):1510–1517. Available via http://www.ncbi.nlm.nih.gov/pubmed/25349916

Poldrack RA, Barch DM, Mitchell JP, Wager TD, Wagner AD, Devlin JT, Cumba C, Koyejo O, Milham MP (2013) Toward open sharing of task-based fMRI data: the OpenfMRI project. Front Neuroinform 7(12). Available via http://www.ncbi.nlm.nih.gov/pubmed/23847528

Sato N (2017, to appear) Episodic memory and the hippocampus. In: Ahmed M (ed) Computational models of brain and behavior. Chichester: Wiley-Blackwell

Schultz W (2016) Reward functions of the basal ganglia. J Neural Transm (Vienna) 123(7):679–693. Available via http://www.ncbi.nlm.nih.gov/pubmed/26838982

Sejnowski TJ, Churchland PS, Movshon AJ (2014) Putting big data to good use in neuroscience. Nat Neurosci 17(11):1440–1441. Available via http://www.ncbi.nlm.nih.gov/pubmed/25349909

Shepherd GM (2003) The synaptic organization of the brain, 5th edn. Oxford University Press, New York

Spalding KL, Bergmann O, Alkass K, Bernard S, Salehpour M, Huttner HB, Boström E, Westerlund I, Vial C, Buchholz BA (2013) Dynamics of hippocampal neurogenesis in adult humans. Cell 153(6):1219–1227. Available via http://www.ncbi.nlm.nih.gov/pubmed/23746839

Sporns O (2010) Connectome. Scholarpedia 5(2):5584

Sporns O, Tononi G, Kötter R (2005) The human Connectome: a structural description of the human brain. PLoS Comput Biol 1(4):e42. Available via http://www.ncbi.nlm.nih.gov/pubmed/16201007

Squire LR (1992) Declarative and nondeclarative memory: multiple brain systems supporting learning and memory. J Cogn Neurosci 4(3):232–243. Available via http://www.ncbi.nlm.nih.gov/pubmed/23964880

Stephan KE, Kamper L, Bozkurt A, Burns GA, Young MP, Kötter R (2001) Advanced database methodology for the collation of connectivity data on the macaque brain (CoCoMac). Philos Trans R Soc Lond Ser B Biol Sci 356(1412):1159–1186. Available via http://www.ncbi.nlm.nih.gov/pubmed/11545697

Talairach J, Tournoux P (1998) Co-planar stereotaxic atlas of the human brain: 3-dimensional proportional system: an approach to cerebral imaging. Thieme Medical Publishers, New York

Teyler TJ, DiScenna P (1986) The hippocampal memory indexing theory. Behav Neurosci 100(2):147–154. Available via http://www.ncbi.nlm.nih.gov/pubmed/3008780

Tulving E, Craik FIM (2000) The Oxford handbook of memory. Oxford University Press, Oxford

Van Essen DC, Smith SM, Barch DM, Behrens TE, Yacoub E, Ugurbil K, WU-Minn HCP Consortium (2013) The WU-Minn human Connectome project: an overview. Neuroimage 80:62–79. Available via http://www.ncbi.nlm.nih.gov/pubmed/23684880

Varela F, Lachaux JP, Rodriguez E, Martinerie J (2001) The brainweb: phase synchronization and large-scale integration. Nat Rev Neurosci 2(4):229–239. Available via http://www.ncbi.nlm.nih.gov/pubmed/11283746

Wager TD, Lindquist M, Kaplan L (2007) Meta-analysis of functional neuroimaging data: current and future directions. Soc Cogn Affect Neurosci 2(2):150–158

Part IV
The World of Intelligent Machines and Finiteness

Chapter 6
From Computing Machines to Learning Intelligent Machines: Chronological Development of Alan Turing's Thought on Machines

Katsuhiko Sano and Mai Sugimoto

Abstract The most famous academic contributions of Alan Turing are on Turing machines in 1936 and on the Turing test in 1950. While the motivations of these two works are apparently quite different, this chapter tracks Turing's chronological development between these two contributions and points out how conceptual continuity can be found in Turing's thought on machines.

6.1 Introduction

The most famous academic contributions of Alan Turing are on Turing machines in 1936 and on the Turing test in 1950. Turing (1936) characterized what a human calculator is doing in a computing process in terms of Turing machines and solved the Entscheidungsproblem (the decision problem of the first-order logic) negatively. On the other hand, Turing (1950a) posed a question of "can a computing machine think?", replaced it with a more definite question via the Turing test (the imitation game in Turing's words), and predicted that it would be possible to give an affirmative answer to this question in the future (within "about fifty years" Turing 1950a). Since the motivations and the contributions of these two works are apparently quite different, it may be difficult for a reader to understand a possible connection between these two achievements by Turing. The aim of this chapter is to track Turing's chronological development between these two academic contributions and to point out how conceptual continuity can be found in Turing's thoughts on machines.

K. Sano (✉)
Department of Philosophy, Graduate School of Letters, Hokkaido University, Nishi 7 Chome, Kita 10 Jo, Kita-ku, Sapporo, 060-0810, Hokkaido, Japan
e-mail: v-sano@let.hokudai.ac.jp

M. Sugimoto
Faculty of Sociology, Kansai University, 3-3-35, Yamatecho, Suita, 564-8680, Osaka, Japan
e-mail: msgmt@kansai-u.ac.jp

© Springer International Publishing AG 2017
A.J. Schuster (eds.), *Understanding Information*, Advanced Information and Knowledge Processing, DOI 10.1007/978-3-319-59090-5_6

101

Turing (1936) was concerned with modeling a human calculator who follows an effective or mechanical procedure, and so it was *beyond* his scope at that time to capture a human mathematician's intuition or intelligent behavior of a machine. On the other hand, it was after World War II (WWII) and his moving to the National Physical Laboratory (NPL) that Turing seemed to shift his interest to model intelligent human behavior in terms of machines, i.e., to realize intelligent behavior of a machine. In particular, Turing (1947) sketched some specific requirements for a machine to behave intelligently towards the end of his lecture at the London Mathematical Society. The requirements consist of the following three:

(i)   A machine should be able to learn from the machine's experience.
(ii) A machine may commit a mistake or an error.
(iii) A machine needs to be able to interact with the machine's circumstance.

This chapter extracts these three requirements as a key to track Turing's chronological development and investigates how these three requirements were elaborated and realized in Turing's works on intelligent machinery (Turing 1948) and on the Turing test (Turing 1950a). While there are several objections to the Turing test, the focus of this chapter is in Turing's predicted answer to the test, and so, this chapter will not go into the details of these objections. The reader who is interested in these discussions is referred to, e.g., Shieber (2004).

This chapter proceeds as follows. Section 6.2 goes into the details of Turing machines as well as the universal Turing machine and then explains how Turing machines are used for solving the Entscheidungsproblem negatively. Moreover, Turing's justification of the Church-Turing thesis is outlined. Section 6.3 reviews how Turing, after his work on Turing machines, involved himself in making practical computing machines. Section 6.4 extracts the three requirements for machines to behave intelligently from Turing's lecture at the London Mathematical Society and examines the contents of the requirements in the lecture. While Sects. 6.5 and 6.6 deal with Turing's papers on intelligent machinery and the Turing test, respectively, we also investigate in these sections the development and deepening of Turing's thoughts on machines as he tried to realize the three requirements mentioned before. Our investigation in these sections will concentrate on Turing's specific models of machines, i.e., P-type machines in Sect. 6.5, and the child program in a digital computing machine and the education process for it in Sect. 6.6.

6.1.1 Related Work

The work by Hodges (1992) is an extensive biography of Turing, together with a detailed description of the historical and cultural background to understand Turing's life and work. Copeland (2004b) is a convenient collection of Turing's academic papers. All the papers we deal with in this chapter can be found there. Please note also that each of Turing's papers in Copeland (2004b) is accompanied with a commentary for the reader. Petzold (2008) devotes his volume to explain the content of Turing's 1936 paper (Turing 1936) and its historical and theoretical background. Piccinini (2003), deals with Turing's idea about machines, mathematical methods of proof, and intelligence, with an emphasis on Turing's reaction to "mathematical objection" against the view that a machine could show intelligent behavior. Teuscher (2001), examines and revives the content of Turing's 1948 paper (Turing 1948), which was left unpublished until 1968, from a modern viewpoint. Unlike these related studies, this chapter focuses mainly on the theoretical aspects of Turing's work from Turing machines to the Turing test and tries to understand the conceptual continuity of Turing's thoughts on machines.

6.2   How Can We Model Effective Computation by Human Caclulator?

The Entscheidungsproblem (or decision problem) is a challenge in first-order logic. In 1936, Turing proposed the idea of Turing machines to solve the Entscheidungsproblem negatively, while Church (1936) also, independently, gave a negative answer to the question in terms of the lambda calculus, a mathematically different idea from Turing machines. This section investigates how Turing tackled the question and how the idea of Turing machine contributes to give a negative answer to the question.

6.2.1   The Entscheidungsproblem and Effective or Mechanical Procedure

Let us start with a very short introduction to the first-order logic. We can regard a verb, e.g., "love", as a binary relation or predicate in the sense that the verb "love" needs two arguments x and y such that x is a subject noun and y an object noun of the verb. Let us write $L(x, y)$ to mean "x loves y." Since the sentences "all people love some people" and "some people are loved by all people" have different meanings, their symbolization or formalization should be distinct even if we use a relation $L(x, y)$ for symbolizing both examples. Here the universal and existential quantifiers come into our picture. When we want to bound the argument of a position of the subject (or the object) of $L(x, y)$, we use a variable x (or y) as a bound variable. The symbols "$\forall x.$" and "$\exists y.$" mean "for all x" and "for some y," respectively. Then "all people love some people" is symbolized as $\forall x.\exists y.L(x, y)$ and "some people are loved by all people" by $\exists y.\forall x.L(x, y)$. Now we can understand that a difference of these examples in meaning comes from a difference in the order of the quantifiers. This was an insight of the German mathematician Friedrich Ludwig "Gottlob" Frege on the syntax of the first-order logic.

Let us introduce the implication symbol "→" to capture the implication relation between the sentences. Then it is easy to see that "some people are loved by all people" implies "all people love some people" and so

$$\exists y.\forall x.L(x, y) \rightarrow \forall x.\exists y.L(x, y) \tag{6.1}$$

seems to hold. In our ordinary linguistic intuition, however, the converse implication

$$\forall x.\exists y.L(x, y) \rightarrow \exists y.\forall x.L(x, y) \tag{6.2}$$

seems to fail. Even if we change our reading of "$L(x, y)$" into an arbitrary one (say "x is a parent of y"), we can still say that (6.1) seems to hold. This seems still true if we change the total individual objects under consideration in an arbitrary way.

A *formula* is a symbolized sentence which may contain logical symbols such as $\forall$, $\exists$, $\rightarrow$, etc. Let us say that a formula is *valid* if the symbolized sentence is true for any choice (or set) of total individual objects and for any interpretation of relation or predicate symbols. Then (6.1) becomes valid but the converse implication (6.2) is not valid. Is it possible for us to *decide* if a given formula is valid or not? This is what the original formulation of the Entscheidungsproblem concerns.

Now we can look at what the Entscheidungsproblem (originally posed by the German mathematicians David Hilbert and Wilhelm Ackermann) actually is.

> The Entscheidungsproblem is solved if one know a procedure which will permit one to decide, using a finite number of operations, on the validity, respectively the satisfiability of a given [first-order] logical expressions. (Hilbert and Ackermann 1928, p.73, English translation from Gandy 1995, p.58)

It is well-known that Gödel (1930) proved that the set of all valid formulas (i.e., "logical expressions") coincides with the set of all provable formulas in a formal system for the first-order logic, where a *formal system* is understood as a system consisting of finite appropriate axiom schemes and finite appropriate sets of inference rules and a formula is said to be *provable* in the formal system if the logical expression is derived from axiom schemes by finite inference rules.[1]

Therefore, the Entscheidungsproblem can be reformulated as follows:

> By the Entscheidungsproblem of a system of symbolic logic is there understood the problem to find an effective method by which, given any expression Q in the notation of the system, it can be determined whether or not Q is provable in the system. (Church 1936, p.41)

It seemed that Turing first met the Entscheidungsproblem in a lecture by Maxwell (Max) Newman around the spring of 1935 (cf. Anderson 2013, p.30). At that time, Turing attended Newman's "Part III Foundations of Mathematics course."[2]

---

[1] Such a formal system should be found in a standard textbook of mathematical logic, e.g., see Enderton 2001, Section 2.4. Turing (1936) used a formal system "**K**" from Hilbert and Ackermann (1928) for the first-order logic.

[2] The reader may wonder how Max Newman knew the problem. Grattan-Guinness wrote that Newman sent a letter to Bertrand Russell from Italy in September 1928 soon after attending the

One of the keys to understand the Entscheidungsproblem lies in: how do we understand "using a finite number of operations" in the first citation and "an effective method" in the second citation mentioned before. In this context, "effective" is also regarded as synonymous to the term "mechanical." For these words, we employ Copeland's (2008) characterization of an effective or mechanical method as follows.

> A method, or procedure, M, for achieving some desired result is called 'effective' or 'mechanical' just in case
>
> 1. M is set out in terms of a finite number of exact instructions (each instruction being expressed by means of a finite number of symbols);
> 2. M will, if carried out without error, produce the desired result in a finite number of steps;
> 3. M can (in practice or in principle) be carried out by a human being unaided by any machinery save paper and pencil;
> 4. M demands no insight or ingenuity on the part of the human being carrying it out.

Related to item 4, it is sometimes required that any effective procedure "cannot rely upon the outcomes of random processes (for example, rolls of a die)" (cf. Detlefsen et al. 1999, p.4). It should be remarked that this characterization is *not* mathematical, because any mathematical definition of "insight" nor "ingenuity" in item 4 are not given in the above and moreover it seems impossible for us to give any mathematical definition to these terms. In order to solve the Entscheidungsproblem *negatively*, we need to show that there is *no* effective method for determining whether a given logical expression is provable in a fixed formal system (say, by Hilbert and Ackermann) for the first-order logic. This is what Turing did in 1936 (Turing 1936). We will go into its details in the next section.

6.2.2 Turing Machine in 1936: Computing Machine

In most of the modern textbooks on computability theory (e.g., Boolos et al. 2007), Turing machines are often introduced to define the notion of computable *function* on the natural numbers. Turing (1936), however, proposed the notion of Turing machine to compute a *real number* (say, π, e, etc.) in its binary expansion. Thus "numbers" in the title "on computable numbers" of Turing (1936) mean real numbers. For Turing, a computing machine introduced in Turing (1936) was an *idealized human calculator* in terms of effective or mechanical methods. A human calculator ("computer") is a person reckoning with paper, a pencil, an eraser, and perhaps a mechanical calculator (cf. Piccinini 2003, p.25). Turing introduces the

---

conference (see Grattan-Guinness 2012, p.19). So Newman might know at least the problem of "completeness" of a formal system of the first-order logic, which was solved by Gödel in 1930, at the International Congress of Mathematicians at Bologna in 1928, because David Hilbert explained the problem in his talk there.

distinction between *automatic* and *choice* machines and focuses on the automatic machines in the paper:

> If at each stage the motion of a machine (in the sense of §1) is completely determined by the configuration, we shall call the machine an "automatic machine" (or *a*-machine). For some purposes we might use machines (choice machines or *c*-machines) whose motion is only partially determined by the configuration (hence the use of the word "possible" in §1). When such a machine reaches one of these ambiguous configurations, it cannot go on until some arbitrary choice has been made by an external operator. (Turing 1936, p.232)

A Turing machine is an abstract machine that manipulates (read, write, erase, etc.) symbols on an infinitely long tape according to a given table of rules. The infinitely long tape is divided into sections called *squares*, and it has an initial square and continues in the right direction but not in the left direction. An abstract machine has a head which can scan a square and a symbol in it, erase the symbol, and write a new symbol in the square. For the tape, Turing used a convention that we have two kinds of square alternately called F-, and E-squares, where we can erase and rewrite a symbol in an E-square but we cannot do so for any F-square. While E-squares are for the necessary "rough work" (cf. Turing 1936, p.242), F-squares are intended to write a binary expansion of a real number. We note that the initial square is an F-square. To specify a table of rules (let us say that it is a *Turing machine program*[3] in what follows), we need to fix the following three components: (i) a finite set Σ of symbols where Σ is assumed to contain 0 and 1 at least, (ii) a finite set $Q = \{q_1, \ldots, q_n\}$ of machine configurations (abbreviated as *m*-configurations), and (iii) a finite list of quadruples of the following form:

- $q_i X R q_j$, which means "when the head reads a symbol $X \in \Sigma$ in *m*-configuration q_i, then the head is moved to *right* and the *m*-configuration is changed into q_j";
- $q_i X L q_j$, which means "when the head reads a symbol $X \in \Sigma$ in *m*-configuration q_i, then the head is moved to *left* and the *m*-configuration is changed into q_j";
- $q_i X X' q_j$, which means "when the head reads a symbol $X \in \Sigma$ in *m*-configuration q_i, then the symbol is erased, a new symbol $X' \in \Sigma$ is overwritten and then the *m*-configuration is changed into q_j."

When we set $\Sigma = \{0, 1, B\}$ ("B" means a blank) and $Q = \{q_1, q_2, q_3, q_4\}$, Fig. 6.1 (left) is an example of a Turing machine program, which will generate a sequence $01010101010 \cdots$ in F-squares of the tape (this is left for the exercise of the reader).[4] Note also that Fig. 6.1 (right) illustrates a so-called state transition graph for the program. Since Turing's main interest is in real numbers as binary decimals, i.e., an infinite sequence consisting of 0s and 1s, he focuses on the Turing machine programs that generate such infinite sequences in the F-squares and calls such programs *circle-free* programs. It is clear that a Turing machine program of Fig. 6.1

---

[3] We note that Turing himself did not use the term "program" in Turing (1936). For this point, the reader is referred also to Copeland 2004a, pp.30–2.

[4] This example is not exactly the same as that which is given in Turing (1936). We note that state transition graphs were not used in Turing (1936).

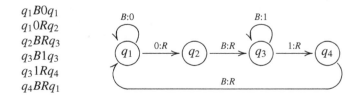

$$q_1 B 0 q_1$$
$$q_1 0 R q_2$$
$$q_2 B R q_3$$
$$q_3 B 1 q_3$$
$$q_3 1 R q_4$$
$$q_4 B R q_1$$

Fig. 6.1 A circle-free program (*left*) and its representation in a so-called state transition graph (*right*)

is circle-free. It should be noted that such a circle-free program does not terminate or halt. Now we can check Turing's definition of a computable sequence and number.[5]

> The real number whose expression as a binary decimal is obtained by prefacing this sequence by a decimal point is called the *number computed by the machine*. [...] A sequence is said to be computable if it can be computed by a circle-free machine. A number is computable if it differs by an integer from the number computed by a circle-free machine. (Turing 1936, pp.232–3)

6.2.3 Universal Computing Machine

Turing (1936) also presented the details of the *universal computing machine*, i.e., a universal Turing machine program U in the sense that, for every Turing machine program P, once we input the information of the quadruples of P onto the tape, U can simulate the behavior of the program P and so U can generate the same sequence as that of P on the F-squares of the tape. The main difficulties for realizing such a universal Turing machine program consist in the following two points. Firstly, we need to have a trick of how to input the information of the quadruples of a Turing machine program. Secondly, we need to "implement" the behavior of the universal Turing machine program U. Let us see the outline of these two points step by step below.

As for the first point, it suffices for us to have a method of converting the quadruples of a program into a sequence of symbols or a natural number (as a binary decimal, if necessary), where such a sequence or a natural number can be read as an input by the universal program. From the modern viewpoint, either way is fine as far as we can "recover" the quadruples of a program uniquely from the converted natural number or the converted sequence of symbols. Let us recall a program of Fig. 6.1 and explain Turing's way of converting the quadruples of a program. For a

---

[5]Unfortunately, there is a flaw in Turing's definition of computable numbers in the sense that, even if x and y are computable real numbers, $x + y$ may not be computable (for more detail, the reader is referred to Gherardi 2011, pp.404–6). Therefore, Turing revised his definition of computable number in Turing (1937).

finite set Σ of symbols, we prepare $S_0, S_1, S_2, \ldots$, and stipulate that S_0, S_1, and S_2 are used for B, 0, and 1, respectively. Then we replace S_i by the letter "D" followed by the letter "C" repeated i times. For m-configuration q_i, we replace it by the letter "D" followed by the letter "A" repeated i times. By this convention, "$q_1 B 0 q_1$" of Fig. 6.1 is converted into $DADDCDA$ and "$q_1 0 R q_2$" of Fig. 6.1 into $DADCRDAA$. With the help of the semicolon ";", we can now convert the program of Fig. 6.1 into:

$$DADDCDA; DADCRDAA; DAADRDAAA; DAAADDCCDAAA;$$

$$DAAADCCRDAAAA; DAAAADRDA.$$

Such a converted symbol is called the *standard description* in Turing (1936). Furthermore, when we replace A, C, D, L, R, and ; with 1, 2, 3, 4, 5, 7, respectively, then we can obtain the following number called a *description number*:

31332317313253117311353111773111332231117311132253111173111113531.

Turing defines that a *satisfactory number* is a description number of a circle-free Turing machine program.

For the second point above, a universal Turing machine program should be able to do the following two tasks:

- the program "recovers" the information of the quadruples of a given program from its standard description on the tape; and then
- the program reads the recovered quadruples and writes an output successively on the F-squares.

An implementation of the universal program should be regarded as a large-scale programming in the modern sense. Turing spent the whole of one section (cf. Turing 1936, Section 7) to explain the details of the universal program.[6]

6.2.4 Unsolvable Problems in Turing's 1936 Paper

Since we can assign distinct natural numbers (description numbers as in the previous section) with distinct Turing machine programs, the cardinality (or number) of all the Turing machine programs is less than or equal to the cardinality of the set $\mathbb{N}$ of all natural numbers. We know that the cardinality of $\mathbb{N}$ is less than the cardinality of the set $\{0, 1\}^{\mathbb{N}}$ of all (countably) infinite sequences consisting of 0s and 1s (this is due to the German mathematician Georg Cantor). This implies that there *exists* an uncomputable sequence (and so a real number) in terms of a Turing machine

---

[6]Turing's implementation of the idea of the universal Turing machine is so large-scale that it cannot avoid containing some "bugs" or programming errors, though Davies (2004) describes how to fix these errors.

program, because the cardinality of the set of all circle-free programs is less than the cardinality of the set $\{0, 1\}^{\mathbb{N}}$.

But, what is a concrete example of an uncomputable or unsolvable problem? The reader might consider that the halting problem (a problem determining if a given program halt at a given input) is such an example and Turing proposed the problem in Turing (1936).[7] This is not the case. Turing (1936) considers the following three unsolvable problems (cf. Copeland 2004a).

- The printing problem: The problem determining if any given Turing machine program ever prints "0" (in F-squares) in its computation.
- The circle-freeness problem: The problem determining if any given Turing machine program is circle-free, i.e., if a program generates an infinite sequence of 0s and 1s in F-squares.
- The enumeration problem: Is there a Turing machine program that enumerates all the computable sequences (consisting of 0s and 1s)?

What is a relationship between these three problems? Turing (1936) showed that the printing problem is unsolvable in the following steps:

(Step1) If the printing problem is solvable by a Turing machine program, then the circle-freeness problem is also solvable by a Turing machine program.
(Step2) If the circle-freeness problem is solvable by a Turing machine program, then we can solve the enumeration problem positively.
(Step3) If we can solve the enumeration problem positively, this implies a contradiction.

It is immediate to see that these three steps imply that the printing problem is not solvable by any Turing machine program.

Here we would like to see the outline of Turing's argument for (Step 3), where Turing employs Cantor's diagonal argument to establish the statement of the step. The argument proceeds as follows. Suppose that we can solve the enumeration problem positively. That is, there exists a Turing machine program that enumerates all the computable sequences. Let us write the n-th computable sequence by $r^{(n)}$ and use $r^{(n)}(k)$ to mean the k-th component of the sequence $r^{(n)}$. By combining the universal Turing machine program, the following "diagonal" sequence:

$$(r^{(n)}(n))_{n\in\mathbb{N}} = r^{(0)}(0), r^{(1)}(1), r^{(2)}(2), \ldots$$

is shown to be computable (Turing constructed a circle-free program generating this sequence under the supposition). Now let us consider the sequence $s := (1 - r^{(n)}(n))_{n\in\mathbb{N}}$, which is also shown to be computable. When we let, for example,

---

[7]Martin Davis, who is a student of Alonzo Church, thinks it likely that he first used the term "halting problem" in a series of lectures at the University of Illinois in 1952 (cf. Copeland 2004a, p.40). After the publication of the textbook by Davis (1982) on computability, it seems that the term "halting problem" has been widely known (cf. Petzold 2008). The book by Davis (1982) is a well-written introduction to the computability in terms of Turing machines.

$(r^{(n)}(n))_{n \in \mathbb{N}} = 1, 0, 0, \ldots$, then our new sequence becomes: $s = 0, 1, 1, \ldots$. Because the sequence s is computable, s itself should also appear in the enumeration of our supposition. So let the m-th sequence be the sequence s, i.e., $r^{(m)} = s$. When we consider the m-th *component* of this m-th sequence, it is $r^{(m)}(m)$ but, at the same time, it should be $1 - r^{(m)}(m)$ by our definition of s. Therefore, $1 - r^{(m)}(m) = r^{(m)}(m)$, hence $r^{(m)}(m) = \frac{1}{2}$, a contradiction with the fact that the component should be either 0 or 1. This finishes to establish (Step 3).

6.2.5 How Did Turing Solve the Entscheidungsproblem Negatively?

Let us now move back to the Entscheidungsproblem. This section outlines how Turing solved the Entscheidungsproblem negatively. Turing's argument is to reduce the unsolvability of the Entscheidungsproblem in terms of effective methods to the unsolvability of the printing problem in terms of Turing machine programs. Let us see the detail below in this section.

Let **K** be a formal system for the first-order logic. For example, such a system was found in Hilbert and Ackermann (1928) at that time and it was employed by Turing (1936). Suppose for the sake of contradiction that there is an effective or mechanical method E such that E can decide if any given formula is provable in **K** or not. Given any Turing machine program P, Turing constructed a special formula UN(P) in the syntax of the first-order logic such that the following two are equivalent:

- the program P prints "0" at some point in the computation;
- UN(P) is provable in **K**.

By our supposition, our effective method E can check if UN(P) is provable in **K**. Because of the equivalence above, now we can say that our supposed effective method E can be also used for solving the printing problem. If we can justify the claim that:

> any effective method is computable by a Turing machine program   (CT)

then now we conclude that the printing problem is solvable in a Turing machine program. This is a contradiction with what we have discussed in the previous section.

So, Turing's negative solution to the Entscheidungsproblem depends on the claim (CT). This claim is now called the *Church-Turing Thesis*. This is why Turing needed to provide several arguments for (CT) in Turing (1936). While the notion of computability in terms of Turing machine programs is mathematically defined, the notion of effective calculability is not mathematically defined, as we have seen in the first subsection of this section. So any argument for (CT) needs to justify the implication from the non-mathematical but conceptual definition to the purely mathematical definition. Thus it is unavoidable that an argument for (CT) becomes philosophical or conceptual. Turing's arguments for (CT) consist of the following three kinds (see Turing 1936, p.249):

(a) A direct appeal to intuition.
(b) A proof of the equivalence of two definitions (in case the new definition has a greater intuitive appeal).
(c) Giving examples of large classes of numbers which are computable.

Here we focus on Turing's argument of item (a), where he analyzes in detail what a human calculator is doing when the calculator computes a number in terms of effective or mechanical methods. Turing's analysis of the human calculator proceeds as follows (cf. Sieg 1993, pp.89–97). For a human calculator, two-dimensional character of a paper is not essential, so a tape of one dimensional character is sufficient for the computation. We can suppose that the behavior of the calculator is determined by symbols she observes and a state of her[8] mind at that moment. Then it is natural to impose the following two conditions:

(F1) The number of symbols and squares the calculator can immediately recognize is finite;
(F2) The number of states of the calculator's mind is finite.

The operations of the calculator should be so elementary that they could not be divided into a simpler operation. Then the operations are restricted to the following (cf. Turing 1936, p.250):

(O1) Changes of the symbol on one of the observed squares;
(O2) Changes of one of the squares observed to another square within a fixed number of squares of one of the previously observed squares.

Each of the operations may involve a change of a state of the calculator's mind. To sum up, Turing's analysis of a human calculator is that her behavior is determined by finite symbols she observes and a state of her mind (the number of such states is finite) and furthermore it should satisfy the four conditions (F1), (F2), (O1) and (O2) above. So, Turing states that an abstract machine satisfying his analysis of the calculator does "not differ very essentially from computing machine" (cf. Turing 1936, p.252). Therefore, he concludes that "corresponding to any machine of this type a computing machine can be constructed to compute the same sequence, that is to say the sequence computed by the computer" (cf. Turing 1936, p.252).

We would like to add that the Church-Turing thesis is widely accepted now. One of the reasons for this is that several conceptually different definitions for computability all turn out to be equivalent (cf. Turing 1939, p.166). For example, these include Gödel's notion of "general recursive functions," Alonzo Church's notion of "λ-definability," Turing's notion of computability in terms of Turing machines, etc.

---

[8] We use "she" or "her" as a gender-neutral singular pronoun in this chapter.

6.3 From the Universal Computing Machine to Practical Computing Machines

6.3.1 Turing's Dissertation at Princeton: Oracle Machine

Turing (1936) "characterized" the notion of effective procedure ("effective calculability" in his word) in terms of Turing machines. In his dissertation at Princeton University under the supervision of Alonzo Church, Turing's interest moves to the exploration of the *uncomputable* (cf. Hodges 2011). One incentive for this motivation was in the first incompleteness theorem by Gödel (1931). Hodges (2011) summarized that Turing's dissertation (later appeared as Turing 1939) "considered the mind when seeing the truth of one of Gödel's true but formally unprovable propositions, and hence going beyond rules based on the axioms of the system." When he tackled this problem, Turing introduced the notion of "oracle", which is incorporated into a Turing machine, as follows:

> Let us suppose that we are supplied with some unspecified means of solving number-theoretic problems; a kind of oracle as it were. We shall not go any further into the nature of this oracle apart from saying that it cannot be a machine. With the help of the oracle we could form a new kind of machine (call them o-machines), having as one of its fundamental processes that of solving a given number-theoretic problem. More definitely these machines are to behave in this way. The moves of the machine are determined as usual by a table except in the case of moves from a certain internal configuration o. If the machine is in the internal configuration o and if the sequence of symbols marked with l is then the well-formed formula A, then the machine goes into the internal configuration p or t according as it is or is not true that A is dual. The decision as to which is the case is referred to the oracle. (Turing 1939, pp.172–3)

It is noted in this citation that "A is dual" means that A holds provided A is supposed to formalize a number-theoretic problem. We can investigate if a number-theoretic problem is solvable or not relatively to the ability of a given oracle. Thus, the oracle allows us to investigate the *relative* computability, while Turing (1936) is regarded as studying the *absolute* computability. Max Newman stated that the oracle "resembles stages in the construction of a proof by a mathematician where he 'has an idea', as distinct from making mechanical use of a method" (cf. Newman 1955, p.259). So the reader might regard the oracle as incorporating the place for mathematicians' intuition, as a black box, into the notion of Turing machine. We should, however, note that the ability of the oracle may go beyond the ability of any human mathematician and so the oracle could be "too powerful" in this sense (cf. Hodges 2011).

6.3.2 Turing and Practical Computing Machines

It was during WWII that Turing started engaging in design and operation of working machines for computing. From 1939, after coming back from Princeton, he participated in cryptanalysis as wartime research for the United Kingdom. It is well-known that Turing contributed to the decryption of various cryptography of Axis at Bletchley Park. He worked for the early design of Bombe, which was machinery for decryption of Enigma, and later conducted research on an electronic enciphering system for a speech at Hanslope Park (cf. Hodges 1992, chapter 5). During this period, Turing deepened his knowledge of electrical engineering.

After the war had ended, Turing moved to NPL. Scholars at the NPL had been interested in Turing's work on computability. Since the late 1930s the implementation of the universal Turing machine of Sect. 6.2.3 had been discussed in the laboratory, and in the early 1940s, it was suggested to design a large-scale computing machine using equipment for automatic telephone exchanges (cf. Copeland 2004b, pp.363–4). Turing came to NPL to work for this computing machine called Automatic Computing Engine (ACE). In late 1945, Turing wrote a report titled "Proposed Electronic Calculator," which describes the technical details of the computing machine he planned at NPL. This report was submitted and accepted to NPL in February 1946, as Turing (1946).

Turing himself regarded the digital computing machine ACE as a "practical version" of the universal Turing machine, which "can be made to do any rule of thumb process" (cf. Turing 1947), where "rule of thumb" can be regarded as synonymous with "effective" (cf. Copeland 2004a, p.42). Turing (1950b) described that rule of thumb process "could have been done by a human operator working in a *disciplined* but unintelligent manner" (emphasis by the authors) and "Electronic computers are intended to carry out any definite rule of thumb process." It is noted that the word "discipline" will be one of the key terms to capture intelligent behavior of a machine in Sect. 6.5. He seemed to recognize the analogy between his universal machine model and the practical digital computing machines. Turing's previous work on computability would have influenced his later policy that the complexity of practical computing machines should be concentrated in programs. For example, Turing (1947) said that it was unnecessary to add a binary-decimal converter as hardware to ACE, and explained the reason as follows:

> There are many fussy little details which have to be taken care of, and which, according to normal engineering practice, would require special circuits. We are able to deal with these points without modification of the machine itself, by pure paper work, eventually resulting in feeding in appropriate instructions. (Turing 1948, p.385)

It would be natural to consider his analogy as the result of combining Turing's preceding career on computability and his experience on the working machines for cryptography during WWII.

Turing eventually left NPL in 1948, since the ACE project did not make progress smoothly (cf. Hodges 1992). Turing started working in the Mathematics Department at the Victoria University of Manchester, where Manchester Small-Scale Experimental Machine, commonly referred to as Manchester Baby, was already developed, and in 1949 Manchester Automatic Digital Machine, also called Manchester Mark I, was completed. Turing was appointed Deputy Director of the Computing Machine Laboratory, and on Manchester Mark I he conducted computing experiments on various topics such as chess games and morphogenesis (Turing 1952). The well-known project on morphogenesis was also carried out in Manchester.

6.4   Three Requirements for Intelligent Behavior of Machines at Lecture to the London Mathematical Society

During his days in NPL and then in Manchester, Turing described his idea on the analogy between a machine and a human brain. From this section, we will see the development of Turing's ideas on intelligent behavior of machines.

Turing (1947), was written as a draft of Turing's presentation at the London Mathematical Society on ACE proposed at NPL.[9] This paper shows his design concept of the proposed digital computing machine together with the mathematical properties of each mechanical part. It also mentions the significance of "being digital" (cf. Turing 1947, p.378), the analogy between digital computing machinery and Turing machines, desired characteristics of memory storage including acoustic delay lines, and the role of "subsidiary table" (Turing 1947, p.389), which is in fact similar to the subroutine.

Moreover, Turing (1947) includes Turing's initial statements on the intelligence of machinery. Discussing the properties of memory storage, Turing mentions "intelligence" of machinery for the first time in this article, as follows:

> I have spent a considerable time in this lecture on this question of memory, because I believe that the provision of proper storage is the key to the problem of the digital computer, and certainly if they are to be persuaded to show any sort of genuine intelligence much larger capacities than are yet available must be provided. (Turing 1947, p.383)

How could we make machines to show "any sort of genuine intelligence"? From Turing (1947), we can extract the following three requirements to realize machines that can show their own intelligence:

(R1) A machine needs to learn from experience,
(R2) We must allow a machine to make mistakes,
(R3) A machine needs to interact with circumstance.

Turing presented these three points successively in the last several paragraphs of Turing (1947), and they are frequently revisited in his later discussions in the late 1940s and the 1950s. It is immediate to see that these three requirements are not independent but interrelate with each other. For example, the learning process of a machine possibly involves interaction with circumstance or interference from out-

---

[9]This paper was never published in Turing's lifetime. We could access the digitally scanned copy via The Turing Digital Archive (http://www.turingarchive.org/). Reprints are published in Carpenter and Doran (1977) and Copeland (2004b), and they provide different revisions at some points. In this chapter, we use page numbers of Copeland (2004b).

side, and a learning process under a teacher presupposes that the machine may make mistakes. Let us see the detail of our three requirements in Turing (1947) below.

Firstly, let us discuss (R1). Turing stated "What we want is a machine that can learn from experience" (cf. Turing 1947, p.393). For a machine to behave intelligently, however, what does the machine learn from experience? This should be compared to what the machine is intended to do initially. Turing described a very basic idea of learning machines, using an analogy of a relationship between a student and a teacher, as follows:

> Let us suppose we have set up a machine with certain initial instruction tables, so constructed that these tables might on occasion, if good reason arose, modify those tables. One can imagine that after the machine had been operating for some time, the instructions would have altered out of all recognition, but nevertheless still be such that one would have to admit that the machine was still doing very worthwhile calculations. Possibly it might still be getting results of the type desired when the machine was first set up, but in a much more efficient manner. In such a case one would have to admit that the progress of the machine had not been foreseen when its original instructions were put in. It would be like a pupil who had learnt much from his master, but had added much more by his own work. When this happens I feel that one is obliged to regard the machine as showing intelligence. (Turing 1947, p.393)

A teacher (or a "master") thinks her students (or "pupil"s) are making progress or "showing intelligence" when the students add much more to what they learnt directly from the teacher. Analogous to this case, a human would regard a machine as intelligent when the machine adds much more (or something new) by its own work. The contents of "much more" at least include a more efficient way of doing calculations to get the same result as the initial setup of the machine. In order for a machine to "learn from experience," Turing also assumed that the machine should be able to modify its initial instructions.

Secondly, let us move to (R2). Turing stated "if a machine is expected to be infallible, it cannot also be intelligent" (cf. Turing 1947, p.394). This requirement is pointed out with considering an argument against the idea of a machine with intelligence. The argument is explained as follows:

> It has for instance been shown that with certain logical systems there can be no machine which will distinguish provable formulae of the system from unprovable, i.e. that there is no test that the machine can apply which will divide propositions with certainty into these two classes. Thus if a machine is made for this purpose it must in some cases fail to give an answer. On the other hand if a mathematician is confronted with such a problem he would search around a[nd] find new methods of proof, so that he ought eventually to be able to reach a decision about any given formula. (Turing 1947, pp.393–4)

Here, Turing employed his own negative solution to the Entscheidungsproblem (recall Sect. 6.2) as an example to explain the argument that there is a problem such that a human mathematician can solve it but any machine could not do that. Turing opposed this argument by taking into consideration a possibility of making a mistake. When a human mathematician tries out a new technique for a problem beyond the scope of the effective procedures, he could not avoid making errors. Therefore, if machines are expected to solve a problem beyond the effective procedures and to be intelligent like humans, Turing claims that they should be fallible.

Finally, let us examine (R3). As we have seen it for item (R2), Turing seems to admit that a human mathematician can show intelligent behavior. But how does a human mathematician develop her intelligence? This should be through "an extensive training" (cf. Turing 1947, p.394). It is obvious that such a training could not be done without an interaction with others, including a teacher. So, in order for a machine to behave intelligently, Turing continues as follows:

> This training may be regarded as not unlike putting instruction tables into a machine. One must therefore not expect a machine to do a very great deal of building up of instruction tables on its own. No man adds very much to the body of knowledge, why should we expect more of a machine? Putting the same point differently, the machine must be allowed to have contact with human beings in order that it may adapt itself to their standards. (Turing 1947, p.394)

Turing regards that the training to be a human mathematician may be like setting an instruction table (or a program) into a machine and also that this training of a machine should not be done by the machine itself. In this sense, a machine needs to interact with circumstance.

Turing did not provide any specific model to realize the three requirements in this article. In later articles, these ideas are described in a more sophisticated form. We will see how Turing developed the ideas on the intelligence of machines by examining two articles: Turing (1948, 1950a).

To finish this section, we stress the possible continuity of Turing (1947) from Turing (1936, 1939) in terms of machines. We may regard that Turing (1947) left the idea of the oracle machine (discussed in Sect. 6.3.1) aside and went back to the idea of the choice machine (discussed in Sect. 6.2.2) to realize intelligence of a machine, where we recall that the choice machine was described as a machine "whose motion is only partially determined by the configuration" (cf. Turing 1936, p.232).

6.5   Learning Process to Organize Intelligent Machinery

Turing (1948) was submitted to Sir Charles Galton Darwin, the director of NPL, and never published during Turing's lifetime.[10] This is one of the earliest articles which Turing wrote about the intelligence of machines in detail and could be useful to learn the background of the famous article (Turing 1950a) on the Turing test. In this section, we examine the content of Turing (1948) from our perspective of the three requirements (R1), (R2), and (R3), discussed in the previous section.

The outline of the article is summarized well by Turing himself as follows.

---

[10]We could access the digitally scanned copy of the original typescript via The Turing Digital Archive (http://www.turingarchive.org/). Reprints are published in Robinson and Evans (1968) and Copeland (2004b). In this chapter, we use page numbers of Copeland (2004b).

> The possible ways in which machinery might be made to show intelligent behaviour are discussed. The analogy with the human brain is used as a guiding principle. It is pointed out that the potentialities of the human intelligence can only be realised if suitable education is provided. The investigation mainly centres round an analogous teaching process applied to machines. The idea of an unorganised machine is defined, and it is suggested that the infant human cortex is of this nature. Simple examples of such machines are given, and their education by means of rewards and punishments is discussed. In one case the education process is carried through until the organisation is similar to that of an ACE. (Turing 1948, pp.431–2)

Following this summary, we shall examine Turing's argument in (1948) for intelligent behavior of machines.

What kind of "machinery" does Turing have in mind in his summary? To specify it, Turing classified machines that existed at the time (cf. Turing 1948, p.412). Turing distinguished between "discrete" and "continuous" machinery, where a machine is discrete when "it is natural to describe its possible states as a discrete set" and it is continuous when its possible states "form a continuous manifold." For example, ACE, the automatic computing engine, is a discrete machine and a differential analyzer is a continuous machine. Moreover, he distinguished between "controlling" and "active" machinery, where a machine is said to be controlling if "it only deals with information" and it is active when it is intended to "produce some definite physical effect." For example, ACE is a controlling machine and a bulldozer is an active machine. Based on these introduced categories, Turing (1948) was mainly concerned with discrete controlling machinery. In addition, Turing emphasized the importance of a memory capacity as: "The memory capacity of a machine more than anything else determines the complexity of its possible behaviour" (cf. Turing 1948, p.413). Therefore, a machine should have enough memory capacity to show intelligent behavior.

6.5.1 How to Obtain Machine with Discipline and Initiative

As we have seen in our explanation of (R2) in Sect. 6.4, Turing's (1948) goal was not the machines which only use an effective method but the machines which have the ability also beyond the limit of the effective methods. To explain these points, Turing (1948, p.429) introduced two concepts, "discipline" and "initiative." He called the routines that would be rules for effective methods as "discipline," and emphasized its importance as "[w]ithout something of this kind one cannot set up proper communication." Turing stated, however, that "discipline is certainly not enough in itself to produce intelligence." Then Turing described "initiative" as follows: "That which is required in addition we call initiative" (cf. Turing 1948, p.429).

Hence, we can say both discipline and initiative are necessary for intelligence. Moreover, the description above implies that "initiative" is an ability to execute operations which humans could do but the universal Turing machines could not do. Turing said that initiative is particularly required when coping with problems of "search" such as a search for a solution to a problem of the form "find a number n such that ..." (cf. Turing 1948, p.430). We will come back to this point later in the end of this section (see Sect. 6.5.3). Then, how could we obtain a machine with both discipline and initiative? Turing (1948, pp.429–30) suggested two methods:

(M1) Grafting some initiative onto the universal Turing machine, which has discipline in advance,
(M2) Bringing both discipline and initiative into an unorganized machine at once.

Turing noted that both approaches should be tried. The outline of the method (M1) is described by Turing as follows:

> This [the method (M1)] would probably take the form of programming the machine to do every kind of job that could be done, as a matter of principle [...]. Bit by bit one would be able to allow the machine to make more and more 'choices' or 'decisions'. One would eventually find it possible to programme it so as to make its behaviour be the logical result of a comparatively small number of general principles. When these became sufficiently general, interference would no longer be necessary, and the machine would have 'grown up'. (Turing 1948, pp.429–30)

This method (M1) seems to be adopted to obtain an intelligent machine later in Turing (1950a), while Turing (1948) seemed to try the second method (M2) *partially* in the sense that he argues how to bring the *discipline* into an "unorganized" machine. Turing (1948) discussed a machine composed of simple input-output units which are randomly connected to each other and then introduced a model called "P-type machine". He argued how to "organize" this P-type machine into a machine with discipline through a learning process which involves a random process and interferences from the outside. It is noted that Turing's idea of the method (M2) seems to come from the analogy with the human brain, where Turing also regards the cortex of the infant as "an unorganised machine, which can be organised by suitable interfering training" (cf. Turing 1948, p.424).

6.5.2 P-Type Machines

This subsection goes into the details of Turing's idea of P-type machines via Turing's (1948) specific example of it, called "a small P-type machine." As stated above, P-type machine is intended to acquire discipline. Turing compared P-type machines with Turing machines (referred as "L.C.M." in the citation below) and summarized the idea of P-type machines as follows.

> The P-type machine may be regarded as an L.C.M. [logical computing machine] without a tape, and whose description is largely incomplete. When a configuration is reached for which the action is undetermined, a random choice for the missing data is made and the appropriate entry is made in the description, tentatively, and is applied. When a pain stimulus occurs all tentative entries are cancelled, and when a pleasure stimulus occurs they are all made permanent. (Turing 1948, p.425)

Table 6.1 A table of Turing's small P-type machine

Situation s	Input	Externally visible action	A value to memory unit
1	P	A	
2	P	B	$M_1 = 1$
3	P	B	
4	S_1	A	$M_1 = 0$
5	M_1	C	

Table 6.1 provides an example of a table which specifies the behavior of a P-type machine. With the help of this example, let us see the details of the P-type machines. A configuration of P-type machine is called a *situation* in Turing (1948). The number of situations is defined to be finite for each P-type machine. When the number of situations is N, let us write the situations as 1, 2, ..., N. It is easy to see that we can set $N = 5$ in Table 6.1.

What can each P-type machine do in each situation? The actions consist of the following:

- To do one of the externally visible actions that are pre-determined;
- To set one of the memory units (say $M_1, ..., M_R$) either into the "1" condition or into the "0" condition.

When the memory unit M_i is in the "0" (or "1") condition, let us say that M_i has the value 0 (or 1) and write it as $M_i = 0$ (or $M_i = 1$, respectively). These two actions are noted to be not mutually exclusive, i.e., a machine could do both. For example, the set of memory units in Table 6.1 is a singleton of M_1 and the machine did a visible action in all its situations.

How can a given P-type machine change its situation? Recall that we have defined that the number of possible situations is N. Depending on whether the value which the machine chooses is 0 or 1, the next situation of the machine is calculated as follows. Let $s \in \{1, 2, ..., N\}$ be the current situation. When the value is chosen to be 0 (or 1) at the situation s, then the next state of s is the reminder of $2s$ (or $2s + 1$, respectively) by division of the total number N of situations. For example, when the current situation is $s = 2$ in Table 6.1 and the chosen value is 0 (or 1), the next state is 4 (or 5, respectively), where recall that $N = 5$ in Table 6.1.

Now we need to know how the machine chooses one of the values of 0 and 1. It is immediate to see that the memory unit is one of the sources of such value. According to Turing, which value the machine uses is pre-determined by either:

(a) One of the memory units of the machine,
(b) A sense stimulus of the machine, or
(c) The pleasure-pain arrangements of the machine,

where "[t]he sense stimuli are means by which the teacher communicates 'unemotionally' to the machine, i.e. otherwise than by pleasure and pain stimuli"

(Turing 1948, p.426) and cases (b) and (c) are intended for communicating with the teacher. It is noted that such communication channels are presupposed for our requirements of (R1) and (R3) at least.

The word "pre-determined" means that which of (a), (b), and (c) the machine uses is determined or specified by a table (such as Table 6.1) for the machine, and also means that such a pre-specified table will *not* be changed in the process of computation. When a given situation is specified to use one of the memory units (a) or a sense stimulus (b), we can say that the action of the situation is *completely determined*. The situations 4 and 5 of Table 6.1 are examples of completely determined situations where M_1 is the unique memory unit of the machine and S_1 is the unique sensor which can receive a stimulus. Otherwise, we can say that the action of the situation is *not* completely determined ("undetermined" in Turing's summary of P-type machine). The situations 1, 2, and 3 of Table 6.1 are examples of such situations. According to Turing, interference does not have any effect in the cases (a) and (b) but it matters in case (c), where our requirement (R3) is reflected.

But then what is the machine supposed to do in such an undetermined situation (e.g., one of the situations 1, 2, and 3)? This is a place where random process and interference process (such as punishments and rewards) play an important role. Let us see the details. The letter "P" of Table 6.1 is one of the following letters: U (uncertain), T0 (tentative 0), T1, D0 (definite 0), D1. Depending on which letter is in the entry at the current situation, the machine proceeds as follows:

- The case where U (uncertain) is on the entry: the value 0 or 1 is chosen from a given random process, and the letter in the entry is changed into Ti (tentative i), where i is the chosen value.
- The case where T0 or T1 is on the entry: when a pleasure stimulus (i.e., reward) occurs, Ti (tentative i) is changed into Di (definite i) and so the tentative input becomes the definite one. When a pain stimulus (i.e., punishment) occurs, Ti is changed into U and so the tentative input is cancelled and the entry is moved back to the uncertain status U.
- The case where D0 or D1 is on the entry: the value i of the letter Di is used by the machine.

A teacher of a P-type machine observes the sequence of the "externally visible action" and provides a pleasure stimulus or a pain stimulus as an interference if necessary. Turing provided an illustration of how the machine behaves in terms of Table 6.1. In the illustration, a teacher used a pain stimulus to break an undesired repetitive cycle of externally visible actions such as BABAB (see Turing 1948, p.427).

Now let us see how our three requirements are satisfied in P-type machines. Since the interference from a teacher plays a role in case (c) above, (R3) is naturally satisfied. In terms of (R3), Turing (1948) "compare[d] the circumstances of our machine with those of a man" and says:

It would be quite unfair to expect a machine straight from the factory to compete on equal terms with a university graduate [...] [who] has had contact with human beings for twenty years or more [...] [a human] is in frequent communication with other men, and is continually receiving visual and other stimuli which themselves constitute a form of interference. (Turing 1948, p.421)

It is noteworthy that the errors made by P-type machines under the learning process have to be "visible." While the internal situations of a machine cannot be seen directly from outside, all actions or behavior are visible, and the teacher makes a decision whether she will provide reward or punishment, based on what she saw.

For (R1), by providing a pleasure or pain stimulus to a machine, an education process or a learning process of the machine is implemented, where it is noted that a sense stimulus may be also regarded as an "unemotional" communication channel from the teacher to the machine. We also note that Turing (1948) used the analogy between the education process for human students and the learning process for machines, as described in Turing's summary of the article. Turing said that he was "following the human model" and suggested "by applying appropriate interference, mimicking education, we should hope to modify the machine until it could be relied on to produce definite reactions to certain commands" (cf. Turing 1948, p.422). Turing noted, however, that "[t]he actual technique by which the 'organising' of the P-type machine was [...] not sufficiently analogous to the kind of process by which a child would really be taught", just because it is "too laborious at present." Still Turing "feel[s] that more should be done on these lines" (cf. Turing 1948, p.428).

Finally for (R2), Turing (1948) claims that "the condition that the machine must not make mistakes [...] is not a requirement for intelligence" (cf. Turing 1948, p.411). How is this requirement reflected in P-type machines? When a teacher provides a pain stimulus, a machine is regarded as making an error. However, we remark that (R2) is originally required for a machine to solve a problem beyond effective procedures or discipline.

6.5.3   The Scope of P-Type Machines and Beyond

Recall from the end of Sect. 6.5.1 that Turing (1948) *partially* tried the method (M2) to realize intelligent behavior of a machine. Why partially? This is because P-machines are intended to organize and to obtain discipline at least, and the discipline is, for Turing, a necessary but insufficient condition for intelligence of a machine. According to Turing, "[t]o convert a brain or machine into a universal machine is the extremest form of discipline" (cf. Turing 1948, p.429). In the summary of the article, Turing stated that "[i]n one case the education process is carried through until the organisation is similar to that of an ACE", where ACE is a practical computing machine, which has the essential properties of the universal Turing machine. In particular, Turing said a P-type machine with external memory, which means a tape, could be organized into the universal Turing machine (cf. Turing 1948, 427–8). Therefore, we can say that Turing (1948) tried to organize a P-type machine into the universal Turing machine, by the learning process with the interference of a teacher. However, we should add that it is not immediately clear from Turing (1948) if a P-type machine could be organized to obtain both discipline and initiative, i.e., if the method (M2) of Sect. 6.5.1 is possible.

How can we organize the machine to have initiative? Let us briefly look at this point. We saw in Sect. 6.5.1 that, for Turing, initiative was required for a problem of the form "find a number n such that ....", since it is possible for Turing to reduce a wide variety of problems into this form. One of the naivest ways of dealing with such a question is by brute force, i.e., to check if each of the positive integers satisfies the required property, though it is often quite time consuming. So, Turing claims "[f]or practical work therefore some more expeditious method is necessary." Turing's idea of an expeditious method first employs a universal practical computing machine in which a program corresponding to a logical system is built-in, where Turing seems to employ his first method (M1). Then the machine's behavior is not *deterministic*, i.e., "at various stages more than one choice as to the next step would be possible." Thus it becomes important to determine how choice is made by the machine. How the original problem is solved expeditiously depends on how the machine makes a choice. Therefore, Turing states:

> Further research into intelligence of machinery will probably be very greatly concerned with "searches" of this kind. We may perhaps call such searches 'intellectual searches'. They might very briefly be defined as 'searches carried out by brains for combinations with particular properties'. (Turing 1948, p.430)

Related to this importance of searching, Turing picks up two other kinds of search: evolutionary search and cultural search. In terms of our three requirements, the second search is concerned with (R3). After Turing noted that "the isolated man does not develop any intellectual power", he continues:

> It is necessary for him to be immersed in an environment of other men, whose techniques he absorbs during the first 20 years of his life. He may then perhaps do a little research of his own and make a very few discoveries which are passed on to other men. From this point of view the search for new techniques must be regarded as carried out by the human community as a whole, rather than by individuals. (Turing 1948, p.431)

To sum up, Turing (1948) proposed two methods (M1) and (M2) to realize intelligence of a machine, i.e., both discipline and initiative of a machine, and he tried the method (M2) partially in the sense that he proposed the idea of P-type machines to organize a machine to obtain discipline at least. Even if we restrict our attention to discipline alone, we saw that our three requirements (R1), (R2) and (R3) are naturally satisfied in P-type machines. Turing (1948), however, specifies that initiative is required for a problem of searching a value and outlined how the method (M1) will be employed to reduce such a searching problem to a problem of choosing an appropriate alternative in a non-deterministic behavior of the machine.

6.6 How Can We Construct an Intelligent Machine to Pass the Imitation Game?

Turing (1950a), published in *Mind*, is well-known as the paper of the Turing test. It deals with various issues on the intelligence of machines including those which were discussed in the previous articles. This article consists of topics such as the setting of the Turing test, the architecture of digital computing machines, the universality of digital computers, Turing's refutations to the objections for the question "Can machines think?", and the discussion on learning machines. In particular, Turing (1950a) seems to employ the method (M1) from Sect. 6.5.1 to realize intelligent behavior of a machine, i.e., the method of grafting some initiative onto the universal Turing machine, which has discipline in advance. This section first checks the setting of the Turing test and Turing's answer to the test, and then elucidates Turing's perspective for the future of the intelligence of machines from our three requirements (R1) to (R3).

6.6.1 The Imitation Game

At the very beginning of the article, the question "Can machines think?" is presented. To cope with this question, Turing avoided giving definitions of the words such as "machine" and "think" and suggested replacing this question itself with another question that "is closely related to it and is expressed in relatively unambiguous words" as follows[11]:

> It is played with three people, a man (A), a woman (B), and an interrogator (C) who may be of either sex. The interrogator stays in a room apart from the other two. The object of the game for the interrogator is to determine which of the other two is the man and which is the woman. He knows them by labels X and Y, and at the end of the game he says either 'X is A and Y is B' or 'X is B and Y is A'. The interrogator is allowed to put questions to A and B [...] It is A's object in the game to try and cause C to make the wrong identification. [...] In order that tones of voice may not help the interrogator the answers should be written, or better still, typewritten. [...] The object of the game for the third player (B) is to help the interrogator. [...] We now ask the question, 'What will happen when a machine takes the part of A in this game?' Will the interrogator decide wrongly as often when the game is played like this as he does when the game is played between a man and a woman? These questions replace our original, 'Can machines think?' (Turing 1950a, pp.433–4)

---

[11]This was not the first time that Turing presented this kind of game. In the last part of Turing (1948), a prototype of the Turing test is presented, as follows:

> Now get three men as subjects for the experiment A, B, C. A and C are to be rather poor chess players, B is the operator who works the paper machine. [...] Two rooms are used with some arrangement for communicating moves, and a game is played between C and either A or the paper machine. C may find it quite difficult to tell which he is playing. (Turing 1948, p.431)

This is called the "imitation game" in Turing (1950a), which is now well-known as the Turing test. To rephrase this question again into a more detailed one, Turing starts clarifying what kind of machine could pass the game. Turing's answer is a digital computer. This "digital computer" is described as a computing machine, with an enormous number of discrete states, as consisting of three components: "Store" (memory storage), "Executive unit," and "Control" (cf. Turing 1950a, p.437). In particular, Turing emphasizes that a digital computer has the special property that it "can mimic any discrete state machine" and so it can be called a universal machine (cf. Turing 1950a, pp.441–2, recall Sect. 6.2.3):

> The existence of machines with this property [the special property above] has the important consequence that, considerations of speed apart, it is unnecessary to design various new machines to do various computing processes. They can all be done with one digital computer, suitably programmed for each case. It will be seen that as a consequence of this all digital computers are in a sense equivalent. (Turing 1950a, pp.441–2)

Based on this clarification, Turing rephrases the question of the imitation game again as follows.

> 'Let us fix our attention on one particular digital computer C. Is it true that by modifying this computer to have an adequate storage, suitably increasing its speed of action, and providing it with an appropriate programme, C can be made to play satisfactorily the part of A in the imitation game, the part of B being taken by a man?' (Turing 1950a, p.442)

We can admit that the digital computer C in the citation is a universal Turing machine, which has discipline in advance. So Turing's question is also regarded as: Is it possible to use the method (M1) of Sect. 6.5.1 to equip a universal Turing machine with initiative to pass the imitation game? Now the question becomes a matter of program.[12] Turing made a prediction about when a well-programmed digital machine will pass the imitation game as follows:

> [...] in about fifty years' time it will be possible to programme computers, with a storage capacity of about 10^9, to make them play the imitation game so well that an average interrogator will not have more than 70 per cent. (Turing 1950a, p.442)

How can Turing make quantitative judgements such as "about fifty years" and "a storage capacity of about 10^9" in this answer? As for the storage capacity, 10^9 binary digits would be enough for the machine because "[e]stimates of the storage capacity of the brain vary from 10^{10} to 10^{15} binary digits" and "[m]ost of it is probably used for the retention of visual impressions" (cf. Turing 1950a, p.455). "About fifty years" is coming from Turing's speed of programming at that time (about a thousand digits of programme a day)[13] as follows:

> [...] about sixty workers, working steadily through the fifty years might accomplish the job, if nothing went into the waste-paper basket. (Turing 1950a, p.455)

---

[12]Note that Turing believed a computing machine which can play the imitation game well is obtained by programming, not by tinkering hardware. Turing said "[o]ur problem then is to find out how to programme these machines to play the game" (cf. Turing 1950a, p.455).

[13]We note that in a script of BBC radio program "Can Automatic Calculating Machines Be Said to Think," Turing said it would be "at least 100 years" for a machine to play the imitation game sufficiently. See Newman et al. (1952) in Copeland (2004b, p.495).

Turing's answer with the quantitative judgments above implies that an intended program would be quite complex. Then, how could we obtain such a complex program? First of all, Turing said that, in order to make such a program for the machine which can play the imitation game, "[a] storage capacity of 10^7 would be a very practicable possibility even by present techniques" and "[i]t is probably not necessary to increase the speed of operations of the machines at all" (cf. Turing 1950a, p.455). Explaining the reason to the latter half, Turing uses the analogy between a human brain and a machine: Turing said "Parts of modern machines which can be regarded as analogues of nerve cells work about a thousand times faster than the latter."

Turing's idea to obtain a complex program which can play the imitation game is not to try "to imitate adult human mind" directly but rather to analyze the process of reaching the adult human mind into the following three components (cf. Turing 1950a, p.455):

(a) The initial state of the mind, say at birth,
(b) The education to which it has been subjected,
(c) Other experience, not to be described as education, to which it has been subjected.

Then Turing states that "there is so little mechanism in the child-brain that something like it can be easily programmed" (cf. Turing 1950a, p.456) and suggests the problem into two parts:

the child-program and the education process.

But how much education do we need? Turing's approximation is: "The amount of work in the education we can assume, as a first approximation, to be much the same as for the human child" (cf. Turing 1950a, p.456). While Turing provided such approximation on the amount of the education for a machine, the education or teaching process itself is not quite the same as the process for the human child. So, Turing said "It will not be possible to apply exactly the same teaching process to the machine as to a normal child. It will not, for instance, be provided with legs, so that it could not be asked to go out and fill the coal scuttle" (cf. Turing 1950a, p.456). Let us see Turing's details of two parts of the child-program and the education process in the next subsection.

6.6.2 Learning Process for Child Program

The details of Turing's idea of the child-program and the education process are discussed in the section "Learning Machines" in Turing (1950a). To pass the imitation game, a machine needs to be able to show intelligent behavior after the learning process. Turing characterizes intelligent behavior as follows.

> Intelligent behaviour presumably consists in a departure from the completely disciplined
> behaviour involved in computation, but a rather slight one, which does not rise to random
> behaviour, or to pointless repetitive loops. (Turing 1950a, p.459)

This citation explains, from the viewpoint of behavior, why Turing claimed that both discipline and initiative are needed for intelligence. Recall that "initiative" is defined as "that which is required in addition [to discipline] we call initiative" in Turing (1948, p.429). In the above citation, Turing provides a further analysis of initiative in terms of behavior of a machine. In order for a digital machine with the universal property to pass the imitation game, Turing's idea of the child-program and the education process for it should be able to realize a slight departure from "the completely disciplined behavior involved in the computation." Now let us examine the detail of the child-program and the education process in Turing (1950a) in terms of our three requirements (R1), (R2), and (R3).

Let us start with (R1). From the side of a machine, the education or teaching process is a *learning* process. How can a digital machine with a child-program learn from experience? Or, in other words, what kind of function is a child program supposed to have? Let us suppose that a digital machine with a child-program has "a complete system of logical inference 'built in'," which means that "the logical system will not have to be learnt." Then in this case,

> [...] the store [of a machine] would be largely occupied with definitions and propositions.
> The propositions would have various kinds of status, e.g. well-established facts, conjectures,
> mathematically proved theorems, statements given by an authority, expressions having the
> logical form of proposition but not belief-value. Certain propositions may be described as
> 'imperatives.' (Turing 1950a, p.457)

Turing continues "The machine should be so constructed that as soon as an imperative is classed as 'well-established' the appropriate action automatically takes place." How is this possible? Turing illustrates this point as follows.

> [...] suppose the teacher says to the machine, 'Do your homework now'. This may cause
> "Teacher says 'Do your homework now'" to be included amongst the well-established facts.
> Another such fact might be, "Everything that teacher says is true". Combining these may
> eventually lead to the imperative, 'Do your homework now', being included amongst the
> well-established facts, and this, by the construction of the machine, will mean that the
> homework actually gets started, but the effect is very satisfactory. (Turing 1950a, pp.457–8)

This explains a very rough idea of how the requirement (R1) is satisfied. Moreover, recall that Turing assumed for (R1) that the machine should be able to modify initial instructions. How can the initial instructions of a machine change? Turing describes it as follows:

> The idea of a learning machine may appear paradoxical to some readers. How can the rules
> of operation of the machine change? They should describe completely how the machine
> will react whatever its history might be, whatever changes it might undergo. The rules are
> thus quite time-invariant. This is quite true. The explanation of the paradox is that the rules
> which get changed in the learning process are of a rather less pretentious kind, claiming
> only an ephemeral validity. The reader may draw a parallel with the Constitution of the
> United States. (Turing 1950a, p.458)

It should be noted that, when an amendment is to be made to the Constitution of the United States, the original constitution is kept as it is and the amendment added to the constitution. Similarly to this, we may keep the initial instructions of a machine through the learning process but add an "amendment" to the instructions to modify behavior of a machine.

Even if the machine can learn from experience as discussed in the above, the machine needs to interact with circumstance, i.e., the machine should satisfy (R3). Otherwise, it may be impossible for a machine to show intelligent behavior. Similarly to the discussion in Turing (1948), Turing (1950a) uses the teacher-student analogy to describe the learning process with "unemotional" channels to communicate with a machine as well as punishments and rewards from a teacher. What is the importance of the "unemotional" channels of communication? They are needed to make a teaching process more efficient as follows.

> If these ['unemotional' channels of communication] are available it is possible to teach a machine by punishments and rewards to obey orders given in some language, e.g. a symbolic language. These orders are to be transmitted through the 'unemotional' channels. The use of this language will diminish greatly the number of punishments and rewards required. (Turing 1950a, p.457)

Finally, we also add that Turing related the learning process with a problem of searching as "a search for a form of behaviour which will satisfy the teacher (or some other criterion)" (Turing 1950a, p.459).

How can we realize a "slight departure" from completely disciplined behavior by the learning process satisfying (R1) and (R3) as in the above? Here our requirement of (R2) becomes important, i.e., we need to allow a digital machine with a child program to make an error or a mistake. Turing classifies the errors of machines into two groups: "errors of functioning" and "errors of conclusion" (cf. Turing 1950a, p.449). The former errors are caused by some mechanical trouble of the hardware, where Turing assumes that such errors never happen in the learning process for a child-program. The latter errors occur because the machine does not operate only with an effective method but "it might have some method for drawing conclusions by scientific induction" (cf. Turing 1950a, p.449). If a machine uses methods other than the effective procedures, it might lead a wrong answer. Therefore, we must allow such errors to obtain machines which show intelligent behavior. Turing (1950a) suggested again that not only the discipline but the initiative, as discussed in Turing (1948), are important for the intelligence.

The machine of fallibility is mentioned in another way. In the learning process of the machines with the built-in system of logic, imperatives which "regulate the order in which the rules of the logical system concerned are to be applied" (cf. Turing 1950a, p.458) are critical, and Turing said that the machine itself can produce them with scientific induction. The scientific induction, which is not deductive reasoning, may lead to a false conclusion. Hence the machine which uses the scientific induction may make mistakes. "We must expect such a method to lead occasionally to erroneous results" (cf. Turing 1950a, p.449) said, Turing.

Based on the above observations in terms of the three requirements (R1), (R2), and (R3), we may summarize that: A machine which can play the imitation game is described as a learning machine. Turing seems to employ his first method (M1) to realize intelligence, i.e., both discipline and initiative. In particular, such a machine could be implemented first as a child mind program in a digital computing machine and then would go through the learning process. Similarly to (1948), Turing kept discussing the interferences from outside during the learning process and the visible behavior of machines. The errors possibly made by a machine are classified into two groups, and Turing regarded that "errors of conclusion," such as errors caused by scientific induction, should be allowed if we expect intelligence of the machine.

6.7   Conclusion

Let us summarize the development of Turing's idea between his papers (Turing 1936, 1950a).

Turing (1936) characterized what a human calculator is doing in her computation (i.e., an effective or mechanical procedure) in terms of Turing machines (computing machines in Turing's term) and, at the same time, Turing (1936) demonstrated that there is an uncomputable problem by any Turing machine, i.e., the printing problem and the Entscheidungsproblem, while a human mathematician may find a way to cope with such a problem with the help of intuition, etc. It might be argued from these that a machine could not be intelligent. Turing (1947) rejected the argument by allowing a machine to make an error or a mistake (the requirement R2) and considered a possibility that a machine may show intelligent behavior. For such a possibility, Turing (1947) posed two more requirements: a machine can learn from the machine's experience (the requirement R1) and a machine needs to interact with circumstance (the requirement R3).

Turing (1948) first specifies which kinds of machine we should take into consideration. A machine that could show intelligent behavior should be a discrete and controlling machine with enough memory storage, where "discrete" means that the machine's possible states are described as a discrete (not continuous) set and "controlling" means that the machine deal with information alone. Then, Turing (1948) claimed that not only discipline but also initiative are needed for a machine to produce intelligence. What is the discipline here? From Turing's (1948) description, it should contain effective or mechanical methods by a human calculator at least. Moreover, he suggested two methods of making such a machine: First, we make a universal Turing machine (supposed to have discipline) learn initiative; Second, we make an unorganized machine to learn discipline and initiative at once. Turing (1948) seems to choose the second method and proposed an idea of P-type machines to capture discipline, at least, by a learning process involving interference of reward and punishment from a teacher. We have examined how the above three requirements are elaborated in P-type machines, where we note that discipline was regarded as *necessary* (but not sufficient) for a machine to produce intelligence. Turing (1948), however, did not have any concrete model for making a machine have initiative.

In order for a machine to pass the imitation game, Turing (1950a) seemed to assume that the machine needs to have discipline as well as initiative. For a machine to pass the game, how is the machine supposed to behave? Here is Turing's answer: "Intelligent behavior presumably consists in a departure from the completely disciplined behavior involved in computation, but a rather slight one, which does not rise to random behavior, or to pointless repetitive loops." To realize such a "rather slight departure" from "the completely disciplined behavior," Turing employed the first method above of making a universal computing machine learn initiative. In particular, Turing (1950a) proposed a method by a child machine and the education process for it, where our three requirements are naturally satisfied.

Acknowledgements The work of the first author was partially supported by JSPS KAKENHI Grant-in-Aid for Young Scientists (B) Grant Number 15K21025 and JSPS Core-to-Core Program (A. Advanced Research Networks).

References

Anderson D (2013) Max Newman: forgotten man of early British computing. Commun ACM 56(5):29–31

Boolos GS, Burgess JP, Jeffery RC (2007) Computability and logic. Cambridge University Press, Cambridge

Carpenter BE, Doran RW (1977) The other Turing machine. Comput J 20(3):269–279

Church A (1936) A note on the Entscheidungsproblem. J Symb Log 1(1):40–41

Copeland BJ (2004a) Computable numbers: a guide. In: Copeland BJ (ed) The essential Turing. Oxford University Press, Oxford, pp 5–57

Copeland BJ (2004b) The essential Turing: seminal writings in computing, logic, philosophy, artificial intelligence, and artificial life plus the secrets of Enigma. Oxford University Press, Oxford/New York

Copeland BJ (2008) The Church-Turing thesis. In: Zalta EN (ed) The stanford encyclopedia of philosophy, Fall 2008 edn. Available via http://plato.stanford.edu/archives/fall2008/entries/church-turing/. Accessed 23 Mar 2017

Davies DW (2004) Corrections to Turing's universal computing machine. In: Copeland BJ (ed) The essential Turing: seminal writings in computing, logic, philosophy, artificial intelligence, and artificial life plus the secrets of enigma, chapter 2.4. Oxford University Press, Oxford/New York, pp 103–124

Davis M (1982) Computability and unsolvability. Dover, New York

Detlefsen M, MacCarty DC, Bacon JB (1999) LOGIC from A to Z. Routledge, London/New York

Enderton EB (2001) A mathematical introduction to logic, 2nd edn. Academic Press, San Diego

Gandy R (1995) The confluence of ideas in 1936. In: Herken R (ed) The universal Turing machine. Springer, New York

Gherardi G (2011) Alan Turing and the foundations of computable analysis. Bull Symb Log 17(3):394–430

Gödel K (1930) Die Vollständigkeit der Axiome des logischen Functionenkalküls. Monatshefte für Mathematik und Physik. 37:349–360

Gödel K (1931) Über formal unentscheidbare Sätze der Principia Mathematica und verwandter Systeme, I. Monatshefte für Mathematik und Physik. 38:173–98

Grattan-Guinness I (2012) Logic, topology and physics: points of contact between Bertrand Russell and Max Newman. J Bertrand Russell Stud 32:5–29

Hilbert D, Ackermann W (1928) Grundzüge der theoretischen Logik. Springer, Berlin

Hodges A (1992) Alan Turing: the enigma. Vintage Books, London

Hodges A (2011) Alan Turing. In: Zalta EN (ed) The stanford encyclopedia of philosophy, Summer 2011 edn. Available via http://plato.stanford.edu/archives/sum2011/entries/turing/. Accessed 23 Mar 2017

Newman MHA (1955) Alan Mathison Turing. Biogr Mem Fellows R Soc 1:253–263

Newman MHA, Turing AM, Jefferson G, Braithwaite RB (1952) Can automatic calculating machines be said to think? Radio interview, recorded 10 Jan 1952 and broadcast 14 and 23 Jan 1952. Turing Archives reference number B.6.

Petzold C (2008) The Annoteated Turing. Wiley, Indianapolis

Piccinini G (2003) Alan Turing and the mathematical objection. Mind Mach 13:23–48

Robinson ADJ, Evans C (1968) Cybernetics: key papers. Butterworths, London

Shieber S (2004) The Turing test: verbal behavior as the hallmark of intelligence. MIT Press, Cambridge

Sieg W (1993) Mechanical procedures and mathematical experience. In: George A (ed) Mathematics and mind, chapter 4. Oxford University Press, New York, pp. 71–117

Teuscher C (2001) Turing's connectionism: an investigation of neural network architectures. Springer, London

Turing AM (1936) On computable numbers with an application to the Entscheidungsproblem. Proc Lond Math Soc 42:230–265. Reprinted In: Copeland BJ (ed) The essential Turing: seminal writings in computing, logic, philosophy, artificial intelligence, and artificial life plus the secrets of Enigma. Oxford University Press, Oxford/New York (2004)

Turing AM (1937) On computable numbers, with an application to the Entscheidungsproblem. A correction. Proc Lond Math Soc 43:544–546. Reprinted In: Copeland BJ (ed) The essential Turing: seminal writings in computing, logic, philosophy, artificial intelligence, and artificial life plus the secrets of Enigma. Oxford University Press, Oxford/New York (2004)

Turing AM (1939) Systems of logic defined by ordinals. Proc Lond Math Soc 45:161–228

Turing AM (1946) Proposal for development in the mathematics division of an automatic computing engine (ACE). Reprinted In: Carpenter BE, Doran RW (eds) A.M. Turing's ACE report of 1946 and other papers. MIT Press, Cambridge, pp. 20–105, c.1946. Available via http://www.turingarchive.org/browse.php/C/32. Accessed 23 Mar 2017

Turing AM (1947) Lecture to L.M.S. [London Mathematical Society] (20 Feb 1947). In: The Papers of Alan Mathison Turing. King's College Archive Centre, Cambridge. AMT/B/1. Also In: Copeland BJ (ed) The essential Turing: seminal writings in computing, logic, philosophy, artificial intelligence, and artificial life plus the secrets of Enigma. Oxford University Press, Oxford/New York. Available via http://www.turingarchive.org/browse.php/B/1 (2004). Accessed 23 Mar 2017

Turing AM (1948) Intelligent machinery. In: The Papers of Alan Mathison Turing. King's College Archive Centre, Cambridge. AMT/C/11. Also In: Copeland BJ (ed) The essential Turing: seminal writings in computing, logic, philosophy, artificial intelligence, and artificial life plus the secrets of enigma. Oxford University Press, Oxford/New York. Available via http://www.turingarchive.org/browse.php/C/11 (2004). Accessed 23 Mar 2017

Turing AM (1950a) Computing machinery and intelligence. Mind 59:433–460. Reprinted In: Copeland BJ (ed) The essential Turing: seminal writings in computing, logic, philosophy, artificial intelligence, and artificial life plus the secrets of enigma. Oxford University Press, Oxford/New York (2004)

Turing AM (1950b) Programmers' handbook for Manchester electronic computer. University of Manchester computing laboratory. Available via http://www.turingarchive.org/browse.php/B/32. Accessed 23 Mar 2017

Turing AM (1952) The chemical basis of morphogenesis. Philos Trans R Soc B 237(641):37–72

Chapter 7
Finite Information Agency

Alfons Josef Schuster

Abstract This chapter describes in more detail our work on so-called 'finite information spaces'. Loosely speaking, finite information spaces include any kind of information agent existing in any type of information environment. From this point of view, human beings, robots, or books represent finite information agents, while a library or the Internet may represent finite information environments. The chapter describes, analyzes, and interprets finite information spaces and related concepts. The chapter also provides an interesting measure called 'autonomy index'. This index provides an opportunity to attribute a degree of autonomy to any finite information agent. We believe that our findings could be relevant in a wide range of areas.

7.1 Introduction

Today, information is increasingly recognized as a fundamental concept across a wide range of science domains. For instance, the interest and intensity in which information is studied and investigated ranges from the physical world (Frank 2002) to the biological kingdom (Marois and Ivanoff 2005), to the modern world of the Internet and computer games (Henschke 2010; Silver et al. 2016), up to the sublime realm of the mind (Floridi 2011). In a sense, the work presented in this chapter relates to any of these fields in a rather general way.[1] More specifically, our work is inspired by the observation that there are some fundamental limits in which we can determine, or comprehend, or interact with the objects in 'the world around us'.[2] In

---

[1] From a historical perspective, this chapter is a substantial extension of our first contribution (Schuster 2014) in the area of finite information spaces.

[2] It is not a trivial affair to define, exactly, what we mean by the expression 'the world around us'. In this chapter, it is helpful to envisage the world around us as the everyday world of our experiences or, likewise, as the world that covers everything that physically exists. This does not necessarily

Dr A.J. Schuster (✉)
(Assistant Professor in Information Studies), School of International Liberal Studies, Waseda University, 4F, Building 11, 1-6-1 Nishi-Waseda, 169-8050, Shinjuku-ku, Tokyo, Japan
e-mail: a.schuster@aoni.waseda.jp

© Springer International Publishing AG 2017
A.J. Schuster (eds.), *Understanding Information*, Advanced Information and Knowledge Processing, DOI 10.1007/978-3-319-59090-5_7

a similar vein, Goldstein (2006, pp. 13–51) mentions three fundamental discoveries, developed in the early twentieth century within the mathematical sciences, that challenge our intuitions about the world around us to the current day, namely: (i) Einstein's theory of relativity, (ii) Heisenberg's uncertainty principle, and (iii) Gödel's incompleteness theorems. Unfortunately, for various reasons, a deeper exploration of these extraordinary discoveries of the human mind is beyond the scope of this work.

In this work, we would like to propose another fundamental property in the world around us, namely that of 'finiteness'. Finiteness is one of those properties that are so omnipresent, familiar, and common to us that we usually do not question their value and meaning too much. Proposition 1 below challenges this everyday view. The proposition tries to indicate that finiteness could be a much more embracing concept than many of us may have thought it is. Indeed, the proposition suggests that on a deeper layer of inspection, finiteness might be a property that lies behind many observable phenomena in the world around us.

Proposition 1 *Finiteness is a fundamental concept in the world around us. The property of finiteness provides an opportunity for interpreting and understanding many physical (and potentially nonphysical) phenomena in the world around us in a fundamental way.*

In order to support this proposition, the chapter describes and analyzes fundamental challenges finite information agents (e.g., biological organism, or software agents) that are equipped with finite information processing capacity (e.g., memory, or lifespan) may encounter in interactions with other finite information agents in various types of finite information environment (e.g., a biosphere in the case of biological agents, or a virtual reality world in the case of software agents). Entities such as finite information agents, finite information sources, finite information environments, or finite information universes are more generally referred to as 'finite information spaces'. When there is no ambiguity involved, we refer to these entities simply as (information) agents, sources, environments, universes, or spaces.

Perhaps, one of the first things that comes to mind when contemplating an information environment may be a society of human beings living on planet Earth. However, it is important to understand that there are various other possibilities. For example, it is possible to consider an information environment consisting of an individual agent engaged in a self-referential process. This agent could be a human being residing in a state of contemplation or meditation. Likewise, it could be a robot or some other form of artificial intelligence (AI) system querying a database or some other form of knowledge repository. The environments where biological agents and artificial agents interact in a collaborative manner are possible, too. Imagine the case of an on-line role playing game on the Internet where teams of human players and software agents team up in virtual worlds. In these environments, a human player

---

imply that this chapter neglects or excludes, de facto, the world of the mind (Feser 2006). Actually, the chapter considers this possibility with great interest. It only means that from the position of this work, the term 'the world around us' provides a somewhat more solid grounding for our arguments than the world of the mind does.

may not always use a software agent in the same manner as a puppeteer manipulates a marionette. On the contrary, some of the software agents developed today (e.g., in computer games or other virtual reality environments) flourish in exhibiting increasing degrees of sophistication (Kang and Tan 2013). In terms of topology, it is also possible to imagine nested information environments where larger, more encompassing environments, may be conceived as super-environments or universes. One such universe could be that of all the people playing on-line role playing games on the Internet at a particular moment in time.

Our work takes its motivation from these ideas. Section 7.2 in this chapter describes and defines various elementary information space scenarios. These scenarios are going to generate an understanding about the fundamental challenges finite information spaces contain. Section 7.3 captures these basic scenarios in a simple mathematical model. The somewhat longer Sect. 7.4 provides various interpretations of this model. These interpretations allow us to evaluate the relevance of our work in modern-day, high-density information environments, and beyond. Section 7.5 ends the chapter with a summary.

7.2 Information Space Scenarios

The aim in this section is to clearly define the main concepts of finite information spaces (agents, sources, environments, etc.) and to extract a set of fundamental properties and behaviors that apply to all finite information spaces. Forthcoming sections are going to further analyze and interpret this set of properties and behaviors.

7.2.1 Scenario 1

Figure 7.1 illustrates a first, basic scenario. This scenario includes a universe (u), an information environment (e), an information agent (a), and an information source (s). In order to provide a better understanding about the various elements in Fig. 7.1, let us first clarify a few general assumptions that apply to all agents, sources, environments, and universes.

Definition 1 Agents, sources, environments, and universes.

- Every agent, source, environment, and universe, has an information capacity referred to as c_a, c_s, c_e, or c_u, respectively.[3]

---

[3]Information capacity may be envisaged as the size of a computer memory (e.g., 300 TB [terabyte]), or as the number of unique words in a work of literature (e.g., with 4024 lines, *Hamlet* is the longest play by Shakespeare Dunton-Downer and Riding 2004, pp. 324–335).

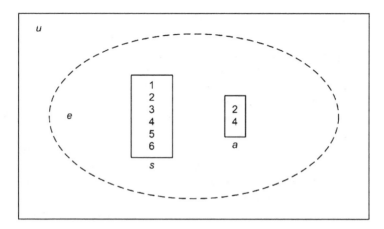

Fig. 7.1 Scenario 1: A universe (u) including (*dashed line*) an information environment (e), an information source (s) and an information agent (a)

- The information capacities c_{a_i}, c_{s_j}, c_{e_k}, and c_{u_l} of all agents a_i, sources s_j, environments e_k, and universes u_l is finite ($i, j, k, l \in \mathbb{N}$).[4]
- The information capacity of an environment c_e is always equal to the sum of the information capacities of all agents and sources existing in this environment. That is: $c_e = \sum_{i=1}^{n} c_{a_i} + \sum_{j=1}^{m} c_{s_j}$, where n and m are the number of agents and sources in the environment c_e ($n, m, i, j \in \mathbb{N}$).[5]
- An empty information environment cannot exist. That is, if E is the set of all environments e then $\forall e \in E : e \neq \emptyset$.
- The information capacity of a universe c_u is always equal to the sum of the information capacities of all environments existing in this universe. That is:

---

[4] Although it is possible to consider infinite information capacities for agents, sources, environments, and universes, this work avoids such considerations. Instead, this work considers the familiar world of our everyday life experiences where biological agents and sources (e.g., humans, or the genetic code of a human being), as well as artificial agents and sources (e.g., a robot, or a database this robot may access) exist. One argument for assuming finite information capacities for all these entities could be the following. When we think about information existing in a human body then we may assume that this information will cease to exist when this human life ends (Krauss and Starkman 2000; Marois and Ivanoff 2005). Likewise, as long as there are no computers or data stores with infinite memory (capacity), it is reasonable to consider the information capacity of a robot or that of a database to be finite too (Frank 2002; Hilbert and López 2011). In short, this chapter considers the information capacity of all agents, sources, environments, and universes as limited (finite) in space and time.

[5] An environment may be envisaged as a mathematical set containing one or more agents and sources. Note that, depending on the context, it is possible for one information environment to include several other information environments.

$c_u = \sum_{i=1}^{n} c_{e_i}$, where n is the number of environments in the universe c_u $(n, i \in \mathbb{N})$.[6]

- An empty universe cannot exist. That is, if U is the set of all universes u then $\forall u \in U : u \neq \emptyset$.

With Definition 1 in mind, imagine now a Fig. 7.1 scenario, where the source s exhibits a behavior similar to that of casting a dice. Simply imagine the source s sequentially emitting numbers between 1 and 6. Remember that agents, sources, etc., are finite in space and time. The term sequentially, therefore, does not necessarily imply infinity. In terms of the information capacity of agent a, it is helpful to consider a finite memory (e.g., the finite memory of a personal computer). In addition, imagine that agent a commands over a set of input-output operations such as 'read', 'write', 'delete', and 'store'. Since the information capacity of any agent is limited, let us further assume that agent a can maximally store only two numbers emitted by the source s. There are no restrictions as to when the agent stores a number in memory or deletes a number from this memory. As an example, let the source emit the following sequence of numbers [2, 2, 5, 1, 6, 4, 5, 3]. In this case, the agent may have ignored the first 2, but stored the second 2 (underlined). The agent then may have stored the 1, then deleted this 1 again, and instead stored a 4 (underlined). At the end of this process, the memory of the agent looks as follows: {2, 4}. Let us stop here briefly to provide a few more clarifications.

Definition 2 Event, history, and recording.

- An *event*, refers to the emission of data or information by a source.[7]
- The *history* of a source, refers to the sequence of all events emitted by a source over a certain period of time.
- A *recording*, refers to events stored in a memory.

Some initial observations for Scenario 1 in Fig. 7.1 could be the following:

Observation 1

- In case the source s emits only two numbers and the finite information agent a records these numbers, then agent a has access to the complete history of the source s, the environment e, and the universe u.
- In case the source s emits more than two numbers than it is impossible for the finite information agent a to have access to the complete history of the

---

[6]A universe may be envisaged as a kind of superset containing all agents, sources, and environments existing in this universe. Depending on the context, it is possible for one information universe to include several other information universes.

[7]Data and information are not the same thing. In this chapter, we adopt the widely shared view that data constitutes information. Data needs to have (or acquire) a particular syntax in order to generate (meaningful) information (Floridi 2010, 2011).

information environment e (universe u). In this case, agent a may have access to only a fraction of the complete history of the information environment e (universe u).

- It is possible for the agent a to take no recordings at all. In such a case, no historical records exist in the environment e (universe u).
- A recording, taken by the agent a at time t_2 may be exactly the same as a recording taken by the agent at an earlier time t_1. For instance, given the sequence $[\ldots, 2, 4 \ldots, \underline{2}, \underline{4}, \ldots]$ the agent a: may have decided to record the first 2 and the first 4 in the sequence; delete these recordings again; then record the 2 and 4 that are underlined in the sequence. In such a case, the present recordings of agent a describe a state that is indistinguishable from a prehistorical state. In a sense, history has repeated itself for agent a.
- Fundamentally, we can distinguish the following states for the finite information agent a: no history, incomplete history, complete history, and repetitive history.

It is possible, of course, to argue that these observations directly result from the various definitions we introduced earlier on. Although this is correct in principle, we would like to reemphasize our intention here, which is to produce models that relate well to our everyday world. From this perspective, the model in Fig. 7.1, the definitions, as well as our interpretations, appear reasonable. This does not mean, however, that our models exclude situations where an agent may be able to record all events emitted by a source. For instance, imagine an agent with a memory that can store eight or more numbers. If the sequence [2, 2, 5, 1, 6, 4, 5, 3] is all the source in Fig. 7.1 ever emits then this agent has the potential to record the entire history of source s. The following definition embraces such considerations.

Definition 3 Local agents, global agents, and super agents.

- A *local agent* is an agent with the capacity to record all events emitted by a single source. (Remember that all agents, sources, etc., are finite in space and time.)
- A *global agent* is an agent with the capacity to record all events emitted by all sources in a single environment.
- A *super agent* is an agent with the capacity to record all events emitted in a single universe.

From Definition 3, it is only a small step to Definition 4:

Definition 4 Local memories, global memories, and super memories.

- A *local memory* is a recording of all events emitted by a single source.
- A *global memory* is a recording of all events emitted by all sources in a single environment.
- A *super memory* is a recording of all events emitted in a single universe.

Please note that our observations so far, trivial as they may be, already lead to interesting questions. For instance, if the agent in Fig. 7.1 is a human being and the universe in the same figure represents our everyday world then the complete history of this world is not accessible – and never will be accessible – to a single

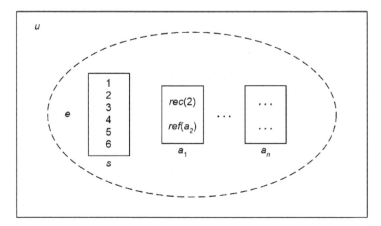

Fig. 7.2 Scenario 2: A universe (u) including an information environment (e), an information source (s), and n information agents ($a_1 \ldots a_n$, where $n \in \mathbb{N}$)

human being. The forthcoming sections consider this dilemma from the perspective of multiple agents (Sect. 7.2.2) and different memory organizations (Sect. 7.2.3).

7.2.2 Scenario 2

Scenario 2 in Fig. 7.2 differs from Scenario 1 in two main ways. The first, more obvious difference is that the universe u now contains more than one agent (agent a_1 to agent a_n, where $n \in \mathbb{N}$). The second difference is that the memory of an individual agent in Fig. 7.2 is now partitioned into two sections. One section allows an agent to record an event (e.g., the outcome of a cast of a dice), while the second section holds a reference to the agent recording the next event (e.g., the outcome of the next cast of the dice). For instance, the record section of the memory of agent a_1 in Fig. 7.2 holds the number 2, while the reference section of the memory of the same agent holds a reference to agent a_2.[8]

Let us now replay Scenario 1, where the source emitted the eight number sequence [2, 2, 5, 1, 6, 4, 5, 3]. If the source in Fig. 7.2 emits the same numbers then it is possible for eight agents to record the complete sequence. For instance, agent a_1 may record the first number (2) plus a reference to agent a_2, while agent a_2 may hold the second number (2) and a reference to agent a_3, and so on, until

---

[8]Of course, the memories of the agents in Scenario 1 (two numbers) and Scenario 2 (one number and one reference) could be different. It could be n numbers in Scenario 1, and m numbers and k references in Scenario 2 ($k, m, n \in \mathbb{N}$). Likewise, it does not really matter in a scenario, whether the memory size is the same for every agent involved. In Scenario 2, it is no problem to imagine one agent with a capacity c_{a_i} and another agent with capacity c_{a_j}, such that $c_{a_i} \neq c_{a_j}$ ($i, j \in \mathbb{N}, i \neq j$). Essentially, what really matters is that the information capacity of any agent is finite.

agent a_8 holds the final number (3), and maybe a reference to agent a_1. This simple example leads to the following definition and observations:

Definition 5 Collective memory.

- Multiple agents can combine their individual memories into a so-called *collective memory*.

Observation 2

- A collective memory may or may not be able to record the entire history of a source (environment, etc.). For example, in case the source in Fig. 7.2 emits more than eight numbers, say nine, then eight agents cannot record the entire history of the source.
- There may be situations where the complete history of a source (environment, etc.) may be recorded in a collective memory. However, even in such situations, it may be the case that none of the finite information agents involved in forming this collective memory, individually, has a record of the complete history of this source. In our example, the collective memory generated by all agents forms a recording of the entire history of the source s. However, none of the agents involved commands over a recording of the entire history of the source s.
- It is possible again to distinguish the following states in a collective memory that is generated by multiple finite information agents: no history, incomplete history, complete history, and repetitive history.

7.2.3 Scenario 3

Scenario 3 extends the previous two scenarios through the introduction of a new type of finite information space, namely that of a finite 'external memory'. Figure 7.3 illustrates a more general Scenario 3 constellation.

For our understanding, it is helpful to think about this constellation as a situation involving agents and sources that are similar to those mentioned for Scenario 2 (Fig. 7.2). The inclusion of multiple sources in the figure does not necessarily complicate matters as we are going to see shortly. However, in comparison to agents, the external memories in the figure should be considered as a different type of finite information space.

Definition 6 External memories.

- *External memories* are information stores.

The following example should help to understand this difference. Imagine the environment of a university. In this environment, several professors may be lecturing to the students. Some students may take notes during lectures. In addition, some students may also visit the university library for their study. In this example, the notebooks and the university library represent external memories. This example leads us to the following definitions for external memories:

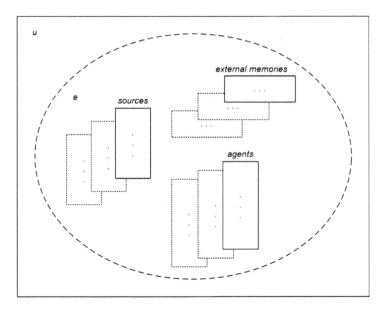

Fig. 7.3 Scenario 3: A universe (*u*) including (*dashed line*) an information environment (*e*) consisting of several information sources, information agents, and external memories

Definition 7 Local external memories, global external memories, and super external memories.

- A *local external memory* is a recording of all events emitted by a source.
- A *global external memory* is a recording of all events emitted by all sources in an environment.
- A *super external memory* is a recording of all events emitted in a universe.

In addition to this definition we need to mention that there is no need to introduce a new type of collective memory. However, it is important to understand that collective memories can include external memories, too.

We also need to understand the difference between two types of memory: 'active memory' and 'passive memory'. It is obvious that in order for an agent to use an external memory (or vice versa), there must be a relationship between these two entities. Such a relationship could be realized in the form of a 'reference'. The memory of an agent, or that of an external memory for that matter, therefore, contains two partitions. One partition holds references to other information spaces, while the second partition holds the actual information the agent requires for internal information processing. For instance, in a class, the aforementioned students may be taught a formula for solving a particular type of problem. A case of active memory would be a situation where a student memorizes, and later in an exercise, remembers and applies this formula successfully. On the other hand, a situation where a student needs to consult a notebook or the university library would be an instance of passive memory usage. The following definition captures this type of reasoning:

Definition 8 Active memory and passive memory.

- *Active memories* contain information that is typically used in some form of internal processing. We refer to the size of such a memory as *active information capacity* ($c_{s,a}$), where s is an information space (agent, environment, etc.).
- *Passive memories* contain references to other information spaces. We refer to the size of such a memory as *passive information capacity* ($c_{s,p}$), where s is an information space (agent, environment, etc.).

7.3   Mathematical Modeling

This section presents a simple mathematical model in order to express a possible relationship between active information capacity and passive information capacity. The model consists of the two equations below.

$$c_s = c_{s,a} + c_{s,p} \qquad (7.1)$$

$$A_I = \frac{c_{s,a} - c_{s,p}}{c_s} \qquad (7.2)$$

Equation 7.1 defines the information capacity (c_s) of an information space as the sum of the active information capacity ($c_{s,a}$) and the passive information capacity ($c_{s,p}$) of this information space. We assume that active and passive information capacities are always positive (i.e., $c_{s,a}, c_{s,p} > 0$) and that it can never be the case that $c_{s,a} = c_{s,p} = 0$ (i.e., active and passive information capacity are never both zero at the same time). Equation 7.2 introduces an index we call 'autonomy index' (A_I). Figure 7.4, which is an illustration of Equation 7.2, aims to explain the rational for this name.

In order to understand Fig. 7.4, let us distinguish three specific cases.

- *Case-1*: Imagine an information agent consisting of passive memories only (i.e., the memory of the agent holds references only). In this case Equation 7.1 produces: $c_s = c_{s,p}$, because $c_{s,a} = 0$. Hence, $A_I = -1$, according to Equation 7.2.
- *Case-2*: Imagine an information agent consisting of active memories only (i.e., the memory of the agent does not contain any references to any other information spaces). Here, Equation 7.1 produces $c_s = c_{s,a}$, because $c_{s,p} = 0$. Equation 7.2, therefore, produces: $A_I = 1$.
- *Case-3*: Imagine an information agent where active and passive information capacity are equal. In this case we have: $c_{s,a} - c_{s,p} = 0$, hence $A_I = 0$.

The forthcoming section is going to provide several interpretations for this model.

Fig. 7.4 Dynamic behavior
of the autonomy index A_I

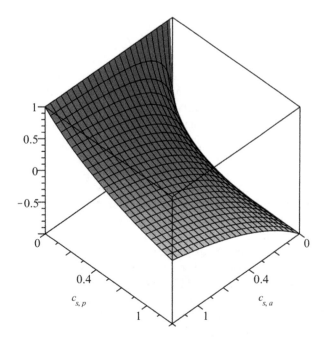

7.4 Interpretations of Finite Information Spaces

For the sake of clarity, we divide this somewhat longer section into three parts. The first part tries to generate a more general, intuitive understanding of the mathematical model introduced before. The second part moves our model and its interpretations into the context of a modern 'information society'. The final, third part, establishes a link between finite information spaces and classical computer theory (in particular Turing machines).

7.4.1 The General Value of the Model

In the context of our work, it is possible to interpret the aforementioned three cases as follows.

Case-1, $A_I = -1$: An entity with references only could be an old-style telephone-book. Such a telephone-book does not do any reasoning or processing by itself. It is an entirely static entity that is consulted by dynamic agents (human beings) for whatever intention such a dynamic agent may have in mind. An example in the IT (information technology) domain could be a relational database system (Codd 1970; Connolly and Begg 2014). The relational database model was invented by Edgar Frank "Ted" Codd (1923–2003). The model is so important that Codd received the

1987 *ACM A.M. Turing Award* for this contribution.[9] For instance, on the Internet, the open source MySQL relational database system is used on many widespread websites (e.g., Facebook, Twitter, or Wikipedia) that are challenged by processing huge data volumes in real-time. From the point of view of our work, such a database represents a passive component (external memory) that is accessed by other information spaces (e.g., humans, or computers) only. By itself, the database does not really act as an active agent (e.g., by initiating actions related to the outside world). It seems to be fair to assign an autonomy index of $A_I = -1$ to such a component.

Case-2, $A_I = 1$: This case describes an agent that is able to do some internal processing, but is unable to access any external sources, because the agent does not have (or cannot access) any references itself that would direct it to any other (outside) resources (e.g., other agents, external memories). In a way, this agent is kind of locked up in itself. For instance, a person who is not able to access or cannot use a telephone-book cannot make a phone-call (in this particular, old-fashioned way). Likewise, a person who does not know how to operate, or does not have access to, a web-browser/Internet cannot access Facebook, Twitter, or Wikipedia. Similarly, an autonomous robot assembled from cutting-edge AI technology cannot function adequately if it cannot interact with its environment meaningfully (e.g., in case its sensors are enabled or malfunctioning).

Case-3, $A_I = 0$: This case portrays a situation in which an agent commands over a set of passive memory as well as active memory in a balanced way. In this way, the agent can do some meaningful (internal) processing as well as interacting with the outside world by accessing external memories. Obviously, such a setup would be desirable in a learning environment. Indeed, we think that this kind of setup is a fundamental feature of the larger human body. It enables humans to exist and survive and evolve in this world. (Note that Sect. 7.4.2 is going to elaborate on this point in more detail.)[10]

The previous interpretations involve the domains of telephone-books, databases, and robots. There are, however, also examples that associate the idea of active/passive memory to various forms of human condition. Consider the cases of Alzheimer's disease and anterograde amnesia. Ultimately, people with Alzheimer's disease suffer memory loss. This experience involves the decline (or

---

[9]ACM A.M. Turing Award. http://amturing.acm.org/. Accessed: 2016-11-28. This award is an annual prize given by the Association for Computing Machinery (ACM). It is the highest recognition awarded in the field of computer science and often referred to as the *Nobel Prize of computing*.

[10]Here, we would like to, briefly, refer back to *Case-1* and *Case-2* again. *Case-1* may have generated an impression of the Internet as an altogether passive environment. Actually, this is not entirely correct. There are already various active elements on the Internet (search engines or so-called web crawlers, for instance). Arguably, the degree of intelligence or autonomy these agents demonstrate is still a bit limited. It is not too difficult, however, to imagine the Internet as a platform where virtual reality worlds get enriched by AI, deep learning networks empower 'big data', and humanoid robotics, autonomous cars, and other technologies merge into a multidimensional 'Internet of Things' (e.g., see Silver et al. 2016; Kajita et al. 2016; Anderson et al. 2014; Zanella

malfunctioning) of passive memories (references to the outside world). On the other hand, people affected by anterograde amnesia may have lost the ability to create new memories, or suffer varying degrees of forgetfulness. In a sense, these people are all kind off time-warped into their former self. It is not the place here to go into the details of these challenging physiological conditions. However, it is clear that these conditions severely impact those people who are affected by them by preventing them from functioning fully (autonomously) in our society. A negative autonomy index A_I, where $-1 \leq A_I < 0$, would capture this type of autonomy deficiency in a meaningful way.

For the second case, we may conjure some hypothetical *Kaspar Hauser* type of situation (Kitchen 2001). Imagine a person locked up in a room. The person shall be 'well' overall (i.e., the person does not suffer lack of nutrition, sleep, exercise, etc.). However, the person cannot access the world outside this room at all. Further, although a teacher shall teach this person every day, the locked up person cannot (and is not allowed to) take any notes. If at all, the person may memorize things. In this way, we could say that the active memory of the person changes (increases) constantly, while the passive memory does not really change. Although passive memories (references) may be generated, they are restricted, because the person is denied access to any outside resources. It seems fair, therefore, to say that the person has access to active memory only. We think that it could be reasonable to use a positive autonomy index A_I, where $0 \leq A_I \leq 1$, to express such a situation.

Lastly, in *Case-3*, we may consider a 'normal' human being existing in this world. This person shall command over active memory and passive memory in a balanced way. In this case, we would think that the reasons why this person functions well (normally) overall, include the facts that the person (i) has sufficient resources (active memory) to act (reason) independently, and (ii) has the freedom to reference, access, and use other external resources in a meaningful way. An autonomy index A_I around zero would expresses this situation well.

7.4.2 The Model from an Information Society and Evolutionary Point of View

This section examines the relevance of our work in the context of modern information society. The section also includes an interpretation that considers finite information capacity as a driving force of evolution. Of course, information society

---

et al. 2014). Contemplating such a development, we could say that the current Internet is passive at large, while the Internet of the future strives to be more active (autonomous). Or, in the language of our work, the current Internet has an autonomy index around $A_I = -1$, while the Internet of the future may have an autonomy index around $A_I = 0$. In such a case, we may wonder about the similarity between humans and the Internet. If the autonomy index for both is around zero, then what does that mean? Are humans and machines essentially the same type of information space?

is one of those terms again that are extremely difficult do define. Nevertheless, out of a large number of definitions, the Wikipedia[11] entry for information society provides the following text:

> ...An information society is a society where the creation, distribution, use, integration and manipulation of information is a significant economic, political, and cultural activity. Its main drivers are digital information and communication technologies, which have resulted in an information explosion and are profoundly changing all aspects of social organization, including the economy, education, health, warfare, government and democracy. The people who have the means to partake in this form of society are sometimes called digital citizens.
> ...

To have access (passive memory, references) to information, and to be able to process (active memory) information, therefore, is essential in information society. For instance, the term 'digital divide' expresses an economic and social inequality with regard to access to information and communication technology (often the Internet) (Norris 2009). The autonomy measure introduced in Sect. 7.3 relates to this topic in a meaningful way. Imagine a situation where it is possible to define active and passive memories for a group of individuals in terms of their access (no access) to some information and communication technology. In such a situation it could be meaningful to use the autonomy index A_I to express a degree of autonomy, or digital divide, for this group.

Another view relates the model in Sect. 7.3 to us humans in a very elementary way. Assume a finite information capacity for humans. That is, humans are indeed finite information agents. Let us further imagine a partitioning of this capacity into active and passive memories. We saw earlier how important a certain balance between these two components can be. But how can such a balanced state be achieved? How can a human agent create an equilibrium between active and passive memory, if the capacity for these memories is limited and the information in an environment increases over time, or is beyond an agent's capacity in the first place? For instance, we do not know whether our universe is finite or infinite. What we know, however, is that our understanding about our universe increases permanently (e.g., through research, study, etc.). One solution (for a second solution see Sect. 7.4.3) to the problem is straightforward, namely – 'outsourcing' (i.e., to produce, reference, and use external memories). A human being can do this by maintaining a small number of references that act as links to external entities that may contain huge amounts of other references to other information sources. A telephone-book or a traditional library are old-fashioned examples, while the World Wide Web (WWW) with its exorbitant number of hyperlinks, hypertexts, and

---

[11] Information society. https://en.wikipedia.org/wiki/Information_society. Accessed: 2016-11-20. Please note that we are aware about the issues involved when using information from sources such as Wikipedia, or, for that matter, any other source that is freely available on the new media environment today. In this particular case, we refer to Wikipedia to indicate its standing as a powerful tool in the modern-day information environment. For a broader exploration on the concept of an information society, we refer the reader to the more academic works of Press and Williams (2010), or Han (2015), who investigate various aspects of this large field of study.

hyperresources is the outstanding example of our time. In the case of the WWW, we only need to maintain one reference, namely that which connects us to the Internet. From there, we can use the external (virtual, i.e., non-physical) information space called WWW. From this perspective, the Internet/WWW[12] suddenly appear as evolutionary information space concepts. This perspective also provides a novel view on big data. Big data is often, rather casually, perceived as a problem of dealing with huge volumes of data. This is true, of course. However, we also believe that big data touches upon a much deeper problem. We suggest that in its core, big data is a problem of human evolution. First of all, it is well-known that a key characteristic of any human society is their accumulation and sharing of experiences and knowledge (Spinney 2012). From a historical point of view, therefore, one of the first things that had to go for humans was the 'sole' reliance on individual memory – hence groups and societies of humans. Second, it is obvious today (as it was in the past) that, in the information age, storage capacity is a fundamental problem. For instance, a white paper published by the International Data Corporation mentions that "In 2007 the amount of information created will surpass, for the first time, the storage capacity available." (Gant et al. 2007). These facts allow us to look at the history of recording (ranging from stone carvings, cave-paintings, papyrus, the printing press, etc., up to – the Internet (Taylor and Joudrey 2008, pp. 67–85)) from the following perspective: We may feel, rightly, that each of the aforementioned developments triumphantly promulgates a victory of human genius – however, each of these steps forward in the human endeavor also symbolizes a defeat to finite information capacity. We need to accept that we humans just struggle to stay abreast with the information influx that has been happening through the ages up to our modern times.

7.4.3   The Model from a Computational Point of View

The previous section discussed the possibility of outsourcing for establishing an equilibrium between active and passive memory. This section considers another, potentially fundamental (evolutionary, survival) mechanism in a world where humans have to deal with finite information capacity. The approach relates to the domain of classical computer theory, in particular the study of so-called automata. Let us first explain the problem in detail (Fig. 7.5).

Figure 7.5a illustrates the finite information capacity c_a of an agent a via a (solid line) square. The agent a exists in an information environment e (circle, dashed line). We assume that some of the total available (finite) information capacity of agent a is already in use for some purposes. The rectangle with the diagonal line pattern in Fig. 7.5a captures this assumption. Further, the black dot in the same

---

[12]Please note that unless a clear distinction is required, from now on, we use the term Internet synonymously for both expressions.

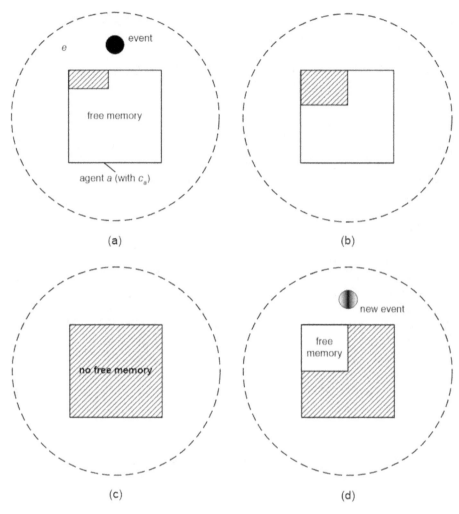

Fig. 7.5 Various situations regarding an agent a with a finite information capacity c_a (*large square*) in an information environment e (*dashed circle*)

figure shall be an event happening in the environment e. Imagine now that agent a can recognize, and process, and store (record) some of the information related to this event. Suppose that storing this information uses some of the remaining (free) information capacity of agent a. Let us also assume that the total memory (passive and active memory) in use by agent a increases overall in this process. The increased rectangle (diagonal line pattern) in Fig. 7.5b captures these changes. It is clear that if this process continues that there is no space available for agent a to record any new events – the finite information capacity of the agent is simply used up. Figure 7.5c illustrates this borderline case. Obviously, in case the agent *a* wants to record any new events (symbolized by the shaded dot in Fig. 7.5d), then the agent must free (delete) some of the recorded information. Figure 7.5d demonstrates this situation. In a way, the entire process is circular, because the situation in Fig. 7.5d is similar (but not identical) to that in Fig. 7.5a. It is necessary to emphasize the circular nature of this process. Although agent *a* suffers some information loss, the agent may not (and should not) loose all the information it may need to exist and operate meaningfully in the environment *e*. It is important to understand here that the perpetual addition/deletion of information is a fundamental (evolutionary, survival) strategy the agent *a* applies in order to make itself 'robust' in its surrounding environment (Schuster 2008; Schuster and Yamaguchi 2009).

At this point, one might argue that the situation is similar to what has been discussed in earlier sections. We agree that this argument has its value. At this point, however, we ask a different question. We are wondering about the following: How is it possible for an agent to process events, which may be familiar or new, in the first place, and, what kind of setup or mechanism could be supportive for such a challenge? These questions lead us to the domain of computer theory including 'Turing machines' (TMs) and the ultimate classical computing device, the so-called 'universal Turing machine' (UTM).[13]

Perhaps, it is helpful to imagine a TM as an extremely powerful sorcerer in a hypothetical wizard universe. Let's say you want to challenge the power of this wizard by asking him to conjure a wormhole. This is no problem for the wizard, of course. It takes him only a split-second with his magic wand until you can see the wormhole (including a little worm wiggling out of it) right in front of your toes. You are confused now, and so is the wizard, when he realizes your confusion. Suddenly, you understand, and explain to the wizard that what you actually wanted him to do was to conjure an 'Einstein-Rosen bridge', a hypothetical topological feature that would allow you to connect, and travel between, two separate points in space-time. This puts the wizard slightly on the edge. Nevertheless, with a grumpy murmur and sparkling eyes, he starts to fulfill your wish. He expertly conjures pirate copies of several classic physics courses from the Internet, browses in them with great curiosity, asks you here and then a few questions, and – there you go – with another wink of his wand, the wizard catapults you into a wormhole. Although you tremendously enjoy the ride down the wormhole, there is also a feeling that you had been lucky that the wizard did not transform you into a wiggling worm.

So, what's the point. The point is to understand that TMs are similar to our wizard. They are servants (machines, computers) that, when given a clear set of instructions (an algorithm, a program), 'always' can execute that algorithm/program. In the modern world, imagine a tablet computer referred to as TC_1. In order to work, this TC_1 needs an operating system (Windows, Linux, etc.). This

---

[13]Note that it is outside the scope of this text to provide a detailed understanding about these machines. For readers interested in these topics, we would like to mention that Schuster (2007) provides a general investigation to the topic of computing, while the work by Cohen (1996) provides a solid introduction to the formal underpinnings of the classical theory of computing.

operating system (say OS_1) allows us to install and run new software (e.g., a new computer game) on TC_1. The important thing to grasp here is that the tablet's operating system (which is a piece of software) allows us to run another piece of software (the game). This is exactly what TMs do. TMs are machines on which 'any' other (clearly specified) programs can run. An UTM is just one step up the ladder. We already mentioned that the operating system of the tablet TC_1 is just a piece of software. Assume now that we have the operating system of another tablet computer. This second tablet (call it TC_2) shall be from a different maker and use a different operating system (say OS_2). It is possible to imagine that we can install (and run) the software OS_2 (because it is just another piece of clearly defined software) on the tablet TC_1 which uses OS_1. Here, the important observation is that it is possible for one machine (TC_1) to 'simulate' another machine (TC_2). In computer theoretic terms we could say that an UTM is a TM that can simulate 'any' other TM. In a nutshell, the previous discussion can be summarized in one of the most powerful and fundamental statements in the world of theoretical computer science, the so-called 'Church-Turing thesis' (Cohen 1996, p. 610):

> ...It is believed that there are *no* functions that can be defined by humans, whose calculation can be described by *any* well-defined mathematical algorithm that people can be taught to perform, that *cannot* be computed by Turing machines. The Turing machine is believed to be the ultimate calculating mechanism. ...

So much for the world of tablets, operating systems, TMs, and UTMs. We can speculate now whether the human brain and mind (if it exists Feser 2006) are devices that operate similarly in their relationship with the world around us. We might reason that the world around us has some clearly defined structure or form.[14] We may think of this form as some kind of 'description of reality'. Such a description of reality would be similar to a program (algorithm) that can be read by machine – here a brain/mind (which would be similar to a TM/UTM according to our previous example). The idea that the brain is a computer is not a novelty in itself. Indeed, this idea has been around in various fields, including AI, neuroscience, and several other fields.[15] However, as far as we know, these other works did not put as much

---

[14]For instance, in physics one goal is to find a so-called 'theory of everything' from which the behavior of all matter and energy in the universe could be derived. In order to be meaningful, this endeavor must rely on the idea that there is some structure, pattern, or order in the world around us.

[15]At this point, it might be interesting to diverge into the work of the philosopher Edmund Gustav Albrecht Husserl (1859–1938). In his phenomenology, Husserl introduces terms such as: 'innerer Horizont' (inner horizon), 'äußerer Horizont' (outer horizon), 'Regionen menschlicher Erkenntnis' (regions of human cognition), or 'Intentionalität' (space of potentiality) (Lutz 1999, pp. 208–215). From the point of view of these terms, the square in Fig. 7.5, which we used to demonstrate an agent's finite information capacity, could be an agent's inner horizon (something similar to a snapshot taken by the agent, expressing the agent's state of affairs in environment e). This gives the environment e the character of a (potential) region of cognition. There is a potentiality for the agent a to explore this region of cognition. Everything the agent may be able to experience (sense, understand, comprehend), could be equivalent to an agent's outer horizon. Whether it is possible for an agent to experience (sense, understand, etc.) everything that exists in environment e is an open question. From our work, however, we understand that finiteness, is intrinsically linked to this question.

emphasis on the property of finiteness as we do in this chapter. For instance, in an article related to the fields of quantum computing and cosmology, Lloyd (2012) mentions that:

> ...The question of whether or not infinite memory space is available is not so serious, as one can formulate notions of universal computation with limited memory. After all, we treat our existing electronic computers as universal machines even though they have finite memory (until, of course, we run out of disc space!). ...

Of course, in this chapter we would argue vehemently that we should consider the finiteness of computer memory (or any memory for that matter) seriously for a variety of reasons – including that of 'running out of space'.

7.5 Summary

From a wider perspective, this chapter continues our work on finite information spaces. We use the chapter to provide various definitions that are necessary to understand the idea of finite information spaces and associated concepts. The chapter presents a simple mathematical model which we use to introduce an interesting measure called autonomy index. Our discussions indicate the meaningfulness of this index in a wide range of contexts. Overall, we feel that our work strongly supports our starting Proposition 1, which mentioned that "*finiteness is a fundamental concept in the world around us*". Indeed, we hope the patient reader of this text would agree with us that finiteness is important and relevant within and beyond the scope of this finite chapter.

References

Anderson JM, Kalra N, Stanley KD, Sorensen P, Samaras C, Oluwatola OA (2014) Autonomous vehicle technology: a guide for policymakers. Rand transportation, space, and technology program, 3rd edn. Rand, Santa Monica

Codd EF (1970) A relational model of data for large shared data banks. Commun ACM 13(6):377–387

Cohen DIA (1996) Introduction to computer theory, 2nd edn. John Wiley & Sons, New York, USA

Connolly T, Begg C (2014) Database systems: a practical approach to design, implementation, and management, global edn. Pearson, Harlow

Dunton-Downer L, Riding A (2004) Essential Shakespeare handbook, 1st edn. Dorling Kindersley, London/New York

Feser E (2006) Philosophy of mind: a beginner's guide. Oneworld Publications, Oxford

Floridi L (2010) Information: a very short introduction. Oxford University Press, Oxford

Floridi L (2011) The philosophy of information. Oxford University Press, Oxford

Frank MP (2002) The physical limits of computing. Comput Sci Eng 4(3):16–26

Gant JF, Reinsel D, Chute C, Schlichting W, McArthur J, Minton S, Xheneti I, Toncheva A, Manfrediz A (2007) The expanding digital universe. White paper, International Data Corporation. Available via https://www.idc.com/

Goldstein R (2006) Incompleteness: the proof and paradox of Kurt Gödel. Great Discoveries, New York, N.Y., USA

Han BC (2015) The transparency society, 1st edn. Stanford Briefs, Stanford

Henschke A (2010) Did you just say what I think you said? Talking about genes, identity and information. Identity Inf Soc 3(3):435–456

Hilbert M, López P (2011) The world's technological capacity to store, communicate, and compute information. Science 332(6025):60–65

Kajita S, Hirukawa H, Harada K, Yokoi K (2016) Introduction to humanoid robotics. Springer tracts in advanced robotics. Springer, Berlin

Kang Y, Tan AH (2013) Self-organizing cognitive models for virtual agents. In: Aylett R, Krenn B, Pelachaud C, Shimodaira H (eds) Proceedings of the 13th International conference intelligent virtual agents (IVA'13). Springer, Berlin, pp 29–43

Kitchen M (2001) Who was Kaspar Hauser? In: Kitchen M (ed) Kaspar Hauser: Europe's child. Palgrave Macmillan, Basingstoke, pp 156–174

Krauss LM, Starkman GD (2000) Life, the universe, and nothing: life and death in an ever-expanding universe. Astrophys J 531(1):22–30

Lloyd S (2012) The universe as quantum computer. In: Zenil H (ed) A computable universe: understanding and exploring nature as computation. World Scientific Publishing Company, e-book. World Scientific, Singapore

Lutz B (1999) Die großen Philosophen des 20. Jahrhunderts. Biographisches Lexikon. dtv

Marois R, Ivanoff J (2005) Capacity limits of information processing in the brain. Trends Cogn Sci 9(6):296–305

Norris P (2009) Digital divide: civic engagement, information poverty, and the internet worldwide. Cambridge University Press, Oxford

Press AL, Williams BA (2010) The new media environment: an introduction, 1st edn. Wiley-Blackwell, Chichester

Schuster A (2007) Intelligent computing everywhere. In: Schuster A (ed) Intelligent computing everywhere. Springer, London, pp 3–25

Schuster A (2008) Robustness in nature as a design principle for artificial intelligence. In: Schuster A (ed) Robust intelligent systems. Springer, London, pp 165–188

Schuster A (2014) Interpretation of finite information spaces. In: Proceedings of the Asian conference on society, education and technology (ACSET'14), poster presentation

Schuster A, Yamaguchi Y (2009) The survival of the fittest and the reign of the most robust: in biology and elsewhere. Minds Mach 19(3):361–389

Silver D, Huang A, Maddison CJ, Guez A, Sifre L, (15 additional authors not shown) (2016) Mastering the game of go with deep neural networks and tree search. Nature **529**, 484–489

Spinney L (2012) Busted! The myth of technological progress. New Sci 215(2884):30–33

Taylor AG, Joudrey DN (2008) The organization of information. Library and information science text series, 3rd edn. Libraries Unlimited, Westport

Zanella A, Bui N, Castellani A, Vangelista L, Zorzi M (2014) Internet of things for smart cities. IEEE Internet Things J 1(1):22–32

Part V
The World of Networks, Clouds, and Big Data Processing

Chapter 8
Distributed and Connected Information in the Internet

Jürgen Vogel

Abstract The Internet has established itself as the universal data and information infrastructure. It is used not only for providing and retrieving data in a diverse range of application domains involving human and machine actors, but also as a distributed processing platform. We investigate Internet data and information with a number of technological questions in mind: In which format should data be represented? Where and how should it be stored? How can data be managed? How can the data relevant to a specific need be found in the vast space of the Internet? How can it be accessed by human and machine users, and how can it be processed into information? We cover the Web including the processing of textual, user-generated and Linked Data, as well as the Internet as a processing platform with data exchange between services and for handling Big Data.

8.1 Introduction

The Internet connects computers from all over the world for a fast exchange of data, e.g., from email or Web applications (Tanenbaum and Wetherall 2011). The last decades witnessed the Internet's exponential growth from a small, elite research network to the dominating communication infrastructure it represents today. Almost half of the Earth's population uses the Internet nowadays (ITU 2016), and, as can easily be observed anywhere around the world, being always 'on-line' is a natural and essential habit to many people in their private and professional lives. This success story of the Internet can largely be attributed to its technological foundations that make it a fast, reliable, scalable and fit-for-all-purposes network (Vogel and Widmer 2008).

J. Vogel (✉)
Engineering and Information Technology Department, Bern University of Applied Sciences, Höheweg 80, 2502, Biel, Bern, Switzerland
e-mail: juergen.vogel@bfh.ch

© Springer International Publishing AG 2017   153
A.J. Schuster (eds.), *Understanding Information*, Advanced Information and Knowledge Processing, DOI 10.1007/978-3-319-59090-5_8

Obviously, another major success factor is the economic opportunities of the Internet, which are intelligently exploited by companies such as Google,[1] Facebook,[2] and Amazon.[3] In addition, the Internet supports a wide range of applications such as file transfer, communication via video, email, and chat, business orders, multi-player games, and machine control. From a technological point of view, these applications are distributed systems where different pieces of application logic are executed at different computers using the so-called *client-server* paradigm where a client requests data or triggers functions on a server (Sommerville 2016). The Internet then transports data generated from such applications in a binary format from the sender to its receiver(s) irrespective of the data itself (Tanenbaum and Wetherall 2011), i.e., the network only needs to know the transmission details such as the receiver's address and does not need to process the transmitted data. Thus, the transmitted data becomes information only by interpretation at the sending/receiving application where the appropriate data format (i.e., *syntax*) such as banana is a `String`, `1,24` is a `Double`, and `true` is a `Boolean` is known and used together with the application-specific data interpretation (i.e., *semantics*) such as banana is a `fruit produce`, `1,24` is a `price`, and `true` means `priority shipment`.[4] Depending on the application, data may be intended for machine and/or human use: For instance, orders sent from a customer's Web browser to Amazon will be processed by the highly automated warehousing system, while emails are still mostly targeted at and read by human users.

Data may also be distinguished as being either structured or unstructured: *Structured data* comes with a detailed definition of its syntax and/or semantics as so-called meta-data. A general software design guideline is that the data processed automatically by a machine indeed should be highly structured in order to simplify parsing and to prevent errors (Sommerville 2016). Probably the most common structured data model in use nowadays is the entity-relationship model where relational data is managed in a dedicated SQL (Structured Query Language) database (Elmasri and Navathe 2016). SQL is used to define complex data objects (i.e., entities) with typed attributes and relations to other entities. Further, higher level constraints can be specified that are enforced when manipulating data, e.g., marking an attribute of an entity type as unique so that each value can be present only once for all entities of this type. The success of SQL is also caused by its expressive declarative query language for retrieving data.

In contrast, *unstructured data* lacks such explicit meta-data and relates to multimedia data (audio, images, and video) and textual data composed of natural

---

[1]Google. https://www.google.com/. Accessed: 2016-09-12.

[2]Facebook. https://www.facebook.com/. Accessed: 2016-09-12.

[3]Amazon. https://www.amazon.com/. Accessed: 2016-09-12.

[4]Please note that we follow the widely used distinction between data and information, where information is structured and interpreted data (Manning et al. 2008).

language such as the one contained in the body of an email.[5] Unstructured data is mostly intended for human usage, and before its content can be used by a machine, dedicated analysis methods are required. In this chapter, we focus on textual data, and analyzing multimedia data is out of scope; an overview of analyzing such data can be found, e.g., in Ohm (2016).

In the forthcoming sections, we investigate Internet data and information with a number of technological questions in mind: In which format should data be represented? Where and how should it be stored? How can data be managed? How can the data relevant to a specific need be found in the vast space of the Internet? How can it be accessed by human and machine users, and how can it be processed into information? We will address these questions by means of the most important state-of-the art technologies and also indicate open research questions. We start with the traditional Web where users are primarily readers of Web pages. In Sect. 8.3, we investigate *social data* that is generated by the mass of Internet users themselves as blogs, wikis, or other forms of communication. Users also implicitly generate data by leaving a history of site visits, which we discuss in Sect. 8.4. A large percentage of data available in the Web nowadays is actually text-based and needs to be processed by specialized analysis methods as described in Sect. 8.5. In contrast to human users, the technological foundations of the Internet can also be used for machine-to-machine communication (Sect. 8.6). Another specific field of interest is methods for handling very large amounts of data (i.e., *Big Data*) that we address in Sect. 8.7. In Sect. 8.8, we discuss how data handling by machines may be improved by so-called *Linked Data*. We conclude the chapter with a summary.

8.2   Web Data

The World Wide Web (WWW) started in the early 1990s on the initiative of Tim Berners-Lee who proposed a linked information system where a 'note' could reference another one via a 'link' embedded in the text of the first note and the notes could reside on any machines connected to the Internet (Berners-Lee 1989). Berners-Lee's reference use case was scientists documenting research projects at CERN.[6] With colleagues, Berners-Lee developed the three main elements of the Web: URIs (Uniform Resource Identifiers) (Berners-Lee et al. 2015) to uniquely identify notes and other Web data (so-called *resources*) such as documents and multimedia files so that they can be referenced via the links (so-called *hyperlinks*), the hypertext document format HTML (HyperText Markup Language) (W3C 2014a) for encoding the Web data itself, and the application-level Internet protocol

---

[5]In a very strict sense unstructured data should rather be called *semi-structured* because some struc-ture is inevitably present, e.g., natural language text follows the language's inherent grammatical rules (Manning et al. 2008).

[6]CERN. https://home.cern/. Accessed: 2016-09-12.

```
<!DOCTYPE html>
<html>
  <head>
    <meta charset="UTF-8">
    <title>Hello, World!</title>
  </head>
  <body>
    <p>Hello <strong>World Wide Web!</strong></p>
    <p>I am Sophie Jones and 34 years old.</p>
    <p>See <a href="https://www.w3.org/">W3C</a>.</p>
  </body>
</html>
```

Fig. 8.1 An example of 'Hello, World!' in HTML

HTTP (Hypertext Transfer Protocol) (Fielding and Reschke 2014) for transporting Web data from a Web server to a client. Remarkably, Berners-Lee also founded the W3C[7] (World Wide Web Consortium) that is still the governing body of the Web and responsible for the standardization of various Web-related technologies.

8.2.1 Web Data Format and Web Applications

The core data format of the Web, HTML, is a textual format where data and meta-data are encoded in the same document. A 'Hello, World!' example is given in Fig. 8.1. In HTML, meta-data is used to specify general properties of a Web document (e.g., `<!DOCTYPE html>`), to define the document's internal structure such as headings and paragraphs (e.g., `<p>`), to influence the visual presentation of selected text such as emphasizing (e.g., `<strong>World Wide Web!</strong>`), or to define hyperlinks to other Web resources (e.g., `<a href="https://www.w3.org/">W3C</a>`) that can then be retrieved on demand by the user. As shown in the example above, meta-data is defined via tags (i.e., *markups*) that are opened (e.g., `<p>`) and closed (e.g., `</p>`) to separate them from the embedded content. Tags may also be embedded in each other so that the document's internal structure is tree-shaped.

Traditionally, Web documents are stored as files on a Web server where they can be requested via HTTP by using their URI (e.g., https://www.w3.org/). The requesting Web client, usually a Web browser, can then interpret the HTML code and present the result to the user.

More sophisticated Web pages may also use CSS (Cascading Style Sheets) (W3C 2011) to define layout and styling, and JavaScript (Brooks 2011) to embed interactive elements such as menus as well as client-side data processing functions. In fact, basically all popular 'modern' Web sites nowadays offer interactive Web

---

[7]W3C. https://www.w3.org/. Accessed: 2016-09-12.

applications, where the available content is actually a combination of prepared, static data and dynamically generated data. For implementing such a Web application, the technological state of the art is to use a combination of HTML, CSS, and JavaScript code (plus multimedia content) on the client side, and to develop the server-side code in a higher programming language such as PHP, Java, C#, or Ruby (Sebesta 2015). Application data is mostly stored at the server side using a database, and client-side data is limited to be stored only temporarily in-memory or as so-called *cookies* in a restricted directory (Barth 2011). The execution of and access to the Web application is then controlled by a Web application server such as Apache Tomcat.[8] Once the user opens a certain Web site via the main URI, the Web browser contacts the Web application server, that forwards the request to the Web application. The Web application then processes and assembles the required content and transmits it back to the Web client for display to the user. Depending on user actions such as filling out forms, zooming and detailing into graphics and maps, and navigating to additional views, new content is continuously being requested from the Web server.

8.2.2 Searching and Finding Data

From a user perspective, the Web offers a sheer unlimited amount of data, so that the main challenge is often to find the exact piece of data that fits one's specific information need. In order to address this *Information Retrieval* (IR) challenge, popular search engines such as Google and Bing[9] solve three core issues (Ceri et al. 2013): First, the user needs to express one's information need in an appropriate format. But information needs can be quite different between users and depend on their current task at hand, which range from navigational tasks, where the user wants to find a certain Web source, transactional tasks, where the user wants to execute a certain activity (e.g., a purchase), to informational tasks, where the user wants to learn about a certain topic, potentially from a diverse number of sources (Broder 2002). Designing a user interface to accommodate these different needs is challenging and ultimately led to the seemingly simple design of a search 'box' where the user enters a few keywords. Because the average Web user is not an IT (Information Technology) specialist, such a 'freestyle' keyword-based search has proven to be better, compared to query languages (e.g., such as SQL mentioned before), that are more formal, expressive, and difficult to use. For the more advanced users, search engines offer additional options, e.g., to specify exact phrases, alternative keywords, a time range for specifying when the content was authored, the media type or language of the result, etc. Another supportive feature is the recommendation of alternative keywords that may be implemented on the basis of the query history from all users collected by the search engine (Baeza-Yates et al. 2004).

---

[8] Apache Tomcat. http://tomcat.apache.org/. Accessed: 2016-09-12.
[9] Bing. https://www.bing.com/. Accessed: 2016-09-12.

The second IR challenge for the search engine is to match the formulated query to those Web documents that potentially contain the wanted content. In the simplest case, documents are selected if they contain (all or some of) the user's keywords. But due to its vast size, the Web, obviously, can not be searched in real-time just when users submit a query. Instead, the search engine pre-processes all known Web pages into a so-called *inverted index* (Manning et al. 2008) that allows a fast lookup of which pages contain a certain keyword. The resulting index is so large that it needs to be constructed, stored, and queried in a distributed cluster of computers, complete with multiple copies of the same index to satisfy the high number of queries a Web-scale search engine has to handle. As a prerequisite, the search engine needs to continuously explore the Web in a process called *crawling* (Burner 1997) by following hyperlinks in documents to discover new pages and by re-visiting pages already known in order to check whether their content has been updated since they were visited the last time.

The third IR challenge is to present the results found to the user in a meaningful and easy-to-understand way, which is difficult due to the potentially very high number of matching documents. The most common visualization is a ranked result list where the best matching documents are displayed first with their title, date, URI, and a short excerpt. This requires a method for determining a matching score for each page so that they can be ordered accordingly. For this, many different methods have been developed, which can be roughly divided into two classes: The first approach is to calculate the *relevance* of a document, i.e., how well the textual content of a Web page matches the entered keywords, by means of a similarity metric. State-of-the-art similarity metrics are often based on the vector space model where, in a comparison, the query keywords and the Web page are interpreted as vectors in the high-dimensional space of all words in the dictionary: in the simplest case, the i-th dimension of a vector has a value of 1 if the corresponding word of the dictionary is present and 0 otherwise. The similarity between these two vectors can then be calculated as the general cosine similarity with results ranging between 1 for vectors with identical content and 0 for vectors that do not share any key word. Because words in natural language are not evenly distributed, it makes sense to incorporate the following two factors: First, a word that is mentioned often in a document is probably more important than a word that is mentioned less frequently, and this factor may be counted via the (logarithmically dampened) *term frequency* tf. Second, a word that is rarely used in the Web overall but does occur in a certain query/page is more distinctive than others that can be found everywhere, and this factor may be calculated as the (logarithmically dampened) *inverse document frequency* idf. For the document vector introduced above, the multiplied tf-idf (Salton and Buckley 1988) weight is then assigned for each dimension.

The second approach for scoring search results is based on the *authoritativeness* of the page, i.e., Web pages that are often referenced by other Web pages receive a higher score than rarely referenced ones. In more detail, the Web is interpreted as a directed graph where the pages are nodes that are connected via their unidirectional hyperlinks. Each page in this graph is assigned a score, which expresses the overall authority of this page to the overall Web: Let $P_p = \{p_1, \ldots, p_n\}$, where $n \in \mathbb{N}$, be the set of all pages that refer to a certain page p on the Web. A page $p_i \in P_p$ that links to page p expresses that p has a certain authority from p_i's point of view. The more pages connect to page p (i.e., the more pages P_p contains), the higher the overall authority of p becomes. At the same time, if page p_i has a high score (authority) itself (e.g., Wikipedia[10]), the link from p_i to p is more important (authoritative) than a link from an unknown page (e.g., John Doe's homepage). Thus, the score of p is calculated as the sum of scores from all pages that link to p. In order to prevent easy link spamming where self-made pages reference each other over and over again to boost their scores, the score of a page is divided by the number of its outgoing links. This recursive formula for score calculation can be solved rather easily by iterative approximation. The overall approach is actually the famous PageRank (Page et al. 1999) algorithm that delivers much better search results than the pure content-based approach described earlier and was the foundation of Google's tremendous success. Intuitively, PageRank calculates for each page p the probability that a person who clicks randomly on a Web link will arrive at p.

8.2.3 Evaluating Information Retrieval Algorithms

The overall result of an IR process, i.e., whether the user's information need can be met or not, depends on the combined performance of all three tasks of a search engine. Because of the many different methods and alternative solutions that engineers may choose for the individual steps and because of the inherent difficulties when judging the personal information need from a few keywords on the one hand and extracting relevant information from natural language text on the other hand, one cannot expect perfect results (more on this aspect in Sect. 8.5). In fact, solving a search task is often an iterative process from the user's perspective requiring a few refinements of the original search question until the result can be found (Bruza and Dennis 1997). The performance of a search engine or a particular IR algorithm can also be evaluated formally using a test set (*gold standard*), where the expected result is known beforehand so that the result of the IR algorithm can be compared to the expected one. The most common evaluation metrics are precision, recall and accuracy (Manning et al. 2008): *Precision* measures how many of the pages classified as relevant by the IR algorithm are also marked as relevant in the gold standard; *Recall* states how many of the relevant pages in the gold standard have also been identified as relevant by the algorithm; And *accuracy* is the overall rate of correct results when the algorithm is executed on a test set. In order to compare the performance of different algorithms (or configurations of the same algorithm), it is advisable to use a standardized, publicly available test set such as the ones from the TREC[11] conferences.

---

[10]Wikipedia. https://en.wikipedia.org/. Accessed: 2016-09-12.
[11]Text REtrieval Conference (TREC). http://trec.nist.gov/. Accessed: 2016-09-12.

8.3   Social Data

In the early days of the Web, the average user was a passive consumer of information prepared by a few select publishers such as news media and other 'official' sources. The reason was that the required technical skills of writing HTML code on the one hand and the necessary infrastructure to run a Web server on the other hand were not widespread. But the appearance of WYSIWYG-(for 'what you see is what you get')-style editors (Vetter et al. 1994) that could even be executed inside the user's browser and automatically update content on the corresponding Web server led to the so-called *Web 2.0* boom where basically everyone who is able to master a Web browser could easily become an active contributor of the Web (O'Reilly 2007). The most prominent application examples that build upon this user-generated data are: (1) Knowledge bases and encyclopedias (*wikis*) such as Wikipedia; (2) Diaries and article collections (*blogs*) such as WordPress[12]; (3) Social networks such as Facebook; (4) Reviews about products, books, music, movies, travel locations, etc. in dedicated sites, e.g., IMDb[13] for movies or within online stores, e.g., Amazon; And (5) specialized communities and discussion forums such as stackoverflow,[14] which focuses on helping with software development issues. From an IT perspective, the same core technologies described earlier in Sect. 8.2.1 are used to develop these rich Web applications, e.g., the MediaWiki (Barrett 2008) software that powers Wikipedia. Best practice nowadays is to speed up and improve the development of Web applications by using one of the many available Web application frameworks that combine a scalable software architecture with standard functionality such as user management and that also provide modern user interface elements as building blocks (e.g., see Johanan 2016).

While being user-friendly is a prerequisite for Web 2.0 applications, the core success factor lies in the so-called *long-tail effect* (Brynjolfsson et al. 2006), which essentially means that the sheer number of Web users are able to collaboratively create very large amounts of high quality information even if the individual contributions are rather minor (Ullrich et al. 2008). Even seemingly superfluous content such as the countless small-talk messages sent via the social network of Twitter[15] may be used to generate valuable information such as sensing the current political opinion, e.g., before elections (Tumasjan et al. 2010) (see Sect. 8.5 for details).

Similar to traditional Web data, finding relevant information in user-generated content is challenging. Depending on the application, such data often suffers from

---

[12] WordPress. https://wordpress.com/. Accessed: 2016-09-12.

[13] IMDb. http://www.imdb.com/. Accessed: 2016-09-12.

[14] Stack Overflow. http://stackoverflow.com/. Accessed: 2016-09-12.

[15] Twitter. https://twitter.com/. Accessed: 2016-09-12.

low quality, ranging from misspellings, unintentional misinformation, to outright spam (Agichtein et al. 2008). An additional challenge lies in the social character of content creation itself, i.e., human behavior in social groups needs to be considered. For instance, despite the popularity of Wikipedia the large majority of users are passive consumers and it is rather difficult to motivate them to become active contributors (Halfaker et al. 2012), which results in many pages being halfdone or important topics completely missing. Providing the right incentives to the users is therefore crucial (Forte and Bruckman 2005). Since content on sites such as Wikipedia is usually co-created by a group of authors, it is also important to understand how these groups self-organize. For instance, a study found groups to have different leadership styles with a large impact on content creation (Zhu et al. 2012). A particular challenge for wikis is also that users should agree on a common version of the content, which is obviously difficult, if not impossible, for controversial topics such as Wikipedia's page about abortion (Viégas et al. 2004).

8.4 User Data

Another major and frequently used source of information on the Web nowadays is data about the users themselves. User data may be in the form of explicitly created user profiles with demographic data or personal preferences. In addition, user data may also be implicitly observed behavior such as a user's page visit history. Creating such a visit history via the user's 'click stream' is relatively straightforward via a session cookie that identifies a user as long as the user is logged into a particular Web site or as long as the user has a cross-site account (e.g., from Google or Facebook), so that the contacted Web site(s) can track which pages were requested together with any other user actions of interest. Without an explicit account, a user can still be tracked to a certain degree via persistent tracking cookies or via the unique characteristics of the user's Web client in a process called fingerprinting (Eckersley 2010).

Collecting user data for different purposes is of high economic interest to many companies (Lawrence 2012) with the most obvious applications being directed marketing (Armstrong and Hagel 2000), collecting feedback for product development and innovation (Prahalad and Ramaswamy 2004), and personalizing products and services, e.g., insurance policies (Coroama and Langheinrich 2006). Indeed, 'virtual' companies such as Facebook draw their economic value almost entirely from their collected user data (Rose et al. 2012).

Analyzing how users connect and interact with each other in social networks such as Facebook reveals highly interesting information, e.g., in order to understand how news or marketing campaigns spread in the network (Lerman and Ghosh 2010) or how colleagues form communities, interact and share knowledge within enterprises (Muller et al. 2012). Because social networks are indeed networks, i.e., graphs with users as nodes and relationships or interactions (Wilson et al. 2009) as directed edges, standard graph algorithms can be used to study them (Mislove et al. 2007). For instance, the breadth-firstsearch algorithm (Sedgewick and Wayn 2011) shows how messages spread in a network and the PageRank algorithm (see Sect. 8.2.2) may be used to discover prominent users in the network (Bonchi et al. 2011).

Many user data analysis methods are based on the comparison between users, i.e., data collected from different users is analyzed to detect groups with similar properties and behaviors such as certain types of customers. Because of the high number of users and the large volume of data to be analyzed, this comparison is usually implemented with statistical machine learning methods that in general can detect patterns in data based on certain data properties (*features*) (Witten et al. 2011).

A widespread and highly successful analysis method is so-called *recommender systems* (Resnick and Varian 1997) that aim to predict (i.e., recommend) which 'items' are of interest to a user based on the interests this user has shown before in other items, where the items may be products, movies, news articles, Web pages, etc., and the user's interests are either expressed explicitly via ratings given on a scale (e.g., 3 out of 5 stars) or derived from observed user behavior such as the page visit history, the recorded time spent on a page, or the products bought previously, as is employed extensively by Amazon (Linden et al. 2003). While many different algorithms for recommender systems have been developed (Bobadilla et al. 2013), *collaborative filtering* (CF) (Resnick et al. 1994) still is the baseline method: the core idea of item-based CF (Sarwar et al. 2001) is to define a similarity function between two items, e.g., based on the users' ratings, the users' shopping cart history, or the items' categories. In the case of user ratings, the cosine similarity (see Sect. 8.2.2) between rating vectors can be used. This similarity function can recommend items to a certain user that (i) are (presumably) unknown to the user, and (ii) are similar to items the user was interested in before. An inherent problem with item-based CF is that it tends to recommend very 'obvious' items from the user's perspective, e.g., all other books written by the same author. This problem may be addressed by methods to diversify the list of recommended items (Ziegler et al. 2005).

Similar to the IR methods discussed in Sect. 8.2.2, the quality of a recommender system implementation is evaluated based on a gold standard to calculate, e.g., the overall accuracy of recommendations (Herlocker et al. 2004). Improving the methods for analyzing user data is currently a very active field of research, e.g., in order to provide recommendations for new users without a history of previous interests, known as the *cold start problem* (Schein et al. 2002) or to incorporate additional information about users from sources such as social networks (Guy 2015). But from the user's perspective, dealing with privacy needs and concerns in particular for the now widely-used covert user tracking (Roesner et al. 2012) may be more important than a small increase in accuracy. In the case of recommender systems, first approaches for privacy preservation do exist, e.g., see McSherry and Mironov (2009).

8.5   Text Data

Many data sources in the Web offer text-based content that is in fact natural language intended for human readers. Such text is not easily accessible for automatic processing, which is required for many higher-level information processing tasks such as IR, content-based recommendations or automatic language translation. For instance, it is not straightforward to retrieve the age of `Sophie Jones` from the document depicted in Fig. 8.1. *Natural language processing* (NLP) (Jurafsky and Martin 2009) has to deal with numerous challenges: on a syntactical level, different forms of the same word (e.g., be, am and `were`), misspellings (e.g., `procesing`), street language (e.g., `hm, dunno! lol ;)`), terminology (e.g., `MapReduce`), and complex sentence structures (e.g., `The movie is very popular, but I did not like it`) have to be handled. On a semantic level, synonyms (e.g., `process` and `compute`), ambiguity (e.g., `Jaguar` as cat or car), implicit contextual information (e.g., `Let it be is still popular` referring to the Beatles song), and hidden meanings (e.g., `My new phone has excellent build quality, it broke after 2 days` expressing irony) all make NLP even more difficult. These challenges are amplified due to the fact that language evolves constantly so that static solutions are likely to be outdated quickly.

In general, linguistic and statistical methods may be used for solving typical NLP tasks (Jurafsky and Martin 2009), for instance identifying so-called *named entities* (NEs) such as persons or places in text. The first approaches to *named entity recognition* (NER) were mostly linguistic ones (Nadeau and Sekine 2007), where hand-crafted rules about syntax and semantics of language were used (e.g., NEs are substantives). But nowadays, NER is usually solved via supervised machine learning, where a machine learning algorithm such as the Naive Bayes classifier (McCallum and Nigam 1998) is trained to create a statistical model of how certain features of the text (e.g., a word is uppercased) determine whether a sequence of words is an NE or not with a certain probability. Given distinctive features and the right amount of representative training data, the performance of such a classifier tends to be far better when compared to the first approaches and is also much more scalable.

More generally, many NLP tasks can be formulated as classification problems and therefore be solved by standard machine learning methods, e.g., with Naive Bayes, Support Vector Machines (SVM), neural networks, Hidden Markov Models (HMM), etc. (Russell and Norvig 2009). In recent years, such methods have become increasingly successful and widespread for practical use (Weiss et al. 2015), mostly due to the easy availability of processing power and large amounts of training data (also see Sect. 8.7). For instance, statistical machine translation methods already produce remarkably high-quality results (Bojar et al. 2014) and Google Translate[16]

---

[16]Google Translate. https://translate.google.com/. Accessed: 2016-09-12.

is able to handle dozens of different languages with at least reasonable results in the more common ones (Tobin 2015).

Another NLP application area that receives considerable attention is *sentiment analysis*, where the users' opinions (sentiments) about a certain product, topic, person, etc. is determined on the basis of written reviews or social network messages (Bing 2015). Sentiment analysis is particularly interesting for companies that want to collect feedback about their (and their competitors') products as well as for politicians and social scientists who want to sense the general public mood. In the simplest case, sentiment analysis is a binary classification task where texts express either a positive or negative sentiment, which can be solved reasonably well with one of the machine learning methods mentioned above (Pang et al. 2002). More detailed analysis aims to infer the source, target, and sentiment type, i.e., who has which opinion about what (Ruppenhofer et al. 2008)? In addition to general statistical and linguistic features, dedicated sentiment lexicons that contain formalized sentiment categories and strength of expression are a vital source of information for sentiment analysis (Feldman 2013). Overall, sentiment analysis is a quite difficult NLP task where many subtleties of natural language text such as sentence structure, irony, and negation (Wiegand et al. 2010) have to be considered.

NLP methods also play an important role in improving IR towards providing concrete answers for the user's information need, rather than a ranked result list of more or less relevant Web documents (Manning et al. 2008). For instance, because the information need of users is often focused on certain persons, places, companies etc., NER can improve question-answering significantly. Some question-answering capabilities are already implemented in state-of-the-art search engines, e.g., Google can answer the question of What is the capital of Switzerland? with Bern or convert a certain amount of money from one currency to another one (2.5 Swiss Francs in Euro). Another example is WolframAlpha,[17] which can solve rather complex problems in different domains such as mathematics, chemistry, and sociology; for example, compare the cost of living index Boulder vs Sacramento delivers detailed statistics and background information.

Taking question-answering one step further, conversational agents aim to provide services and support with natural language text or even speech as interface between human and machine (Wahlster 2007). Despite numerous NLP challenges, personal assistants like Apple's Siri[18] and Microsoft's Cortana[19] have already been deployed and offer innovative features such as proactive recommendations that are calculated on the user's learned profile and her current situation. However, conversational systems that are indistinguishable from humans are still more a vision than reality, but

---

[17]WolframAlpha. https://www.wolframalpha.com/. Accessed: 2016-09-12.

[18]Siri. http://www.apple.com/ios/siri/. Accessed: 2016-09-12.

[19]Cortana. https://www.microsoft.com/en-us/windows/cortana. Accessed: 2016-09-12.

nevertheless relatively significant progress has already been made as the repeated questionanswering challenge of the TREC conference has shown (Agichtein et al. 2015).

8.6 Machine Data

The Internet is not only a distributed platform for content to be produced and consumed by humans, but also for enabling distributed applications with *machine-to-machine* (M2M) communication, e.g., ERP (Enterprise Resource Planning) software for distributed companies, sensor networks, or cloud computing platforms. In the early days of the Internet, many protocols for M2M communication used binary formats for efficiency reasons (Tanenbaum and Wetherall 2011), but nowadays text-based formats that are transmitted over the Web protocol HTTP seem to be dominant due to the widespread availability of tools and programming support for Web technologies. Textbased data needs to be highly structured for M2M communication in order to simplify parsing and prevent errors and ambiguities, and the predominant structured data formats for this are XML (Extensible Markup Language) (W3C 2006) and JSON (JavaScript Object Notation) (Bray 2014). The JSON format encodes data as a hierarchy of key-value pairs and is used in many Web applications for transferring data between server and client. Similar to HTML, data and meta-data are separated via tags in XML to form a tree-shaped data structure.

Figure 8.2 shows a simplified example for a user profile encoded as XML where, e.g., the user's age is encoded in the `age` element (and is much easier to process than the version of Fig. 8.1). The exact names, types, ordering, and nesting of the XML elements in such a tree may be further detailed by an accompanying XML Schema (W3C 2012) definition. In Fig. 8.3, the example XML Schema for a user profile is given and defines, e.g., that `age` is a simple XML element that is a child of `user` and contains content of type `integer`.

XML is used in many Web and even desktop applications (e.g., Microsoft Office), is well-supported in most programming languages and by numerous tools (Flynn 2016). In particular, XML is the basis for M2M communication via WSDL-(Web Services Description Language)-based (W3C 2001) *Web services*: A WSDL

```
<?xml version="1.0" encoding="UTF-8"?>
<user xmlns:xsi="http://www.w3.org/2001/XMLSchema-instance"
      xsi:schemaLocation="http://www.social.net user.xsd">
  <firstname>Sophie</firstname>
  <name>Jones</name>
  <age>34</age>
</user>
```

Fig. 8.2 XML document `user.xml`

```
<?xml version="1.0" encoding="UTF-8"?>
<xs:schema xmlns:xs="http://www.w3.org/2001/XMLSchema">
  <xs:element name="user">
    <xs:complexType>
      <xs:sequence>
        <xs:element name="firstname" type="xs:string"/>
        <xs:element name="name" type="xs:string"/>
        <xs:element name="age" type="xs:integer"/>
      </xs:sequence>
    </xs:complexType>
  </xs:element>
</xs:schema>
```

Fig. 8.3 XML Schema document user.xsd

service offers one or more operation(s) that can be called via a formally described service interface. The service interface (i.e., WSDL), the M2M protocol (i.e., SOAP (Simple Object Access Protocol) (W3C 2007)), the exchanged application data, and numerous service properties such as security (e.g., WS-Security OASIS 2006) are all encoded as XML. While WSDL-based Web services are mostly used for business applications within companies, in the 'open' Web REST services are dominant due to their less complex technology stack and seemingly better fit with the general Web paradigm (Pautasso et al. 2008): rather than being function calls like WSDL services, REST services create, read, update, and delete data on the Web (application) server, just as a browser does with Web pages as described in Sect. 8.2.

The idea of providing application logic as Web services decouples service provider and service consumer technologically, which is also called a *Service-Oriented Architecture* (SOA) (Papazoglou 2012). Further, Web services can be combined and integrated into increasingly complex applications either via programming or higher-level business process modeling (Van der Aalst et al. 2003), which may even be done by 'ordinary' Web users (Lecue et al. 2012). Service provider and consumer may in fact come from different organizations, leading to a flexible *Internet of Services* (IoS) (Soriano et al. 2013) where data, computing platforms (Erl et al. 2013), and application logic are available as services (Garcia-Gomez et al. 2012) (i.e., *Everything-as-a-Service* (XaaS)), may be combined depending on the specific needs of the service consumer, and may even be traded like physical goods via a marketplace (Menychtas et al. 2014).

Continuously smaller and cheaper network-enabled hardware has enabled another recent technological development, the so-called *Internet of Things* (IoT) (Whitmore et al. 2015), where machines, sensors, and everyday 'things' (e.g., medicine, consumer products, and even perishable goods) become active nodes in the Internet as producers and consumers of data, which enables a whole new range of applications, for instance, supply chain monitoring, product fraud protection, and smart homes.

8.7 Big Data

The ever-increasing volume of data that not only Web companies but also companies in other industries face (e.g., manufactures, service providers, financial institutions, etc.) has initiated a huge interest in so-called *Big Data* (Tache 2016).

Big Data technologies aim to store, process, and analyze terabytes of data with relatively cheap commodity hardware when compared to previous solutions such as supercomputing. But maybe even more important than hardware costs is the human skills factor, as parallel processing in general and software development for supercomputers in particular is quite challenging. In contrast, Big Data technologies aim to simplify software development via higher-level programming abstractions and frameworks.

For instance, the 'breakthrough' *MapReduce* approach (Dean and Ghemawat 2008) defines a generic data model and two functional interfaces for data processing: The map() function is called first and used to pre-process, filter, or sort the provided data; next the reduce() function processes and summarizes the data from the previous map() step and produces the final result. Both functions take and produce data in the form of (sets of) key-value pairs. The distribution of this data to a (potentially very large) set of processing nodes, where the map()/reduce() functions are executed on manageable portions of data, is handled entirely by the MapReduce framework and of no concern to the software developer, thus significantly reducing the complexity of parallel processing. While being rather simplistic at a first glance, MapReduce does scale well with respect to data volume and required processing power by adapting the number of active processing nodes, is fault-tolerant by being able to automatically replace failed nodes, and can be used to implement a wide range of data processing algorithms (Miner and Shook 2012). For instance, together with large volumes of training data, machine learning solutions become possible that seemed to be unrealistic just a few years ago, e.g., statistical machine translation (Leskovec et al. 2014).

Another success factor is that many Big Data solutions are available as open source: Hadoop[20] implements MapReduce and has developed into a highly popular, universal parallel processing platform with a large ecosystem of complementing tools and technologies (White 2015). Another popular solution is Spark[21] that, compared to Hadoop, offers both performance enhancements due to in-memory data caching and also a more flexible programming model due to additional parallelized data operations.

---

[20]Hadoop. https://hadoop.apache.org/. Accessed: 2016-09-12.

[21]Spark. http://spark.apache.org/. Accessed: 2016-09-12.

8.8   Linked Data

As discussed in Sect. 8.5, accessing information in HTML or textual data is difficult
and error-prone. But even the structured data format of XML (see Sect. 8.6) has
its limitations: Before using XML data, one first needs to understand the particular
syntax and semantics of the individual elements and their overall structuring, which
often requires substantial domain knowledge. Also, different XML data providers
may even use different syntax and/or semantics for the same type of data, unless
they agree on a common standard. The same holds true for other data formats
commonly used, e.g., SQL and CSV (Comma-separated values). As a result, larger
IT projects that involve several parties and need to combine several data sources
usually require a labor-intensive data integration effort, for instance in the Internet of
Services (see Sect. 8.6). Such manual integration is also very error-prone, and case
studies in different industries have revealed that 5 out of 6 real-world integration
projects suffered from syntax-related issues, and all experienced semantics-related
problems (Schmidt et al. 2010). The core issue with these formats therefore is
that the data is not structured enough, i.e., their meta-data does not reveal enough
syntactical and semantical information.

In contrast, the idea of *Linked Data* (Berners-Lee et al. 2006) is to encode
both data and meta-data more formally as graphs that are both flexible and
expressive. As a result, many data handling tasks may be (semi)-automated (Hitzler
et al. 2009), and in particular large scale data integration becomes much easier (Frischmuth et al. 2012). Technologically, Linked Data is based on the RDF
(Resource Description Framework) (W3C 2014b) data format that uses so-called
statements to express certain pieces of information: A statement relates a data
resource (*subject*) to another one (*object*) via a *property*, i.e., RDF statements are
<subject, predicate, object> triples. For the user profile of Fig. 8.2, a
sample RDF statement is <http://social.net/person/sophiejones,
http://social.net/prop\-erty/age,"34">.

The key 'trick' is that subject, predicate, and object are uniquely identified via
URIs (unless they are unnamed or refer to a literal like 34 in the example), and
that their semantics is 'known' (e.g., via standardization), so that both human and
machine users can interpret the statements. RDF statements may also be embedded
into existing Web (i.e., HTML) documents via RDFa (W3C 2015). While RDF is
for expressing statements, RDF types and their relations may be further specified
via RDF Schema (RDFS) (W3C 2014c), e.g., resources of type person may have
a property age that needs to refer to a literal of type integer. Together, RDFS
and RDF define self-descriptive data structures and instances.

Many RDF statements together, which share at least some resources, create a
connected knowledge graph. This graph can then be analyzed via graph algorithms,
or on a higher level of abstraction, via the SPARQL (W3C 2013) query language:
As the name suggests, SPARQL is inspired by SQL and likewise descriptive to
retrieve certain parts of the Linked Data graph (i.e., subgraphs). For example, the
query   SELECT?pWHERE\{?prdf:type<http://social.net/type/

`person>.?p<http://social.net/property/age>"34"\}`, retrieves
all resources of type `person` that are of `age` `34`.

Linked Data is often mentioned as the appropriate data format for *Open Data*,
i.e., data that is to be published without copyright or other restrictions for the free use
of everyone, as so-called *Linked Open Data* (LOD) (Bauer and Kaltenböck 2011).
Although Open Data is already supported by many countries and organizations, for
instance by the USA,[22] EU,[23] UK,[24] and Switzerland,[25] most datasets published
are actually in different formats than Linked Data. The reason is twofold: The first
important prerequisite for a larger adoption of Linked Data is the availability of
standardized (RDFS) ontologies, which formally describe the syntax and semantics
of a Linked Data graph. Basically, different datasets can be combined seamlessly
when they are based on the same ontologies (or an automatic transformation
between different ontologies exists). While a substantial number of widely-adopted
ontologies have already been defined by large standardization bodies such as the
W3C[26] and academic communities, in many domains appropriate ontologies are
not yet available. The second prerequisite for Linked Data to be successful is the
availability of user-friendly tools and software components that provide the typical
functionalities of the so-called data life-cycle, covering the needs to model, create,
store, publish, search, retrieve, integrate, process, visualize, and manage Linked
Data. For some of these tasks commercial solutions do exist from smaller vendors,
e.g., for RDF databases (so-called *triple stores*), while for others academic, open
source software is widespread, e.g., the Protege Editor.[27] However, often these
components are targeted at experts and specialize on a few dedicated tasks so that
users nowadays have to master several of them. First attempts to provide a more
seamless tool chain have been made in some research projects, e.g., LOD2 (Auer
et al. 2012), but the current level of integration and usability still lacks the quality
of established professional tools (e.g., that of SQL).

The fine-grained encoding of small pieces of information as Linked Data is
actually a realization of the so-called *Semantic Web* that was advocated from early
on by Tim Berners-Lee in his vision to make the Web accessible to both humans
and machines (Berners-Lee et al. 2001). The analog concept can be also applied to
Web services (see Sect. 8.6) that can be turned into *Semantic Web Services* (Fensel
et al. 2011) in order to simplify service discovery (Pedrinaci and Domingue 2010),
integration, and composition (Lecue et al. 2012) – all of which are active areas of
research.

---

[22]Open Data, USA. https://www.data.gov/. Accessed: 2016-09-12.

[23]Open Data, EU. http://open-data.europa.eu. Accessed: 2016-09-12.

[24]Open Data, UK. https://data.gov.uk. Accessed: 2016-09-12.

[25]Open Data, Switzerland. https://opendata.swiss/. Accessed: 2016-09-12.

[26]W3C, semantic Web. https://www.w3.org/standards/semanticweb/ontology. Accessed: 2016-09-12.

[27]Protege Editor. http://protege.stanford.edu. Accessed: 2016-09-12.

8.9 Summary

The Internet has established itself as the universal data and information infrastructure, not only for providing and retrieving data in a diverse range of application domains involving human and machine actors, but also as a distributed processing platform. Web data comes in many different formats, and in particular natural language text embedded in HTML often requires complex and error-prone processing before it can be turned into machine-accessible information. More structured data formats such as XML and RDF enable not only easier information access of Internet applications and services but also improve the results of tasks for human users such as IR and machine translation.

References

Agichtein E, Castillo C, Donato D, Gionis A, Mishne G (2008) Finding high-quality content in social media. In: Proceedings of the 2008 International conference on web search and data mining (WSDM'08). ACM, New York, pp 183–194

Agichtein E, Carmel D, Harman D, Pelleg D, Pinter Y (2015) Overview of the TREC 2015 LiveQA track. In: Proceedings of the twenty-fourth text retrieval conference (TREC'15). National Institute of Standards and Technology (NIST). Available via http://trec.nist.gov/pubs/trec24/trec2015.html

Armstrong A, Hagel J (2000) The real value of online communities. Knowl Commun 74(3):85–95

Auer S, Bühmann L, Dirschl C, Erling O, Hausenblas M, Isele R, Lehmann J, Martin M, Mendes PN, van Nuffelen B (2012) Managing the life-cycle of linked data with the LOD2 stack. In: Proceedings of the 11th International semantic web conference. Springer, Berlin, pp 1–16

Baeza-Yates R, Hurtado C, Mendoza M (2004) Query recommendation using query logs in search engines. In: Lindner W, Mesiti M, Türker C, Tzitzikas Y, Vakali AI (eds) Current trends in database technology–EDBT 2004 workshops. Springer, Berlin/Heidelberg, pp 588–596

Barrett DJ (2008) MediaWiki (Wikipedia and Beyond). O'Reilly Media, Farnham

Barth A (2011) HTTP State Management Mechanism (Internet Request For Comments, IETF, RFC-6265). Available via https://tools.ietf.org/html/rfc6265

Bauer F, Kaltenböck M (2011) Linked open data: the essentials. Edition mono/monochrom, Vienna

Berners-Lee T (1989) Information management: a proposal. (Historical document written in March 1989 by Tim Berners-Lee). Available via https://www.w3.org/History/1989/proposal.html

Berners-Lee T, Hendler J, Lassila O (2001) The semantic Web. Sci Am 284(5):28–37

Berners-Lee T, Chen Y, Chilton L, Connolly D, Dhanaraj R, Hollenbach J, Lerer A, Sheets D (2006) Tabulator: exploring and analyzing linked data on the semantic Web. In: Proceedings of the 3rd International semantic web user interaction workshop, Athens, p 159

Berners-Lee T, Fielding RT, Masinter L (2015) Uniform Resource Identifier (URI): Generic Syntax (Internet Request For Comments, IETF, RFC-398). Available via https://tools.ietf.org/html/rfc3986

Bing L (2015) Sentiment analysis: mining opinions, sentiments, and emotions. Cambridge University Press, Cambridge

Bobadilla J, Ortega F, Hernando A, Gutiérrez A (2013) Recommender systems survey. Knowl Bas Syst 46:109–132

Bojar O, Buck C, Federmann C, Haddow B, Koehn P, (8 additional authors not shown) (2014) Findings of the 2014 workshop on statistical machine translation. In: Proceedings of the 9th workshop on statistical machine translation. Association for Computational Linguistics, Baltimore, pp 12–58

Bonchi F, Castillo C, Gionis A, Jaimes A (2011) Social network analysis and mining for business applications. ACM Trans Intell Syst Tech 2(3):22:1–22:37

Bray T (2014) The JavaScript Object Notation (JSON) Data Interchange Format (Internet Request For Comments, IETF, RFC-7159). Available via https://tools.ietf.org/html/rfc7159

Broder A (2002) A taxonomy of web search. SIGIR Forum 36(2):3–10

Brooks DR (2011) Guide to HTML, JavaScript and PHP. Springer, London

Bruza PD, Dennis S (1997) Query reformulation on the Internet: empirical data and the hyperindex search engine. In: Proceeding of computer-assisted information searching on Internet (RIAO'97). Le Centre De Hautes Etudes Internationale D'Informatique Documentaire, pp 488–499

Brynjolfsson E, Hu YJ, Smith MD (2006) From niches to riches: anatomy of the long tail. Sloan Manag Rev 47(4):67–71

Burner M (1997) Crawling towards eternity: building an archive of the World Wide Web. Web Tech Mag 2(5):37–40

Ceri S, Bozzon A, Brambilla M, Valle ED, Fraternali P, Quarteroni S (2013) Web information retrieval. Data-centric systems and applications. Springer, Heidelberg

Coroama V, Langheinrich M (2006) Personalized vehicle insurance rates–a case for client-side personalization in ubiquitous computing. In: Proceedings of human factors in computing systems. Workshop on privacy-enhanced personalization (CHI'06). ACM, pp 56–59

Dean J, Ghemawat S (2008) MapReduce: simplified data processing on large clusters. Commun ACM 51(1):107–113

Eckersley P (2010) How unique is your web browser? In: Proceedings of the 10th International conference on privacy enhancing technologies (PETS'10). Springer, Berlin/Heidelberg, pp 1–18

Elmasri R, Navathe SB (2016) Fundamentals of database systems. Pearson Education, Hoboken

Erl T, Puttini R, Mahmood Z (2013) Cloud computing: concepts, technology & architecture. Prentice Hall Press, Upper Saddle River

Feldman R (2013) Techniques and applications for sentiment analysis. Commun ACM 56(4): 82–89

Fensel D, Facca FM, Simperl E, Toma I (2011) Semantic web services. Springer, Heidelberg/ New York

Fielding RT, Reschke JF (2014) Hypertext Transfer Protocol (HTTP/1.1): Message Syntax and Routing (Internet Request For Comments, IETF, RFC-7230). Available via https://tools.ietf. org/html/rfc7230

Flynn P (2016) The XML FAQ. Silmaril, Edition v.6.4. Available via http://xml.silmaril.ie/

Forte A, Bruckman A (2005) Why do people write for Wikipedia? Incentives to contribute to open–content publishing. In: Proceedings of GROUP – International conference on supporting group work, vol 5, pp 6–9

Frischmuth P, Klímek J, Auer S, Tramp S, Unbehauen J, Holzweissig K, Marquardt CM (2012) Linked data in enterprise information integration. Semantic Web. IOS Press, Amsterdam, NL, pp 1–17

Garcia-Gomez S, Escriche-Vicente M, Arozarena-Llopis P, Lelli F, Taher Y, (12 additional authors not shown) (2012) 4CaaSt: comprehensive management of cloud services through a PaaS. In: Proceedings of the 2012 IEEE 10th International symposium on parallel and distributed processing with applications, Washington, DC, pp 494–499

Guy I (2015) Social recommender systems. In: Ricci F, Rokach L, Shapira B (eds) Recommender systems handbook. Springer, New York, pp 511–543

Halfaker A, Geiger RS, Morgan JT, Riedl J (2012) The rise and decline of an open collaboration system: how Wikipedia's reaction to popularity is causing its decline. Am Behav Sci 57(5): 664–688

Herlocker JL, Konstan JA, Terveen LG, Riedl JT (2004) Evaluating collaborative filtering recommender systems. ACM Trans Inf Syst 22(1):5–53

Hitzler P, Krotzsch M, Rudolph S (2009) Foundations of semantic web technologies. Chapman and Hall/CRC, Boca Raton

ITU (2016) ICT Facts and Figures 2016. Estimates for key telecommunication/ICT indicators. Available via http://www.itu.int/en/ITU-D/Statistics/Documents/facts/ICTFactsFigures2016. pdf

Joshua J, Talha K, Ricardo Z (2016) Web developer's reference guide. Packt Publishing, Birmingham

Jurafsky D, Martin JH (2009) Speech and language processing. Prentice Hall, Upper Saddle River

Lawrence DB (2012) The economic value of information. Springer, New York

Lecue F, Mehandjiev N, Vogel J, Un P, Neu B (2012) KPI-based service composition modeling and optimization with design time user interaction. In: Proceedings of the 2012 IEEE 9th International conference on services computing (SCC). IEEE, Los Alamitos, pp 692–693

Lerman K, Ghosh R (2010) Information contagion: an empirical study of the spread of news on Digg and Twitter social networks. arXiv:1003.2664 [cs.CY]. Available via https://arxiv.org/abs/1003.2664

Leskovec J, Rajaraman A, Ullman J (2014) Mining of massive datasets. Cambridge University Press, Cambridge

Linden G, Smith B, York J (2003) Amazon.com recommendations: item-to-item collaborative filtering. IEEE Internet Comput 7(1):76–80

Manning CD, Raghavan P, Schütze H (2008) Introduction to information retrieval. Cambridge University Press, Cambridge

McCallum A, Nigam K (1998) A comparison of event models for naive Bayes text classification. In: Proceedings of AAAI/ICML–98 workshop on learning for text categorization. AAAI Press, pp 41–48

McSherry F, Mironov I (2009) Differentially private recommender systems: building privacy into the net. In: Proceedings of the 15th ACM SIGKDD International conference on knowledge discovery and data mining (KDD'09). ACM, New York, pp 627–636

Menychtas A, Vogel J, Giessmann A, Gatzioura A, Gomez SG, Moulos V, Junker F, Müller M, Kyriazis D, Stanoevska-Slabeva K (2014) 4CaaSt marketplace: an advanced business environment for trading cloud services. Futur Gener Comput Syst 41:104–120

Miner D, Shook A (2012) MapReduce design patterns: building effective algorithms and analytics for Hadoop and other systems. O'Reilly Media, Beijing

Mislove A, Marcon M, Gummadi KP, Druschel P, Bhattacharjee B (2007) Measurement and analysis of online social networks. In: Proceedings of the 7th ACM SIGCOMM conference on Internet measurement (IMC'07). ACM, New York, pp 29–42

Muller M, Ehrlich K, Matthews T, Perer A, Ronen I, Guy I (2012) Diversity among enterprise online communities: collaborating, teaming, and innovating through social media. In: Proceedings of the ACM SIGCHI conference on human factors in computing systems (CHI'12). ACM, New York

Nadeau D, Sekine S (2007) A survey of named entity recognition and classification. Lingvisticae Investigationes. 30(1):3–26

OASIS (2006) Web Services Security: SOAP Message Security 1.1 (Technical Report). Available via http://docs.oasis-open.org/wss/v1.1/

Ohm JR (2016) Multimedia content analysis. Signals and communication technology. Springer, Berlin

O'Reilly T (2007) What is Web 2.0: design patterns and business models for the next generation of software. Commun Strateg 1:17

Page L, Brin S, Motwani R, Winograd T (1999) The PageRank citation ranking: Bringing order to the Web. (Technical Report, 1999-66) Stanford InfoLab. Available via http://ilpubs.stanford.edu:8090/422/

Pang B, Lee L, Vaithyanathan S (2002) Thumbs up? Sentiment classification using machine learning techniques. In: Proceedings of the ACL-02 conference on empirical methods in natural language processing (EMNLP'02), vol 10. Association for Computational Linguistics, Stroudsburg, pp 79–86

Papazoglou M (2012) Web services and SOA: principles and technology, 2nd edn. Pearson Education, Harlow

Pautasso C, Zimmermann O, Leymann F (2008) Restful Web services vs. "Big" Web services: making the right architectural decision. In: Proceedings of the 17th International conference on World Wide Web (WWW'08). ACM, New York, pp 805–814

Pedrinaci C, Domingue J (2010) Toward the next wave of services: linked services for the Web of data. J Univers Comput Sci 16(13):1694–1719

Prahalad CK, Ramaswamy V (2004) Co-creation experiences: the next practice in value creation. J Interact Mark 18(3):5–14

Resnick P, Varian HR (1997) Recommender systems. Commun ACM 40(3):56–58

Resnick P, Iacovou N, Suchak M, Bergstrom P, Riedl J (1994) GroupLens: an open architecture for collaborative filtering of netnews. In: Proceedings of the 1994 ACM conference on computer supported cooperative work (CSCW'94), pp 175–186. ACM, New York

Roesner F, Kohno T, Wetherall D (2012) Detecting and defending against third-party tracking on the Web. In: Proceedings of the 9th USENIX conference on networked systems design and implementation (NSDI'12). USENIX Association, Berkeley, p 12

Rose J, Rehse O, Röber B (2012) The value of our digital identity. The Boston Consulting Group. Available via http://www.libertyglobal.com/PDF/public-policy/The-Value-of-Our-Digital-Identity.pdf

Ruppenhofer J, Somasundaran S, Wiebe J (2008) Finding the sources and targets of subjective expressions. In: Proceedings of the 6th International language resources and evaluation (LREC'08)

Russell S, Norvig P (2009) Artificial intelligence: a modern approach, 3rd edn. Prentice Hall Press, Upper Saddle River

Salton G, Buckley C (1988) Term-weighting approaches in automatic text retrieval. IP&M 24(5):513–523

Sarwar B, Karypis G, Konstan J, Riedl J (2001) Item-based collaborative filtering recommendation algorithms. In: Proceedings of the 10th International conference on World Wide Web (WWW'01). ACM, New York, pp 285–295

Schein AI, Popescul A, Ungar LH, Pennock DM (2002) Methods and metrics for cold-start recommendations. In: Proceedings of the 25th annual International ACM SIGIR conference on research and development in information retrieval (SIGIR'02). ACM, New York, pp 253–260

Schmidt A, Otto B, Österle H (2010) Integrating information systems: case studies on current challenges. Electron Mark 20(2):161–174

Sebesta RW (2015) Programming the World Wide Web. Pearson Education, Boston

Sedgewick R, Wayne K (2011) Algorithms. Pearson Education, Boston

Sommerville I (2016) Software engineering. Pearson, Boston

Soriano J, Heitz C, Hutter HP, Fernández R, Hierro JJ, Vogel J, Edmonds A, Bohnert TM (2013) Internet of services. In: Bertin E, Crespi N, Magedanz T (eds) Evolution of telecommunication services: the convergence of telecom and Internet: technologies and ecosystems. Springer, Berlin/Heidelberg, pp 283–325

Tache N (ed) (2016) Big data now, 2015 edn. O'Reilly, Sebastopol

Tanenbaum AS, Wetherall DJ (2011) Computer networks. Pearson Prentice Hall, Boston

Tobin A (2015) Is Google translate good enough for commercial websites? A machine translation evaluation of text from English websites into four different languages. Reitaku Rev 21:94–116

Tumasjan A, Sprenger TO, Sandner PG, Welpe IM (2010) Predicting elections with Twitter: what 140 characters reveal about political sentiment. In: Proceedings of the fourth International AAAI conference on weblogs and social media, vol 10, pp 178–185

Ullrich C, Borau K, Luo H, Tan X, Shen L, Shen R (2008) Why Web 2.0 is good for learning and for research: principles and prototypes. In: Proceedings of the 17th International conference on World Wide Web (WWW'08). ACM, New York, pp 705–714

Van der Aalst WMP, Ter Hofstede AHM, Weske M (2003) Business process management: a survey. In: Proceedings of the International conference on business process management. Springer, Berlin/New York, pp 1–12

Vetter RJ, Spell C, Ward C (1994) Mosaic and the World Wide Web. Computer 27(10):49–57

Viégas FB, Wattenberg M, Kushal D (2004) Studying cooperation and conflict between authors with history flow visualizations. In: Proceedings of the ACM SIGCHI conference on human factors in computing systems (CHI'04). ACM, New York, pp 575–582

Vogel J, Widmer J (2008) Robustness in network protocols and distributed applications of the Internet. In: Schuster A (ed) Robust intelligent systems. Springer, London, pp 61–86

Wahlster W (2007) Smartweb: multimodal web services on the road. In: Proceedings of the 15th ACM International conference on multimedia (MM'07), ACM, New York, pp 16–16

Weiss SM, Indurkhya N, Zhang T (2015) Fundamentals of predictive text mining. Texts in computer science. Springer, London

White T (2015) Hadoop: the definitive guide. O'Reilly Media, Sebastopol

Whitmore A, Agarwal A, Da Xu L (2015) The Internet of things: a survey of topics and trends. Inf Syst Front 17(2):261–274

Wiegand M, Balahur A, Roth B, Klakow D, Montoyo A (2010) A survey on the role of negation in sentiment analysis. In: Proceedings of the workshop on negation and speculation in natural language processing. Association for Computational Linguistics, Stroudsburg, pp 60–68

Wilson C, Boe B, Sala A, Puttaswamy KPN, Zhao BY (2009) User interactions in social networks and their implications. In: Proceedings of the 4th ACM European conference on computer systems (EuroSys'09). ACM, New York, pp 205–218

Witten IH, Frank E, Hall MA (2011) Data mining: practical machine learning tools and techniques, 3rd edn. Morgan Kaufmann Publishers Inc., San Francisco

W3C (2001) Web Services Description Language (WSDL) (W3C, Technical Report). Available via https://www.w3.org/TR/wsdl

W3C (2006) Extensible Markup Language (XML) (W3C, Technical Report). Available via https://www.w3.org/TR/xml11/

W3C (2007) SOAP Version 1.2 Part 1: Messaging Framework, 2nd edn. (W3C, Technical Report). Available via https://www.w3.org/TR/soap12/

W3C (2011) Cascading Style Sheets Level 2 Revision 1 (CSS 2.1) Specification (W3C, Technical Report). Available via https://www.w3.org/TR/CSS2/

W3C (2012) XML Schema Definition Language (XSD) (W3C, Technical Report). Available via https://www.w3.org/TR/xmlschema11-1/

W3C (2013) SPARQL 1.1 Overview (W3C, Technical Report). Available via https://www.w3.org/TR/sparql11-overview/

W3C (2014a) HTML5 (W3C, Technical Report). Available via https://www.w3.org/TR/html5/

W3C (2014b) RDF 1.1 Primer (W3C, Technical Report). Available via https://www.w3.org/TR/rdf11-primer/

W3C (2014c) RDF Schema 1.1 (W3C, Technical Report). Available via https://www.w3.org/TR/rdf-schema/

W3C (2015) RDFa 1.1 Primer (W3C, Technical Report). Available via https://www.w3.org/TR/rdfa-primer/

Zhu H, Kraut R, Kittur A (2012) Effectiveness of shared leadership in online communities. In: Proceedings of the ACM 2012 conference on computer supported cooperative work (CSCW'12). ACM, New York, pp 407–416

Ziegler CN, McNee SM, Konstan JA, Lausen G (2005) Improving recommendation lists through topic diversification. In: Proceedings of the 14th International conference on World Wide Web (WWW'05). ACM, New York, pp 22–32

Chapter 9
Custom Hardware Versus Cloud Computing in Big Data

Gaye Lightbody, Fiona Browne, and Valeriia Haberland

Abstract The computational and data handling challenges in big data are immense yet a market is steadily growing traditionally supported by technologies such as Hadoop for management and processing of huge and unstructured datasets. With this ever increasing deluge of data we now need the algorithms, tools and computing infrastructure to handle the extremely computationally intense data analytics, looking for patterns and information pertinent to creating a market edge for a range of applications. Cloud computing has provided opportunities for scalable high-performance solutions without the initial outlay of developing and creating the core infrastructure. One vendor in particular, Amazon Web Services, has been leading this field. However, other solutions exist to take on the computational load of big data analytics. This chapter provides an overview of the extent of applications in which big data analytics is used. Then an overview is given of some of the high-performance computing options that are available, ranging from multiple Central Processing Unit (CPU) setups, Graphical Processing Units (GPUs), Field Programmable Gate Arrays (FPGAs) and cloud solutions. The chapter concludes by looking at some of the state of the art solutions for deep learning platforms in which custom hardware such as FPGAs and Application Specific Integrated Circuits (ASICs) are used within a cloud platform for key computational bottlenecks.

9.1 Introduction

The exponential growth in technology has fuelled the rise of complex computing applications churning out reams of data and information which in turn needs to be processed using high-performance computing solutions, stored using mammoth

G. Lightbody (✉) • F. Browne
School of Computing and Mathematics, Ulster University, Shore Road, Newtownabbey, Co. Antrim, BT37 0QB, UK
e-mail: g.lightbody@ulster.ac.uk; f.browne@ulster.ac.uk

V. Haberland
Tungsten Centre for Intelligent Data Analytics, Goldsmiths, University of London, New Cross, SE14 6NW, London, UK
e-mail: v.haberland@gold.ac.uk

© Springer International Publishing AG 2017
A.J. Schuster (eds.), *Understanding Information*, Advanced Information and Knowledge Processing, DOI 10.1007/978-3-319-59090-5_9

data centers and managed through the support of refined data governance. Such applications span a broad range of areas and disciplines and this spread is accelerating at a phenomenal rate. The world around us offers endless possibilities of monitoring and gathering data. Our cities, homes and even ourselves are amassed with technology for monitoring, collating and analyzing data. From a vision of smart cities (Townsend 2014) in which the very control of home heating is managed through analytical decisions (ODwyer et al. 2016) through to effective control of power generation (BritishGas 2017), it is clear to see how such analysis opens up the potential for affecting power consumption and ultimately impacts the global fuel crisis.

Through the development of powerful technology such as smart phones, wearable tech and sensors, we are now generating huge amounts of personal data on our daily lives, behavior, health and well-being. We are currently amidst a self-quantification era in which we wear sensors to report back on activity, behavior and well-being.[1] From a non-clinical aspect this enables a tracking of fitness and personal goals with the added dimension of social support through disseminating our personal metric data through social media communities. The direction this is going, is to a more biological level in that we are prepared to share biosignal metrics and signals such as Electroencephalography (EEG) (Terrell 2015) and even our own DNA (AncestryDNA[TM] 2016; 23andMe 2015) in the concerted goal to furthering ourselves and medical science.[2]

Continuing the discussion in the medical domain, a further source of high volume heterogeneous data is with digital records. Such an encompassing term spans far beyond text-based information to mammoth digital files of x-ray images, Magnetic Resonance Imaging (MRI) scans, recordings of EEG and possible Exome or Genome sequences. The image processing required for digital capture again needs to be of a significant quality as not to lose vital information from the record. Furthermore, methods to analyze and quantify what the images are showing indicate a necessity for high-performance computing solutions (Wang et al. 2010).

The result of such generation of huge volumes of data is referred to as big data. However, it is not only the sheer quantity of data created that defines big data, but there are also the four 'V's' (Hashem et al. 2015) that are recognized characteristics:

1. Volume: refers to the sheer amount of data coming from multiple resources.
2. Variety: refers to the heterogeneous nature of the data. That is data of the different types coming from the different collection mechanisms, such as sensors, physiological recordings, speech, video, text, social networks, to name just a few. In addition to the sheer amount of data, a major hurdle is in handling the diversity in data format and whether the data is structured or unstructured.
3. Velocity: refers to the speed at which the data is created and transferred.

---

[1]Quantified Self. http://quantifiedself.com/. Accessed: 2017-02-03.

[2]IGSR: The International Genome Sample Resource. http://www.internationalgenome.org/home. Accessed: 2017-02-03.

4. Value: The benefit of meeting such a challenge is the potential that by gathering such a diverse and large set of data then previously hidden trends and patterns can emerge through analysis.

Big data opens up a range of challenges along every stage of data handling, processing and analysis (Chen et al. 2014). The computational challenges are extreme and as such a range of solutions exists, where each platform is heralding scalability and performance advantages. In this chapter a high-level review is given of the range of common applications in which big data now features. The overview provides some insight into different solutions or examples of how the computational challenges have been met in these applications. A summary is provided of high-performance platforms, ranging from multiple CPU setups, GPUs, FPGAs and cloud solutions. The chapter concludes with a discussion around custom hardware solutions versus scalable on-demand cloud computing solutions, asking the question whether cloud computing holds all the cards? A peek into current technology trends is given suggesting that custom devices may be the support engine for computational enhancements for the cloud, while providing customers with the scalable and on-demand service that they require.

9.2 Applications

The range of applications involving big data is comprehensive and diverse, playing a role in personalized medicine, genomics, self-quantification through to monitoring financial markets or transactions. Smart cities and the Internet of Things (IOT) create a wealth of recordable data from the devices in homes through to cities. This section provides a high-level overview of some of the current big data challenges.

9.2.1 Genomics and Proteomics

In the last decade there has been a seismic shift in the technological advances for sequencing DNA. Edward Sanger developed the Sanger approach in 1975 using capillary electrophoresis and for decades this approach has been the technique employed. It is expensive and slow, limiting the opportunities for use. However, recent technological advances in sequencing has led to it being possible to sequence a whole human genome using a single instrument in 26 h (Miller et al. 2015). The enabler for this has been the development of High-Throughput Sequencing (HTS) which provides massively parallel sequencing power at an accelerated rate yet with significant cost reductions (Baker 2010; ODriscoll et al. 2013).

The reduction in costs has made HTS technologies much more accessible to labs and has facilitated their use in a broad range of applications and experimentation, including diagnostic testing for hereditary disorders, high-throughput polymorphism detections, comparative genomics, transcriptome analysis and therapeutic decision-making for somatic cancers (Van Dijk et al. 2014). A review and comparison of sequencing technologies can be found in Metzker (2009) and Loman et al. (2012).

However, HTS generates enormous datasets, with the possibility of producing >100 gigabases (Gb) of reads in a day (Naccache et al. 2014). For these reasons, coupled with the challenges of integrating heterogeneous datasets, HTS sequencing data can be characterised as big data, and as such there lies a significant computational challenge. High-performance, cloud and grid computing are aspects of computing that have become ubiquitous with processing and analysis of HTS data (Lightbody et al. 2016), generated at ever increasing momentum. As the technologies are ever developing, sequencing could become a routine facet of personalized medicine (Erlich 2015).

9.2.2 Digital Pathology

Traditional microscopy involves the analysis of a sample, for example, a biopsy on a glass slide using a microscope. The domain of virtual microscopy has moved from viewing of glass slides to viewing of diagnostic quality digital images using specialised software. These slides can be viewed on-line through a browser or as recently demonstrated via a mobile device whereby the computational power of mobile devices provide a cost-effective mobile-phone-based multimodal microscopy tool which combines molecular assays and portable optical imaging enabling on-site diagnostics (Kuhnemund et al. 2017). Where more extensive computational power is required, some service providers have opted for cloud based virtual microscopy solutions which offer the promise of in-depth image processing of the tissue samples (Wang et al. 2010).

The drive towards personalized medicine has led to a deluge of personal data from heterogeneous sources. This big data challenge is discussed by Li et al. (2016), in which they highlight that "integrative analysis of this rich clinical, pathological, molecular and imaging data represents one of the greatest bottlenecks in biomarker discovery research in cancer and other diseases". They have developed a framework, Pathology Integromics in Cancer (PICan), to accelerate and support data collation and analysis. This framework connects the tissue analysis to other genomic information, enabling a full and comprehensive understanding to be attained.

9.2.3 Self-Quantification

We are in an era in which society is 'comfortable' with every aspect of their behavior and person being monitored and analyzed. Part of this, has been the birth of a Quantified Self (QS) movement in which the person collates data on their daily life and physiology. It is reported as "self-knowledge through numbers".[1]

The goal of such monitoring is often for self-improvement, whether it is to encourage more physical activity or to improve on lifestyle choices (Almalki et al. 2013). Alternately, it could come from the belief that by gathering enough data from enough people, then trends in the data can be found. This offers the opportunity to impact society's health and well-being, and not just benefit the individual.

The advances in personal devices such as smart phones and sensor technology have promoted the gathering of such vast resources of personal data, which can fall into the category of big data, due to the sheer amount of data, the heterogeneous nature of the data and the speed at which it needs to be processed and managed.

An emerging addition to the QS movement is in collecting and analyzing electrical activity of the brain. Measured using the EEG, evaluation and classification of brain function such as sensory, motor and cognitive processes can be made. With the advancements in electronics,[3] wearable sensors, algorithms and software development kits there has been a shift towards exploring other possible applications in which EEG can play its part. One organization[4] has developed a neuroscience platform to encourage users to perform "routine brain health monitoring". By many users sharing their EEG, it is envisaged that it may be possible to derive critical insight into brain health and disease.

As QS applications evolve, it is expected that advanced machine learning and pattern recognition techniques will be involved in the analysis of data coming from multiple heterogeneous sources such as wearable electronics, biosensors, mobile phones, genomic data, and cloud-based services (Swan 2013).

9.2.4 Surveillance

Surveillance, specifically videos, are becoming ubiquitous in a number of situations for the monitoring of activity. With threats of terrorism, crime events, traffic incidents and governance, we have seen a rise of surveillance across global cites. Alongside this increase, we have seen progress on research in the area of computer vision, whereby processing and understanding surveillance videos can be performed automatically and key tasks such as people segmentation, tracking moving entities, as well as classification of human activities have been undertaken. Big data and the four 'V's' are relevant to the surveillance domain due to the scope and volume of video data captured (Xu et al. 2016). It has been estimated by the British Security Industry Association that there are between 4 and 5.9 million cameras in the UK. A single camera can capture up to 48 GB of high-definition video a day. This results in issues with local storage through to the fusion of data from multiple video streams which may differ in terms of format. These issues lead to the processing of video analytics which has an impact upon terrorist prediction and governance. To address such needs, research has been performed in the area. This includes the study by Xu

---

[3]EMOTIV. https://www.emotiv.com/. Accessed: 2017-02-03.
[4]BrainWaveBank. https://www.brainwavebank.com/. Accessed: 2017-02-03.

et al. (2015) whereby a semantic based model called Video Structural Description was proposed to represent and organize video resources (Najafabadi et al. 2015).

Another application in the area has been work performed by Krizhevsky et al. (2012) where deep convolutional neural networks were applied to classify 1.2 million images in the ImageNet dataset, achieving top-1 and top-5 and error rates of 37.5% and 17.0%, outperforming state-of-the-art classifiers. To speed up the process and improve efficiency, GPU convolution operations were implemented.

9.2.5 Internet-of-Things

IOT has been defined by the radio frequency identification group as "the world-wide network of interconnected objects uniquely addressable based on standard communications protocols" (Gubbi et al. 2013). These objects, such as sensors can be embedded in various devices across diverse domains such as healthcare, environment and astrology and are continually collecting and communicating data. These data are often semi-structured and require processing and analysis to provide useful information (Riggins and Wamba 2015).

An example of IOT and big data analytics is urban planning and smart cities (Kitchin 2014). A smart city can consist of devices built into the urban environment such as utility, communication and transport systems. These devices can be used in real-time to monitor and regulate city flows and processes. The integration and analysis of the data produced from these devices could provide an improved understanding of the city that enhances efficiency and sustainability (Hancke et al. 2013) and further models and predicts urban processes for future urban development (Batty et al. 2012). Examples of such platforms to support the IOT within a smart city include ThingSpeak[5] which provides a cloud-based platform where sensor data can be uploaded and analyzed using MatLab and iOBridge,[6] which provides a hardware solution to connect to the cloud with developed Application Programming Interfaces (APIs) to allow integration with other web services. Multi-nationals such as HP and IBM are also investing in projects such as CeNSE[7] and Smarter Planet,[8] respectively. CeNSE is deploying a vast number of sensors used to track for a range of applications from monitoring use and location of hospital equipment to tracking traffic flow. It then gathers and transmits such data to computing engines for analysis in real-time.

---

[5]ThingSpeak. https://thingspeak.com/pages/learn_more. Accessed: 2017-02-03.

[6]ioBridge. http://connect.iobridge.com/. Accessed: 2017-02-03.

[7]CeNSE.   http://www8.hp.com/us/en/hp-information/environment/cense.html#.WJCsHbaLR0K. Accessed: 2017-02-03.

[8]IBM Smarter Planet. http://www.ibm.com/smarterplanet/us/en/. Accessed: 2017-02-03.

9.2.6   *Finance*

Financial institutions are adopting a data-driven approach with the aim of improving their performance, service and, as seen with the financial crash in 2008, their risks (Fan et al. 2014). Financial data can be in a structured or semi-structured form; such data includes stock prices, derivative trades, transaction records and high-frequency trades (HFT). A study by Seddon and Currie (2017) proposed a model for applying big data analytics in HFT. HFT uses algorithmic software to perform trades built upon advanced technological infrastructure with a focus on speed to process and leverage vast amounts of financial data (Aldridge 2009). This study analyzed big data and its impact upon financial markets. An important discussion, applicable to all application areas is data security and privacy. With high volumes of data used in analysis, questions need to be addressed around data security protection, intellectual property protection, personal privacy protection, commercial secrets and financial information protection (Chen and Zhang 2014).

9.3   Computational Challenges

At the heart of many of the computationally intense applications lies pattern matching and machine learning:

- Machine learning
- Deep learning
- Pattern matching
- Image/video/audio processing
- Sentiment analysis
- Natural language processing

Recent advances in high-performance computing has encouraged the field of deep learning to move out from research laboratories and become a commercial opportunity. Deep learning, driven by research centers and initiatives such as the Google Brain project,[9] has projected to become a multi-billion pound industry by 2024 (Tractica 2015; PR Newswire 2016), finding potential enterprise applications in areas of finance, advertisement, automotive, medical and other end-user applications. An enabler for this projected growth is in research and development of infrastructures, software and hardware technologies optimized for deep learning solutions.

---

[9]Google Brain Team. https://research.google.com/teams/brain/. Accessed: 2017-02-03.

9.4   High-Performance Computing Solutions

A background into different approaches is provided in this section. It should be noted that different application domains will have varied computational demands (Singh and Reddy 2014). The sections below discuss high-performance computing solutions ranging in computational performance.

9.4.1   Graphics Processing Units (GPU) Computing

Graphics processing units as the name suggests, are custom devices consisting of many processing cores or co-processors that have been tailored for processing the vast computational and memory requirements for graphics rendering and image processing. They enable highly mathematical and computationally intense functions to be performed at an accelerated rate due to the parallel computational units at the heart of their structure. The ability to offload computation most suited to parallel operations, while maintaining a great level of flexibility and scalability is a leading benefit of GPU-based computing over sequential oper-ation CPU-based computing (Blayney et al. 2015; Melanakos 2008; Fan et al. 2004). However, the scale of the benefits depends strongly on the nature of the computations.

The application and use of GPUs has gone far beyond computer graphics and gaming, although expansion these markets have certainly reduced the cost of GPUs, making them a more affordable and thus widespread technology (Fan et al. 2004). The terms General-Purpose computation on Graphics Processing Units (GPGPU) and GPU Computing have arisen which signifies that the processors have a broad range of potential applications.

NVIDIA, is a market leader GPU producer, providing a range of GPU pro-cessors, boards and platforms.[10] The power of their GPUs can be harnessed through NVIDIA's own Compute Unified Device Architecture (CUDA) parallel computing platform. This technology has been used in a range of applications spanning gaming, mobile, personal computers through to high-performance com-puting, and deep learning. For example, in bioinformatics there have been a large number of CUDA-based tools developed for accelerating sequence pro-cessing and analysis (Klus et al. 2012; Liu et al. 2012, 2013). Although GPU computing is a promising direction for bioinformatics, memory handling and slow data exchange between CPU and GPU processors can still cause challenges (Starostenkov 2013).

In the area of deep learning, NVIDIA sees a market extending its capabilities in the area of accelerating Artificial Intelligence (AI) algorithms (Azoff 2015)

---

[10]NVIDIA. http://www.nvidia.co.uk/page/home.html. Accessed: 2017-02-03.

in industries such as automotive, internet, healthcare, government, finance and others.[11] They are clearly positioning themselves for the expected growth in the big data market.

9.4.2   Field Programmable Gate Arrays

FPGAs are integrated circuits which enable a level of programmability. Their structure consists of an array of programmable logic blocks containing computational units, memory and interconnections that can be fully preconfigured. They sit between highly programmable digital signal processing chips and custom design ASICs, providing a balance of flexibility with parallel custom designed operations. They offer an experimentation and development platform to design and refine solutions. Yet they also provide enterprise solutions for applications in which a certain degree of reconfiguration may be required. However, unlike CPUs and GPUs this reconfiguration cannot be done totally on the fly and takes a level of reprogramming the device. Where there are advantages is when there is a large number of repetitive operations that are suited to parallel implementation, such examples are in image processing, pattern matching, or routing algorithms. In such cases FPGAs can be orders of magnitude faster compared to other platforms. The content below provides an overview of some examples of FPGAs in use.

FPGAs can offer possible solutions to computational challenges in bioinformatics and molecular biology (Ramdas and Egan 2005). A major computational challenge in genomics is in sequence alignment. The Smith–Waterman algorithm is a database search algorithm suited for protein sequence alignment. However, it is computationally intensive and the complexity increases quadratically as the dataset increases. Dydel and Bala (2004), present an implementation of it on FPGA. Tan et al. (2016) also present a FPGA-based co-processor to speed up short read mapping in HTS, reporting a throughput of 947 Gbp per a day, while providing better power efficiency.

Another aspect that can benefit from computational enhancement is in the image processing component in Genomic Microarrays. In these examples, sequencing is not being performed, however, genetic markers are being looked for that respond to known chemical interactions leading to a change in colour in the array, depending on the level of expression. Rodellar et al. (2007) present such a device, tailored to be portable so to make it applicable in regions remote from core healthcare provision. An implementation of the CAST algorithm used for detecting low-complexity regions in protein sequences is described by Papadopoulos et al. (2012). Significant speed-up in computations in the region of 100× where observed. These examples are

---

[11]NVIDIA: Artificial Intelligence and Deep Learning. http://www.nvidia.co.uk/object/deep-learning-uk.html. Accessed: 2017-02-03.

not in themselves related to big data, however, they have relevance in the context of personalized medicine in which such data can routinely form part of a heterogeneous patient dataset.

9.4.3   Cloud Computing Platforms

The National Institute for Standards and Technology (NIST) defines Cloud computing as "a pay-per-use model for enabling convenient, on-demand network access to a shared pool of configurable computing resources (e.g., networks, servers, storage, applications and services) that can be rapidly provisioned and released with minimal management effort or service provider interaction".

Foster et al. (2001) pioneered an idea of Grid computing which constitutes a large-scale distributed resource sharing under specified rules among the users and/or organizations. This idea was based on other known technologies of the time such as distributed computing. Grid computing proved to be useful in many scenarios, especially, for large-scale scientific computations (Di et al. 2012).

The concept of 'Clouds' as a similar but yet different way of distributed computing has been popularized by Amazon[12] in 2006. Armbrust et al. (2010) compare Cloud computing to other similar computing concepts in their work. Hence, they claim that although Grid computing offers protocols to share distributed resources, Cloud computing has advanced forward by offering "a software environment that grew beyond its community" (referring to the high-performance community).

Cloud computing has become a strong industry enabling a range of different services to be deployed typically by a pay-per-use cost model providing scalability in computing performance, storage and applications. Their expandability and sheer flexibility of services can provide a cost effective option for organizations in which the cost for development and maintenance for in-house solutions does not make business sense. Furthermore, cloud services can provide tools such as project and data management tools to aid in collaborations, provision of security and regulations in accessing shared data and analytical resources for the visualisation and understanding of datasets.

Cloud services fall under three different categories depending on the extent of the service provided:

- Infrastructure as a Service (IaaS) – Providing access to the core computing and storage infrastructure.
- Platform as a Service (PaaS) – Users can develop or build upon libraries and existing core platforms, and these solutions run on the cloud infrastructure.
- Software as a Service (SaaS) – Users access applications that form part of the cloud infrastructure.

---

[12] Amazon About AWS. https://aws.amazon.com/about-aws/. Accessed: 2017-02-03.

Some of the first adopters of big data in cloud computing are users that deployed NoSQL and Hadoop clusters in highly scalable and elastic computing environments provided by vendors, such as Google, Microsoft, and Amazon. An overview of the key market players is summarised as follows.

9.4.3.1 Amazon Web Services

Amazon Web Services (AWS) are the strongest competitors in cloud services (Leong et al. 2016), entering the market in 2006 and offering a range of relatively cost effective solutions. Their Amazon Elastic Compute Cloud (EC2) provides a scalable IaaS cloud service,[13] offering users a simplistic interface to their computing infrastructure. PaaS services are also supported. AWS have added Amazon EC2 Elastic GPUs to their provision allowing performance enhancements.

9.4.3.2 Microsoft Azure

Microsoft Azure provides both PaaS and more recently IaaS services.[14] The Azure platform offers functionality to integrate models, analyze data and visualization tools to scale data analysis. The Microsoft Azure model has been described in Gannon et al. (2014) as "layers of services for building large scale web-based applications". These layers communicate across various levels including the hardware level, utilizing data centers worldwide for computation and content delivery. The 'fabric controller' acts as the kernel of the Azure operating system. It performs tasks such as monitoring and managing the virtual machines and hardware resources that make up the Azure system.

9.4.4 Deep Learning Libraries

Machine learning and, in particular, deep learning have become of immediate interest for companies and researchers alike. Such technology is finding its way into a range of products from speech recognition, image processing, search optimization, through to any application where there is a need or interest to understand behavior, images, speech and sentiment analysis. TensorFlow[TM] and other such systems can be a great enabler to develop such features.[15]

TensorFlow[TM] is an open source machine learning infrastructure originating from Google as part of their Google Brain project started in 2011. It formed part of

---

[13] Amazon EC2. https://aws.amazon.com/ec2/. Accessed: 2017-02-03.

[14] Microsoft Azure. https://azure.microsoft.com/. Accessed: 2017-02-03.

[15] TensorFlow[TM]. https://www.tensorflow.org/. Accessed: 2017-02-03.

Table 9.1 Deep learning libraries

Library	Detail
TensorFlow™	Open source machine learning infrastructure originating from Google as part of their Google Brain project started in 2011 (https://www.tensorflow.org/)
MXNet	Flexible library (http://mxnet.io/) which supports multiple languages (C++, Python, R, Scala, Julia, Matlab and Javascript), can operate on personal CPU/GPU setups through to distributed and cloud platforms (including AWS, Google Compute Engine (https://cloud.google.com/compute/), Microsoft Azure)
Caffe	A deep learning framework developed by the Berkeley Vision and Learning Center (http://caffe.berkeleyvision.org/) (Jia 2014). Offers a competitive high-performance convolutional neural networks solution
Theano	A Python-based library with a focus on enhancing mathematical computation of multi-dimensional arrays (http://deeplearning.net/software/theano/)
Torch	A scientific framework for machine learning (http://torch.ch/)

the Google's Machine Intelligence research organization with its focus on machine learning and in particular deep neural networks. A key feature of TensorFlow™ is its sheer scalability and flexibility. It facilitates distribution of computations over a range of devices and platforms, from mobile devices and desktops, through to large scale infrastructures consisting of hundreds of machines or thousands of GPU devices (Abadi et al. 2015). More recently it has been incorporated within AWS Elastic Cloud (Amazon EC2) provision. It is part of their Deep Learning Amazon Machine Image (AMI) and is just one of a suite of deep learning libraries included (see Table 9.1).

9.5   The Role for Custom Hardware

Do we need to look at big data at the micro level or at the macro level? For example, genetic sequencing, particularly as part of next generation sequencing, requires a substantial computational overhead in the alignment of the small reads coming from the initial sample analysis. From this alignment the DNA sequence of smaller exome components can then be used to determine conditions and states of disease. Opposite to this are huge datasets of genomic data across thousands of people ranging in phenotype and genomic marker such as exome sequences. Gathering such huge expanses of genetic data and combining this with other associated information offers huge opportunities in disease stratification, biomarker discovery and drug development (Raghupathi and Raghupathi 2014). This is clearly big data at the macro level. So the question lies – would the same high-performance computing suit both applications? This particular example is further complicated by the size of even a single DNA sequence. Uploading such a file-size to a cloud-based system in itself presents challenges. Techniques have been developed to look at easing storage of such genetic information. One particular approach is with compression algorithms to find an efficient method to represent the data (Qiao et al. 2012). Such a method needs to be loss-less, fast, and effective.

Another consideration could be the need for secure solutions which keep data local, although cloud services such as AWS take great measures to keep their services secure. Establishing a custom system incurs a significant investment and maintenance overhead, and would be difficult to scale up. However, big data computations pose an ever increasing challenge in meeting performance needs. In particular, deep learning is an area of machine learning showing great commercial prospect. The next sections look at some of the deep learning solutions available.

9.5.1 Deep Learning

TensorFlow[TM] and other deep learning libraries (Table 9.1) combined with cloud services provide a platform to develop and create deep learning solutions, leading on to commercial opportunities. However, despite the great flexibility and scalability advantages of such a system, is there a possibility that a hardware-based solution might provide the better solution? This of course depends strongly on the application at hand and the limitations and challenges associated. Nevertheless, deep learning is a component of machine learning with great commercial interest. fpgaConvNet (Venieris et al. 2016) is a framework for mapping convolutional neural networks, a form of deep learning, onto FPGAs. The authors relate to the computational issues presented in convolutional networks, in particular, the classification computation overhead and the rapid scaling in complexity. CNNLab (Zhu et al. 2016), is another parallel framework for deep learning neural networks that distributes computation to both GPUs and FPGAs. Microsoft Azure has also incorporated FPGAs within their cloud platform (Feldman 2016). Woods and Alonso (2011) have developed an FPGA based framework for analytics on high-rate data streams. The next section looks further at enhancing cloud performance through incorporating custom hardware provision.

9.5.2 ASIC Enhanced Cloud Platforms

Nervana[16] has developed a platform for deep learning that is powered using a custom ASIC engine accessed through a cloud platform. They state that their cloud solution enables industry commercialized deep learning solutions. The platform they provide

---

[16]Nervana. https://www.nervanasys.com/intel-nervana/. Accessed: 2017-02-03.

is described by them as a full stack solution for "AI on demand", optimized at each level.

Nervana Neon is an open source Python-based scalable deep learning library. The Nervana Engine is custom ASIC hardware optimized for machine learning and in particular deep learning. They promote high-speed data access with high bandwidth memory, reaching speeds of 8 Terabits per second for memory access. Additionally, on-chip memory is large (32 GB) to meet the excessive storage requirements for machine learning. The core computational power is achieved through a sea of multipliers supported with local memory, without a reliance on cache memory. Nervana have paid great attention to data transfer across the chip including communication pipelines tailored for machine learning operations. One key aspect of this is the design allowing ASICs to be interconnected directly without reliance on Peripheral Component Interconnect Express (PCIE) buses which cause data flow bottlenecks. Nervana Engine is set to be released in 2017 and hopes to establish a place in the top deep learning technologies (Schneider 2017).

9.5.3 ASIC Deep Learning Processors

However, Nervana are not the only ones interested in this market with others are providing custom machine learning processing engines.

One of the most interesting areas in developing on-chip processing is based on the operation of the human brain, termed Neuromorphic chips. In this field, Spiking Neural Networks (SNN) are used to form the computations. The SpiNNaker Project is one example (Sugiarto et al. 2016) and forms part of the Human Brain Project.[17] The Darwin Neural Processing Unit is another exciting example of an ASIC co-processer based on SNN (Shen et al. 2016). Through the very nature of how SNN operate they may lend themselves more closely to machine learning and therefore show great promise in this area (Elton 2016).

9.6   Discussion

Big data and its analysis have the potential to provide insight into many diverse domains. The wealth of data collected at such a vast scale has led to the need for computationally intensive solutions to find useful information hidden in the chaos. The applications for such analysis are far reaching, from surveillance, finance, IOT, and smart cities through to personalized health. Potential of such applications include clinical decision support systems, personalized medicine for healthcare, distribution and logistics optimization for retail and supply chain planning for

---

[17]Human Brain Project. https://www.humanbrainproject.eu/en_GB. Accessed: 2017-02-03.

manufacturing (Sagiroglu and Sinanc 2013). However, even within each example, applications will have different needs in terms of data growth, infrastructure and governance along with integration, velocity, variety, compliance and data visualization (Intel 2012). A number of challenges still need to be addressed such as handling structured and unstructured data in real/near-time at a volume whereby traditional data storage and analysis approaches are not applicable (Zikopoulos and Eaton 2012). Furthermore, as big data analytics becomes mainstream, important issues such as data governance, guaranteeing privacy, safeguarding security, increased network bottlenecks, training of skilled data science professionals, development of compression technologies and establishing standards will require urgent attention (Intel 2012).

Big data analytics and applications are still in the early stages, however, the continuation of technology and platform improvement such as Hadoop, Spark, NoSQL coupled with the development of new analytical algorithms and infrastructure will contribute towards the maturing of the field. Companies such as Nervana are developing custom hardware to work in tandem with their cloud platform to accelerate deep learning. This is one field in which hardware developers can create impact for cloud computing infrastructure and big data analytics. Recently, Microsoft (Feldman 2016) announced the inclusion of Altera FPGAs within their Azure cloud service with the promise of creating an AI supercomputer. Microsoft does not currently plan to use the FPGAs for training neural networks, using GPUs instead for offline training. At present, they see FPGAs providing effective acceleration for evaluating already trained neural networks.

Qualcomm, recognize that their consumers require on-device solutions that do not rely fully on cloud services. Their machine learning platform is implemented on their Snapdragon Neural Processing Engine. The example here highlights that data analytics is a challenge that may not always be resolved through scalable cloud services, but as applications require more computationally intensive data analytics, some of this workload may need to be shared between on-device and cloud-based services. Other companies are also active in this area (Table 9.2) and seemingly there is a strong market for this level of on-device processing. Furthermore, there have been exciting advances happening in the area of Neuromorphic chips for machine learning. It will be interesting to see how this technology impacts the deep learning market.

Clearly, each computational solution offers unique opportunities for overcoming the challenges of big data. FPGA and ASIC solutions can provide computational benefits under certain conditions and as demonstrated through companies such as Microsoft and Nervana they can form a key part of a high-performance cloud platform. Conversely, they play an important role for on-device big data analytics with companies such as Qualcomm and Intel investing largely in developing the next generation of AI chips. In each example the solutions have been tailored for the ever growing market of big data and deep learning. Meeting these challenges will have great impact to applications in the future, advances in healthcare, smart cities, security, automotive industry among other examples forming part of our daily lives.

Table 9.2 Deep learning ASIC processors

Product	Detail
Qualcomm Snapdragon Neural Processing Engine	Deep learning toolkit for mobile and edge devices from Qualcomm Technologies (https://www.qualcomm.com/invention/cognitive-technologies/machine-learning)
Qualcomm Zeroth SDK	On-device machine learning platform (Vicent 2016)
Google's Tensor Processing Unit	Part of Google's drive for deep learning solutions (Osborne 2016). Accelerator ASIC developed to be accompanied by their TensorFlow™ library
Intel Xeon Phi product family – Knights Mill/Knight Landing/Knights Crest	Family of high-performance custom ASICs for machine learning (Hruska 2016). Their product development includes bringing together Nervana's chip technology (Intel acquired Nervana in 2016) together with Xeon processors to produce their Knights Crest chip

References

23andMe (2015) DNA genetic testing & analysis. 23andme. Available via https://www.23andme.com/. Accessed 06 Feb 2017

Abadi M, Agarwal A, Barham P, Brevdo E, Chen Z, Citro C, Corrado GS, Davis A, Dean J, Devin M, (30 additional authors not shown) (2015) Tensorflow: large-scale machine learning on heterogeneous distributed systems. arXiv:1603.04467 [cs.DC]. Available via https://arxiv.org/abs/1603.04467

Aldridge I (2009) High-frequency trading: a practical guide to algorithmic strategies and trading systems, 2nd edn. Wiley, Somerset

Almalki M, Gray K, Sanchez FM (2013) The use of self-quantification systems for personal health information: big data management. Health Inf Sci Syst 3(Suppl 1):1–11

AncestryDNA™ (2016) DNA tests for ethnicity & genealogical DNA testing. AncestryDNA™. Available via https://www.ancestry.co.uk/. Accessed 06 Feb 2017

Armbrust M, Fox A, Griffith R, Joseph AD, Katz R, Konwinski A, Lee G, Patterson D, Rabkin A, Stoica I, Zaharia M (2010) A view of cloud computing. Commun ACM 53(4):50

Azoff M (2015) Machine learning in business use cases: artificial intelligence solutions that can be applied. NVIDIA. Available via http://www.nvidia.com/. Accessed 06 Feb 2017

Baker M (2010) Next-generation sequencing: adjusting to data overload. Nat Methods 7:495–499

Batty M, Axhausen KW, Fosca G, Pozdnoukhov A, Bazzani A, Wachowicz M, Ouzounis GK, Portugali J (2012) Smart cities of the future. European Phys J Spec Top 214(1):481–518

Blayney J, Haberland V, Lightbody G, Browne F (2015) Biomarker discovery, high performance and cloud computing: a comprehensive review. In: Proceedings of 2015 IEEE International conference on bioinformatics and biomedicine (BIBM), pp 1514–1519

British Gas (2017) How data can personalise your energy. British gas. Available via https://www.britishgas.co.uk/. Accessed 06 Feb 2017

Chen CLP, Zhang CY (2014) Data-intensive applications, challenges, techniques and technologies: a survey on big data. Infor Sci 275:314–347

Chen M, Mao S, Liu Y (2014) Big data: a survey. Mob Netw Appl 19(2):171–209

Di S, Kondo D, Cirne W (2012) Characterization and comparison of cloud versus grid workloads. In: Proceedings of 2012 IEEE International conference on cluster computing (CLUSTER'12), pp 230–238

Dydel S, Bała P (2004) Large scale protein sequence alignment using FPGA reprogrammable logic devices. In: Proceedings of 14th International conference field programmable logic and application (FPL'04), pp 23–32

Elton D (2016) Neuromorphic chips: a path towards human-level AI. Singularity. Available via https://www.singularityweblog.com/. Accessed 06 Feb 2017

Erlich Y (2015) A vision for ubiquitous sequencing. Genome Res 25(10):1411–1416

Fan Z, Qiu F, Kaufman A, Yoakum-Stover S (2004) GPU cluster for high performance computing. In: Proceedings of 2004 ACM/IEEE conference on supercomputing (SC'04), pp 47–47

Fan J, Han F, Liu H (2014) Challenges of big data analysis. Natl Sci Rev 1(2):293–314

Feldman M (2016) Microsoft goes all in for FPGAs to build out AI cloud. TOP500 supercomputer sites. Available via https://www.top500.org/. Accessed 06 Feb 2017

Foster I, Kesselman C, Tuecke S (2001) The anatomy of the grid: enabling scalable virtual organizations. Int J High Perform Comput Appl 15(3):200–222

Gannon D, Fay D, Green D, Takeda K, Yi W (2014) Science in the cloud: lessons from three years of research projects on Microsoft Azure. In: Proceedings of 5th ACM workshop on scientific cloud computing (ScienceCloud'14), pp 1–8

Gubbi J, Buyya R, Marusic S, Palaniswami M (2013) Internet of things IoT: a vision, architectural elements, and future directions. Future Gener Comput Syst 29(7):1645–1660

Hancke GP, de Carvalho e Silva B, Hancke GP Jr (2013) Sensors. Role Adv Sens Smart Cities 13(1):393–425

Hashem IAT, Yaqoob I, Anuar NB, Mokhtar S, Gani A, Ullah KS (2015) The Rise of "big data" on cloud computing: review and open research issues. Inform Syst 47:98–115

Hruska J (2016) Intel announces major AI push with upcoming Knights Mill Xeon Phi, custom silicon. Extreme Tech. Available via https://www.extremetech.com/. Accessed 06 Feb 2017

Intel (2012) Big data analytics Intel's IT manager survey on how organizations are using big data. Intel. Available via http://www.intel.me/. Accessed 06 Feb 2017

Jia Y, Shelhamer E, Donahue J, Karayev S, Long J, Girshick R, Guadarrama S, Darrell T (2014) 'Caffe'. In: Proceedings of 22nd ACM International conference on multimedia (MM'14), pp 675–678

Kitchin R (2014) The real-time city? Big data and smart urbanism. GeoJournal 79(1):1–14

Klus P, Lam S, Lyberg D, Cheung MS, Pullan G, McFarlane I, Yeo GS, Lam BY (2012) BarraCUDA – a fast short read sequence aligner using graphics processing units. BMC Res Notes 5(1):27

Krizhevsky A, Sutskever I, Hinton GE (2012) ImageNet classification with deep convolutional neural networks. In: Proceedings of advances in neural information processing systems 25 (NIPS'12), pp 1097–1105

Kühnemund M, Wei Q, Darai E, Wang Y, Hernández-Neuta I, Yang Z, Tseng D, Ahlford A, Mathot L, Sjöblom T, Ozcan A, Nilsson M (2017) Targeted DNA sequencing and in situ mutation analysis using mobile phone microscopy. Nat Commun 8:13913

Leong L, Petri G, Gill B, Dorosh M (2016) Magic quadrant for cloud infrastructure as a service, worldwide. Gartner. Available via https://www.gartner.com. Accessed 06 Feb 2017

Li G, Bankhead P, Dunne PD, O'Reilly PG, James JA, Salto-Tellez M, Hamilton PW, McArt D (2016) Embracing an integromic approach to tissue biomarker research in cancer: perspectives and lessons learned. Briefings Bioinf bbw044, pp 1–13. Available via https://academic.oup.com/bib/article-lookup/doi/10.1093/bib/bbw044

Lightbody G, Browne F, Zheng H, Haberland V, Blayney J (2016) The role of high performance, grid and cloud computing in high-throughput sequencing. In: Proceedings of 2016 IEEE International conference on bioinformatics and biomedicine (BIBM), pp 890–895

Liu Y, Schmidt B, Maskell DL (2012) Cushaw: a CUDA compatible short read aligner to large genomes based on the Burrows-Wheeler transform. Bioinformatics 28(14):1830–1837

Liu Y, Wirawan A, Schmidt B (2013) CUDASW++ 3.0: accelerating Smith-Waterman protein database search by coupling CPU and GPU SIMD instructions. BMC Bioinf 14(1):117

Loman NJ, Misra RV, Dallman TJ, Constantinidou C, Gharbia SE, Wain J, Pallen MJ (2012) Performance comparison of benchtop high-throughput sequencing platforms. Nat Biotechnol 30(5):434–439

Melanakos J (2008) Parallel computing on a personal computer. Biomedical Computation Review. Available via http://www.biomedicalcomputationreview.org/. Accessed 06 Feb 2017

Metzker ML (2009) Sequencing technologies – the next generation. Nat Rev Genet 11(1):31–46

Miller NA, Farrow EG, Gibson M, Willig LK, Twist G (16 additional authors not shown) (2015) A 26-hour system of highly sensitive whole genome sequencing for emergency management of genetic diseases. Genome Med 7(1):100

Naccache SN, Federman S, Veeeraraghavan N, Zaharia M, Lee D (21 additional authors not shown) (2014) A cloud-compatible bioinformatics pipeline for ultrarapid pathogen identification from next-generation sequencing of clinical samples. Genome Res 24(7):1180–1192

Najafabadi MM, Villanustre F, Khoshgoftaar TM, Seliya N, Wald R, Muharemagic E (2015) Deep learning applications and challenges in big data analytics. J Big Data 2(1):1

O'Driscoll A, Daugelaite J, Sleator RD (2013) 'Big data', Hadoop and cloud computing in genomics. J Biomed Infor 46(5):774–781

O'Dwyer E, De Tommasi L, Kouramas K, Cychowski M, Lightbody G (2016) Modelling and disturbance estimation for model predictive control in building heating systems. Energy Build 130:532–545

Osborne J (2016) Google's tensor processing unit explained: this is what the future of computing looks like. TechRadar. Available via http://www.techradar.com/. Accessed 06 Feb 2017

Papadopoulos A, Kirmitzoglou I, Promponas VJ, Theocharides T (2012) FPGA-based hardware acceleration for local complexity analysis of massive genomic data. Integr VLSI J 46(3):230–239

PR Newswire (2016) $1.77 billion deep learning market 2016 – global forecasts to 2022: Google is among the market. PR Newswire. Available via http://www.prnewswire.com/. Accessed 06 Feb 2017

Qiao D, Yip WK, Lange C (2012) Handling the data management needs of high-throughput sequencing data: speedgene, a compression algorithm for the efficient storage of genetic data. BMC Bioinf 13(1):100

Raghupathi W, Raghupathi V (2014) Big data analytics in healthcare: promise and potential. Health Infor Sci Syst 2(3):1–10. Available via https://link.springer.com/article/10.1186/2047-2501-2-3/fulltext.html

Ramdas T, Egan G (2005) A survey of FPGAs for acceleration of high performance computing and their application to computational molecular biology. In: Proceedings of TENCON 2005 – 2005 IEEE region 10 conference, pp 1–6

Riggins FJ, Wamba SF (2015) Research directions on the adoption, usage, and impact of the Internet of Things through the use of big data analytics. In: Proceedings of 2015 48th Hawaii International conference on system sciences, pp 1531–1540

Rodellar V, Díaz F, Belean B, Malutan R, Stetter B, Gomez P, Martínez-Olalla R, García-Rico E, Pelaez J (2007) Genomic microarray processing on a FPGA for portable remote applications. In: Proceedings of 2007 3rd Southern conference on programmable logic (SPL'07), pp 13–17

Sagiroglu S, Sinanc D (2013) Big data: a review. In: Proceedings of 2013 International conference on collaboration technologies and systems (CTS), pp 42–47

Schneider D (2017) Deeper and cheaper machine learning [Top Tech 2017]. IEEE Spectr 54(1):42–43

Seddon JJJM, Currie WL (2017) A model for unpacking big data analytics in high-frequency trading. J Bus Res 70:300–307

Shen J, Ma D, Gu Z, Zhang M, Zhu X, Xu X, Xu Q, Shen Y, Pan G (2016) Darwin: a neuromorphic hardware co-processor based on spiking neural networks. Sci China Infor Sci 59(2):1–5

Singh D, Reddy CK (2014) A survey on platforms for big data analytics. J Big Data 2(1):8

Starostenkov V (2013) Hadoop + GPU: boost performance of your big data project by 50x-200x? Network World. Available via http://www.networkworld.com/. Accessed 06 Feb 2017

Sugiarto I, Liu G, Davidson S, Plana LA, Furber SB (2016) High performance computing on SpiNNaker neuromorphic platform: a case study for energy efficient image processing. In: Proceedings of 2016 IEEE 35th International performance computing and communications conference (IPCCC), pp 1–8

Swan M (2013) The quantified self: fundamental disruption in big data science and biological discovery. Big Data 1(2):85–99

Tan G, Zhang C, Tang W, Zhang P, Sun N (2016) Accelerating irregular computation in massive short reads mapping on FPGA co-processor. IEEE Trans Parallel Distrib Syst 27(5):1253–1264

Terrell J (2015) Test-driving the brain could reveal early signs of Alzheimer's. The Conversation. Available via http://theconversation.com/. Accessed 06 Feb 2017

Townsend AM (2014) Smart Cities – Big Data, Civic Hackers, and the Quest for a New Utopia. W. W. Norton & Company, Edition Reprint

Tractica (2015) Deep learning software market to surpass $10 billion by 2024. Tractica. Available via https://www.tractica.com/. Accessed 06 Feb 2017

Van Dijk EL, Auger H, Jaszczyszyn Y, Thermes C (2014) Ten years of next-generation sequencing technology. Trends Genet 30(9):418–426

Venieris SI, Bouganis CS (2016) fpgaConvNet: a framework for mapping convolutional neural networks on FPGAs. In: Proceedings of 2016 IEEE 24th annual International symposium on field-programmable custom computing machines (FCCM), pp 40–47

Vicent J (2016) Qualcomm's deep learning SDK will mean more AI on your smartphone. The Verge. Available via http://www.theverge.com/. Accessed 06 Feb 2017

Wang Y, McCleary D, Wang CW, Kelly P, James J, Fennell DA, Hamilton PW (2010) Ultra-fast processing of gigapixel tissue microarray images using high performance computing. Anal Cell Pathol (Amsterdam) 33(5):271–285

Woods L, Alonso G (2011) Fast data analytics with FPGAs. In: Proceedings of 2011 IEEE 27th International conference on data engineering workshops, pp 296–299

Xu Z, Liua Y, Meia L, Hua C, Chen L (2015) Semantic based representing and organizing surveillance big data using video structural description technology. J Syst Softw 102:217–225

Xu Z, Mei L, Hu C, Liu Y (2016) The big data analytics and applications of the surveillance system using video structured description technology. Clust Comput 19(3):1283–1292

Zhu M, Liu L, Wang C, Xie Y (2016) CNNLab: a novel parallel framework for neural networks using GPU and FPGA – a practical study with trade-off analysis. arXiv:1606.06234 [cs.LG]. Available via https://arxiv.org/abs/1606.06234. Accessed 06 Feb 2017

Zikopoulos PC, Eaton C (2012) Understanding big data: analytics for enterprise class Hadoop and streaming data. McGraw-Hill Osborne Media, New York

Part VI
The World of Society and Philosophy

Chapter 10
Information Overload in a Data-Intensive World

Tibor Koltay

Abstract This chapter investigates the complex phenomenon of 'information overload' that, despite controversies about its existence, is a major problem, the symptoms of which have to be alleviated. Its sources and nature in academia, business environments and in everyday life information seeking, its particular features in the data-intensive world are described, not forgetting about the role of information technology. The possible ways of mitigating information overload are specified, underlining the imperative of being critical against information. Potential approaches and tools, described in this chapter include utilizing appropriate information architecture, applying information literacy, data literacy and other literacies, as well as making use of personal information management.

10.1 Introduction

This chapter investigates information overload (IO), a phenomenon that was described by Bawden and Robinson as perhaps the most familiar one from among a recently articulated group of phenomena that can be called 'information pathologies' (Bawden and Robinson 2009).

Examining IO requires some understanding of concepts, such as data, information and knowledge. Among these concepts, perhaps, information is one of the least understood concepts, albeit widely used in its everyday, technical and scholarly meaning. It is typically defined in terms of data, though the implicit challenge is to understand and explain how data is transformed into information, and information into knowledge (Rowley 2007). As to the relationship between data and information, the boundaries between them have never been rigid, and if there are boundaries at all, they are often blurred (Schneider 2013). Nevertheless, these terms are important and will appear in this chapter several times, although with varied frequency. However, since these terms cannot be explained in their entirety in this

T. Koltay (✉)
Faculty of Pedagogy, Institute of Learning Technologies, Eszterházy Károly University,
Rákócziút 53, 5100 Jászberény, Hungary
e-mail: koltay.tibor@uni-eszterhazy.hu

© Springer International Publishing AG 2017   197
A.J. Schuster (eds.), *Understanding Information*, Advanced Information
and Knowledge Processing, DOI 10.1007/978-3-319-59090-5_10

writing for various reasons, questions related to the difficulty of differentiating data, information, and knowledge have been deliberately set aside.

In order to provide a general understanding about the issue of information overload and the various dimensions associated with it, this chapter has the following organization. Section 10.2 describes the general characteristics of information overload (impacting academia), and gives details about its nature in business environments and in everyday life information seeking. The role of information technology is explained, not forgetting about information overload in today's data-intensive world. Section 10.3 charts the spheres of activities, where alleviating the symptoms of information overload can be endeavored. One broad sphere is using the tools and methods of design and information architecture. An even broader sphere of activities is related to different ways of interacting with information, applied by individuals. In this subsection of the chapter, it is explained, how taking a critical stance may help in mitigating information overload, and it is argued that a feasible framework for looking critically at information is provided by a number of different literacies that are described in detail. The prospects of making use of personal information management (PIM) tools and related new, hybrid concepts, operating on this level, are also outlined. Section 10.4 provides a brief discussion, and Sect. 10.5 ends the chapter with a summary.

10.2 Information Overload

Information overload is sometimes qualified by researches as a modern-day myth (Tidline 1999). Some argue that we do not know enough about it (Davis 2012a), among other things, because it often remains unrecognized (Badke 2010). Nonetheless, information overload is a major problem that affects all spheres of our life (Bawden and Robinson 2009). In many cases, the incurring material costs and losses that can be ascribed to IO are estimated to be high (Davis 2011).

Information overload does exist, at least as a perceived difficulty or burden. For instance, the results of a mixed methods quantitative and qualitative study by Benselin and Ragsdell in 2015 found that people in most age groups equally think that they have suffered from IO (Benselin and Ragsdell 2016). Information overload can be defined as an impediment to efficiently using information due to the amount of relevant and potentially useful information available. It can cause delays in decision making. Usually, it is associated with a loss of control over a situation, or with being overwhelmed (Bawden and Robinson 2009). It seems to be obvious that the concept of information overload involves the notion of excess. However, excess in itself is not a sufficient condition for being overloaded. Overload can be defined rather in comparison to some norms, which regulate what is an appropriate amount of information and which pieces of information are undesirable (Himma 2007). These norms are varied, depending on the given task. Therefore they are not fixed, not speaking about being codified in any way.

10.2.1 General Characteristics of Information Overload

Usually, information overload is not caused by a single factor, but has several causes that influence two fundamental (though not exclusive) variables. The first variable is information processing capacity, which is a personal characteristic. The second variable is determined by the nature of the task or process. Thus, IO originates in an environment of information processing requirements, measured in terms of available time, because, usually, a given amount of information has to be processed within a certain time period. If an individual is capable to process only a smaller amount of information than required in the determined timeframe, information overload is present. Therefore, the limitations of an individual's ability to process information, compared to the amount of information received are a decisive factor of IO (Eppler and Mengis 2004).

The three main settings, where IO appears are academia, business and everyday life. Accordingly, we can experience the following types of IO:

- Information overload in academia, impacting faculty, researchers and students;
- Information overload in business environments impacting the employees (decision makers and other members) and customers;
- Everyday information overload of the general public.

Beyond IO, which is experienced on a personal level, there is information overload that impacts organizations (Butcher 1998).

The excessive quantity of information, often labeled as 'Too Much Information' (TMI) represents the macro level of IO (Davis 2011). Caused by the limits of physical storage and processing capacities that impede access to information, this level is identified as one of the major contributing factors of IO (Bawden and Robinson 2009). However, the quantitative growth of information is not only a continuation of the expansion experienced in earlier times. It is also present due to the ease of publishing and storing information on the Internet that is not coupled with incentives to remove unnecessary (i.e. outdated or irrelevant) information (Davis 2012b). In addition to this, we have to handle greater variety of formats and types available, delivered through a limited number of interfaces (Bawden and Robinson 2009). Furthermore, a substantial part of information that we consume and have to manage is becoming utterly volatile (Davis 2012b).

Information overload is often a condition of being overwhelmed and under-informed at the same time. Although this can be qualified as a rare sentiment, it is a state of mind that characterizes our information environment. In this situation, the amount of information may be less critical than the extent to which the information is structured and the form of being structured, in as so much it permits decision making, based on relevance judgments (Hargittai et al. 2012). Essentially, this phenomenon shows similarity to a situation, where we may be overloaded because we are drawn toward information that in the past did not exist or that we did not have access to, but is available now (Hemp 2009).

Conceiving information overload depends to a significant extent on how we understand the nature of information. The three principal uses of the word 'information' are the following ones:

- Information-as-process, i.e. the act of informing;
- Information-as-knowledge, i.e. knowledge communicated concerning some particular fact, subject, or event;
- Information-as-thing, i.e. objects, such as data and documents, which are regarded as being informative (Buckland 2011).

This latter use refers to objective packages of cognitive content in a certain form. Such understanding covers recorded information, which is paramount in generating IO (Kari 2007). Notwithstanding, information-as-thing is associated with practically all forms of IO and is not conceivable without information-as-process and information-as-knowledge.

Complaints about information overload itself are hardly new. Resentment at facing the difficulty to keep up with the amount of information available began early. The growth of information in printed books, scholarly journals, and then by computers, has often been named as the source of IO. Information overload was generally accepted as a problem in the late 1950s and early 1960s, ascribed mainly to the expansion of publication, particularly in science, technology and medicine. By the 1990s references to information overload began to appear in the business world, as well (Bawden and Robinson 2009). In recent times, IO is the result of wide availability and widespread use of social media tools and services. Therefore, social media is largely blamed for the massive increase in information that causes not only abundance, but also raises questions of quality and trust in information (Benselin and Ragsdell 2016).

10.2.2 Information Overload in Business Environments

The impact of IO is usually different in specific (Eppler and Mengis 2004) business areas, yet in business organizations, employees lose productive time when they have to deal with information of limited value (Hemp 2009). Such losses impact organizations far beyond its decision-makers.

The restricted information processing capacity of employees, caused by the complexity of tasks, the need for managing parallel projects or tasks are frequently mentioned (Eppler and Mengis 2004). Frequent interruptions in the work processes represent a serious burden, because employees, interrupted in answering a given message by another one, not only lose time, but have to recover from the interruption and refocus their attention (Hemp 2009).

Managers are typically overloaded by too much information because they have to justify decisions, so they feel the need to collect information in order to indicate their commitment to rationalism and competence, believed to improve decision-making. They receive enormous amounts of unsolicited information, then they seek more information to verify the information that they have already acquired. In many cases, managers collect information because it may be useful, and because they want to acquire all possible information. Last, but not least, they regard information as a currency that may make them indispensable to a certain extent (Butcher 1998).

If organizational design is changed, a higher level of information processing requirements appears, while better coordination through standards, common procedures and rules can reduce these information processing requirements (Eppler and Mengis 2004). Needless to say that overload, produced by the organization is experienced by its individual members.

In cross-cultural business communication, the appearance of IO is related to the ways, how people receive and decode information, mainly in textual form. These differences originate in the variety of professional, corporate and rhetorical styles that are defined by cultural styles, causing differences between varied nations. However, differences within a given culture are less important than the extra cognitive load, caused by having to process information, conceived in a different cultural framework, thus based on different discourse patterns (Ulijn and Strother 2012).

10.2.3 Information Overload in Everyday Life Information Seeking

Besides IO in academic and professional (first of all business) environments, everyday life information seeking also plays a role, even though it received less attention (Hemp 2009). This type of IO is experienced similarly to that in other environments (Savolainen 2007). The concept itself refers to the acquisition of various informational (both cognitive and expressive) elements which people employ to orient themselves in daily life or to solve problems (Savolainen 1995).

Everyday life information seeking is often connected to disposable information, i.e. information that is used once and then discarded. The background to discarding information is that people are only willing to make an effort to get quality information if they foresee further, continued use of that information. Disposable information is usually directed towards satisfying the need for quick answers to minor questions (Mawby et al. 2015). By its very nature, social media, used for everyday use produces masses of disposable information.

While the existence of disposable information seems evident, it is questionable if professional environments produce it or not. It is tempting to say yes, because a given piece of information is often used to provide a base for a unique investigation and/or publication. However, it is rather obvious that research – be it for academic or business purposes – is built on sophisticated processes that allow or require the repeated use of an idea, triggered by a piece of information. Ideas, as we know, have the potential to serve as the rough material of newer investigation and/or publication, albeit their use may be conscious or not.

10.2.4 The Role of Information Technology

As already mentioned, the use and misuse of information technology has been blamed for causing information overload already in the 1980s and 1990s, and it continues to be a major source today.

Actual information and communication technologies make use of information pull and push. Research has shown that either can cause IO and display the symptoms of the loss of control of information (Poirier and Robinson 2014). The pull approach to information stands for the standard method of retrieving information. Push technologies cover automatic delivery based on predefined information profiles. Both have strengths and weaknesses, so the best approach might be to use them in complimentary ways (Savolainen 2007). A somewhat different issue is the (already mentioned) influence of social media, which is tangible in the corporate world, in everyday life information seeking and – to a lesser extent – in scholarly research. Social media is widely characterized by uncontrolled communication, due to the ease of producing information with Web 2.0 tools and the expectation of constant novelty that requires rapid updating and posting of new material. All of them contribute significantly to an enormous growth in the quantity of information.

10.2.5 Information Overload in the Data-Intensive World

In 1996, Bradford and Wurman (Bradford and Wurman 1996) wrote about a 'tsunami of data' that has been more frequently named a 'data deluge', resulting from the existence and availability of high bandwidth networks that have the capacity to store massive amounts of data (Borgman 2012). The prevalence of data in everyday life, in the business world and as research data in the natural sciences, the social sciences and the humanities significantly contributes to IO.

An emergent and important, though not exclusive facet of the data-rich world is 'big data' that is conditioned by the interplay of cultural, technological and scholarly phenomena (Boyd and Crawford 2012). The first and most straightforward measure, by which big data can be defined, is volume, even though views on it also depend on the conceptions in the given field of research. The second measure is variety, which is about managing the complexity of multiple data types. Data is in motion at accelerated speed that causes difficulty in capturing and processing it, thus velocity represents an important dimension (Zikopoulos et al. 2015).

Apparently, information overload, caused by the abundance of data could be called 'data overload'. Whatever the name, it impacts both individuals and organizations in the academic and the business sphere, as well as in everyday settings.

The case of the digital humanities prototypically shows the role and importance of data in today's research. The digital humanities has been led to a substantial extent by the assumption that data can be interpreted as texts, and – conversely –

texts can be interpreted as data. While being interested in recorded information, i.e. information-as-thing, most – if not all – digital humanities projects (Schreibman et al. 2004; Gibbs 2011; Alvarado 2012) rely on some kind of data. Data for the digital humanities is a machine-actionable abstraction that characterizes some aspects of a given object (Schöch 2013). The technology, used by the digital humanities to create new objects for humanistic interrogation (Schmidt 2011) may be extended to media consciousness of the digital age (Piez 2008). This may contribute to the proper understanding of the growing digital infrastructure's effects on all kinds of information. Such thinking also may be broadened to the act of thinking critically about the ways, how knowledge in the 21st century is transformed into information through computational techniques (Dalbello 2011). Consequently, there is a need for acquiring a deeper general understanding of the mutual co-constitution of technology and of the human component and interrogating the possibility of positively influencing the existing cyber-infrastructure (Frabetti 2011; Dillon 2007).

10.3   Alleviating the Symptoms of Information Overload

There is an ever widening gap between information that is available to us and which is usable, because both inbound and outbound flows of information, i.e. information, exploited when consuming and when producing and/or distributing information may not be appropriate to someone's information needs (Davis 2012a). There is no single cure to information overload, because it has several and complex causes. In order to be successful, barriers have to be surmounted and the most efficient measures and tools for discovering, identifying and properly using information have to be found (Bawden and Robinson 2009).

We have pointed out that Too Much Information represents the quantitative side of IO. Arguably, the problem is not that there is too much information. In an information-driven society there cannot be too much information. Information overload represents the challenge to make effective use of information, thus instead of blocking or limiting, there is a need for finding appropriate tools for discovery (Dillon 2007). This can be achieved mainly on the micro-level of overload that is qualitative, because it is essentially caused by a failure to filter information (Davis 2011). Filtering mechanisms provide help in recognizing value-added information to resolve the dilemma of receiving too much information, vs. not receiving the right piece of information, or not getting enough of the right information (Neylon 2011; Katzer and Fletcher 1992).

While IO on the quantitative, macro-level in itself cannot be influenced directly, there are two different broad spheres of activities, where we can venture alleviating the symptoms of qualitative (micro-level) information overload:

1. When designing information;
2. When interacting with information.

10.3.1   Design and Information Architecture

Ill-structured, unclear information causes IO. However, if we can improve the conciseness, consistency and comprehensibility of information, the level of information processing capacity of the individual (Eppler and Mengis 2004) can increase. In other words, the presentation of information, such as its organization, selection, and format, on webpages and in other forms plays an important role in reducing information overload (Blummer and Kenton 2014). This is the reason, why sound reasoning dictates that information architecture (IA) that goes beyond simple design issues, should play an important role in helping people and organizations to successfully mitigate information overload (Tidline 1999), because it can offer solutions to avoid micro-level IO conditions (Davis 2011).

Information architecture explores ways to organize and create semantic and contextual informational relationships that accommodate user goals and behavior (Davis 2010). It addresses information-as-thing, but it is also directed towards facilitating acts of informing (information-as-process) and information-as-knowledge, in the sense of fostering the process of information being transformed into knowledge.

Adequate design of information systems is part of IA and the elimination of IO is not imaginable without it. Designers have to take into account differing motivations and mental models for handling information of different users (Brown 2005). Therefore, the prerequisite of providing adequate design is to have a deep understanding of their users and of their social context among the conditions of growing complexity that emerges in diverse and abundant information choices in almost all fields (Morville 2005).

Organization and representation occupy an important position in IA, and materialize in the concept of findability, which is the art and science of making content findable (Brown 2005). A special, practical field of enabling findability is developing recommendation systems as it was done by Huang et al. (2012), who proposed a personalized guide recommendation system to mitigate IO that encumbers museum learning, i.e. people's use of museums to acquire knowledge, because learners have to decide if certain parts from a mass of information needs to be retained, or discarded.

Sometimes, we may face arguments that there is no need for IA, because users can do the same, what the experts used to do for them (Hinton 2009). In spite of this, architecture is never superfluous, and if we let users manage information for themselves, the information architectures that evolve may have more chance to work inappropriately (Davis 2012a).

This is one of the reasons why proper design also requires an understanding of the differences between professionals and amateurs. Ideally, every information creator would be an expert in producing information (Huvila 2011). However, not everyone has accumulated enough expertise to play this role, because a substantial part of users are amateurs, who love to be engaged in a particular activity, independently of the fact whether they are knowledgeable or not of their respective subject

(Keen 2007). Amateur settings are thus often different from professional environments that foster information use by members of a given profession or discipline. Amateur users, who act as creators, concentrate on their own immediate needs, and do not have a precise idea of other users' needs or the necessity of meeting these needs (Huvila 2011). Certainly, we should not forget about professional amateurs (Pro-Ams), who constitute an intermediate category between amateurs and professionals. They play an important role in fields that are too complex to generate mass popularity, but not sophisticated enough to be removed entirely from the popular realm (Leadbeater and Miller 2004; Reid and Macafee 2007). It comes as no surprise that IO is differently perceived in and by these groups.

In general, combating information overload fits well into the thought of social usefulness of IA, because it describes the process of designing, implementing and evaluating humanly and socially acceptable information spaces (Dillon 2007). Nonetheless, the effects and tools of information architecture alone are limited, because information architects and user experience designers can discover information overload only retrospectively and through indirect means (Davis 2012a). Notwithstanding, information architecture is a useful facet in the complex of interactions that contribute to the user's overall experience with an information resource (Brown 2005).

10.3.2 Interacting with Information

IO is a human experience, thus – being fundamentally propagated by people – technology cannot solve this problem entirely (Davis 2011). Therefore, alleviating the symptoms of IO by individual interactions with information is clearly attached to the micro-level of IO and has at least two sets of approaches:

1. Taking a critical stance on information;
2. Applying personal information management (PIM) tools.

10.3.2.1 Being Critical Against Information

Taking a critical stance is a crucial condition of successfully mitigating information overload. Any critical approach to information presupposes the existence and use of competencies, i.e. the combination of skills, abilities and tools, often not clearly distinguishable from each other.

Being able to recognize the quality of a given message is a key skill. It has become especially important in the present-day information environment, where we experience the prevalence of social media services and tools. The changes in perceiving trust and authority dictate the need for assessing content that involves not only finding authoritative sources, but a self-awareness of someone's own worldview and biases (Association of College and Research Libraries 2015).

Critical thinking materializes to a substantial extent in critical reading, which requires us to do the following:

- Determining the purpose of the text and assessing how the central claims are developed;
- Making judgements about the intended audience of the text;
- Distinguishing the different kinds of reasoning in the text;
- Examining the evidence and sources of the writing (Jones 1996).

If we want to be efficient and successful information users, searching for information has to be critical in the sense that it is based on having a clear picture about the information and data landscape of the given discipline or profession. It has to be understood that in many cases there is a need to determine the validity of the information created by different authorities and to acknowledge that some sources of authority are privileged over others. Therefore, complex search strategies can make a difference to the breadth and depth of information found. Searching for new tools to solve new questions may be required, so it has to be understood that relying always on familiar resources is not appropriate in all cases (SCONUL Working Group on Information Literacy, London 2011). It is crucial to understand that first attempts at searching do not always produce adequate results. It is similarly important to remain persistent when facing search challenges, then recognizing when there is enough information to substantiate a decision if the given information task has been completed or not. Efficient searching presupposes utilizing divergent and convergent thinking that is exemplified by brainstorming and selecting the best source, respectively. Based on search results, needs and further search strategies can be refined. This has to be done despite the reputation of general search engines, first of all the sweeping popularity of Google, and the widespread beliefs about the straightforward and uncomplicated nature and easiness of searching for information. There may be also a need to identify specialist search tools, appropriate to each individual information need and to understand the value of controlled vocabularies and taxonomies in searching. Formats should not be equated with the underlying creation process, because the ambiguity that surrounds the potential value of information in emerging formats and modes has to be taken into consideration. Making informed choices regarding someone's on-line actions in full awareness of issues related to privacy and the commodification of personal information is also desirable, but fairly difficult, because the spirit of social media does not support critical approaches to information (Association of College and Research Libraries 2015).

Influencing the speed of access to information and its consumption also pertains to being critical against information. The accelerated pace of life brought with it an increase in the speed of accessing and using information, resulting in rapid consumption of information that causes IO. Nonetheless, this kind of overload could be mitigated by applying slow principles. Being slow is not identical with doing something less rapidly. It is rather being concerned with control by judging the right speed and tempo for a given activity and the context, with a reflective attitude. Slow principles provide a framework for making balanced choices appropriate to a given situation by creating enough time and space to make choices that may prove beneficial (Bawden and Robinson 2009). However, this may seem impractical and impossible because of the constant pressure to consume and produce information. Instead of completely 'unplugging', the purposive withdrawal from some informational activities, like declining to publish Twitter updates, while still maintaining an account might be suitable. Reading deeply and exclusively from one source, or just doing the opposite, i.e. browsing web material without a predefined direction or need, may provide breathing spaces outside the dominant social tempo. Apparently, there are situations, where a slow approach is undesirable, as for instance when we check trivial facts (Poirier and Robinson 2014). Slow principles clearly demonstrate the importance of time sensitivity that is related to the perception of being overloaded due to the limitation of time for reviewing available information. Time constraints become even more profoundly obstructing in the case of decision making, especially if critical decisions have to be made (Hargittai et al. 2012).

10.3.2.2   Making Use of Varied Literacies

A feasible framework, for looking critically at information is provided by a number of different literacies that help to understand the digital world better and to take meaningful courses of action, because what is digital, is subject to human agency and to human understanding (Association of College and Research Libraries 2000).

The term literacy is closely related to literature, which originally combined the meaning of being knowledgeable with the body of writing of aesthetic merit. Later it began to cover skills by wide masses to handle texts disregarding if they are part of the literary canon or not. In any way, literacy seemed to be well understood and properly defined. However, the growing role of digital technologies changed its meaning (Livingstone 2004; Livingstone et al. 2008; Buschman 2009). Therefore, literacy is contingent on social and cultural practices, thus not limited to cognitive factors. This is one of the reasons, why literacies are often called 'new' by being identified within varying social and technological contexts (Street 2008; Lankshear and Knobel 2004).

Despite considering the influence of technology, the complex and broad forms of literacies are not restricted to any particular technology and foster understanding, meaning and context, and they cannot be conceived without taking notion of reading literacy, which can be defined as an individual's ability to understand printed text and to communicate through print. In a broader sense, literacies involve the integration of listening, speaking, reading, writing, and numeracy and are closely tied to functional literacy that most commonly denotes the ability to read and use information essential for everyday life (Bawden 2001). Literacies clearly encompass and emphasize efficient information retrieval (Ji et al. 2014), but they should go beyond caring for the abilities of finding information, thus include the creation of information, mainly, though not exclusively, in the form of writing (Huvila 2011). Let us add that information architects do not negate that functioning in modern society requires the mastery of written communication (Morville 2005).

If we understand culture as a complex of codes and meanings, on which human communication depends (Buckland 2011), any kind of literacy is cultural knowledge, because it enables us to recognize and use language that is – as stated earlier – appropriate to different social situations (Campbell 1990). Literacies also build a foundation for higher-level skills and abilities of recognizing, analyzing and understanding the context and relationship between language, information and knowledge (D'Angelo and Maid 2004). In other words, they help to "transform information into knowledge and knowledge into judgment and action" (Association of American Colleges and Universities 2004).

Information literacy (IL) is one of the standard literacies, which refers to the use of information and communication technologies to retrieve and disseminate information, to the competences to find and use information in information (re)sources, as well as to the process of recognizing information need, finding, evaluating, and using information to acquire or extend knowledge. By its breadth and by being associated with lifelong learning, it enables the efficient processing of all types of information content. It has been relevant to, and supportive of activities in personal, social and economic spheres. Information literate people are able to recognize when information is needed. They are equipped with skills to identify, locate, evaluate, and use information in order to solve a particular problem (Nazari and Webber 2012; Boekhorst 2012; Association of College and Research Libraries 1989).

Originally information literacy was dominated by questions of access, because it has been dealing with media that have been far from accessible (Association of College and Research Libraries 2000). This has changed now, as there is overabundance of information. Therefore, presently we suffer from information overload in a higher extent than ever. This circumstance substantiates the need for adjusting IL to the properties of the digital environment (Špiranec and Banek Zorica 2010). This is reflected in a newer and up-to-date definition, where IL is characterized as a set of integrated abilities encompassing the reflective discovery of information, the understanding of how information is produced and valued, and the use of information in creating new knowledge and participating ethically in communities of learning (Association of College and Research Libraries 2015).

Besides IL, there are a number of other literacies. Many of them can be qualified as overarching, and share a number of features. For instance, metaliteracy informs other literacy types, while it fosters critical thinking, emphasizes content and participation via social media. It is meant to expand the scope of information literacy as more than a set of discrete skills (Mackey and Jacobson 2011). The newest framework for information literacy, conceived for the higher education draws significantly upon metaliteracy (Association of College and Research Libraries 2015).

Transliteracy comprises the ability to read, write and interact across a range of platforms, tools and media. While being a comprehensive concept, it is not meant to replace any of the format-specific literacies, and it is not tied to any particular technology. It analyses the social uses of technology, by focusing on the relationship between people and technology, most specifically social networking. With this, it also intends to break down barriers between academia and the wider community (Ipri 2010).

Similarly to transliteracy, digital literacy does not lower the standing of traditional literacies, thus it is much inseparable from reading, writing and arithmetic (Murray and Jorge 2010). Accordingly, it is built on both traditional literacy skills, first of all taken from the information literacy domain, while having orientation on understanding of twenty-first century socio-technical systems, thus reflecting that ordinary people became not only receivers, but also senders of messages (Lankshear and Knobel 2004; Martin 2006). Obviously, most up-to-date forms of literacy recognize the role of information production.

Digital literacy serves the identification, access, management, integration, evaluation, analysis and synthesis of digital resources, thus it is made up of awareness, attitudes and abilities, directed towards appropriately using digital tools and facilities. It concentrates on the context of specific life situations. It advances the construction of new knowledge and the creation of media expressions. Therefore, it fosters communication and constructive social action, as well as reflecting on them (Meyers et al. 2013). The distinctive feature of digital literacy is that it is associated with many things or even includes them, without claiming to own them. For instance, it encompasses the presentation of information, without incorporating creative writing and visualization. It includes the evaluation of information, without regarding systematic reviewing and meta-analysis to be its property (Bawden 2008).

Data literacy is not without antecedents, and it is also closely connected to information literacy. Nonetheless, it brings in a new facet to the world of literacies by the fact that it is tied to data, the importance of which is becoming widely accepted. Data literacy appears under different names, such as data information literacy, science data literacy or research data literacy. Nonetheless, the term 'data literacy' is more suitable by being simple and straightforward (Koltay 2015), and does not restrict the concept to research data. Data literacy's closeness to IL becomes evident if we look at one of its definitions that underline the ability to process, sort, and filter vast quantities of information, which requires knowing how to search, how to filter and process, and to produce and synthesize it (Johnson 2012).

In a matrix of data literacy competencies, quality evaluation appears as the perhaps most important activity. It includes assessing data sources for trustworthiness, errors and other problems.

Evaluation appears already when we collect data (Ridsdale et al. 2015). Data quality is determined first of all by trust, which is complex in itself, as it includes the lineage, version and error rate of data (Buckland 2011). Trust depends on subjective judgements on authenticity, acceptability or applicability of the data; and is also influenced by the given subject discipline, the reputation of those responsible for the creation of the data, and the biases of the persons, who are evaluating the data. Quality data can display authenticity, when there is sufficient context in the form of documentation and metadata. Data also has to be usable that presupposes that it is discoverable and accessible. Integrity of data assumes that the data can be proven to be identical, to some previously accepted or verified state (Giarlo 2013).

The need for critical assessment mentioned above, occupies a distinguished place also among the general features of data literacy. Being critical in this environment includes giving emphasis to the version of the given dataset, the person responsible for it (Association of College and Research Libraries 2013), as well as understanding what data means, including how to read graphs and charts appropriately, draw correct conclusions from data, and recognize when data is being used in misleading or inappropriate ways (Carlson et al. 2011). Being familiar with the context in which data is produced and reused can be a decisive factor in evaluation (Calzada Prado and Marzal 2013). A profound understanding of the big data phenomenon (Boyd and Crawford 2012) is an essential aspect of data literacy. Primarily, quality assurance is regarded to be the ability to recognize a pattern or consistency in the data, facilitated or disrupted by the quality of documentation (metadata). In the case of research data, quality assurance requires synthesis, because it is a blend of technical skills, disciplinary knowledge and metacognitive processes (Carlson et al. 2011).

Besides managing quality, data literacy has to give attention to data organization and preservation. Data interpretation is becoming more and more crucial, and clearly shows the mechanisms that also characterize information literacy. As an important technique of interpretation, data visualization comprises creating, evaluating and critically assessing graphical representations of data. Besides visualization, presenting data verbally in a clear and coherent manner is also a crucial data literacy competence (Ridsdale et al. 2015).

All these competencies rely on the ability to translate vast amounts of data into abstract concepts and to understand data-based reasoning, especially if it is coupled with the understanding that data has limitations and we must remain able to act also in the absence of data (Davies et al. 2011).

10.3.2.3 Applying Personal Information Management Tools

The discussion above was built on the idea that there are different levels, where micro-level IO can be mitigated. One of them is given by information architecture that concentrates on the relationship between relatively well-defined actors, i.e. architects and their target audiences. Literacies operate on a more collective, societal level. In addition to these levels, there is a third level, where the creator of information is less visible, or does not play a substantial role. This is the personal level, where the needs and the role of the user appear to be more markedly emphasized than the ones of the creator. Being an activity in which an individual stores personal information items in order to retrieve them later, personal information management (PIM) operates on this level (Bergman 2013).

PIM is "both the practice and the study of the activities a person performs in order to acquire or create, store, organize, maintain, retrieve, use and distribute the information needed to complete tasks (work related or not) and fulfill various roles and responsibilities" (Jones 2008, p. 453).

PIM practices consist of finding information and retaining this information for future re-use. It also includes disposing of information, if it is judged to be unusable or nor worthy of the effort and/or physical space to archive it. These two basic activities (and especially retaining information) are accompanied by meta-level activities, such as measuring, evaluating and organizing information and making sense of it. It is also important to maintain the flow of information and manage privacy (Jones 2008).

PIM tools offer solutions, which can help in decreasing fragmentation that characterizes our information environment. This fragmentation is caused by the ambiguity, novelty, complexity and intensity of information itself and the diversity of formats, applications and tools (Franganillo 2009). As popular interest in personal digital information grows, personal information management has to be explored for its potential as a service, offered by different institutions, first of all, by libraries (Cushing 2016).

By its origin, information, managed through PIM activities, can be either public, or produced by people themselves. Both types can be present in the PIM environment of the same person at the same time. For instance, researchers receive or collect information, produced by others, while they also conserve their own publications. In other words, consuming novel resources is often supplemented by conserving large amounts of information for future consumption. This means that people extensively preserve and curate information. Usually, they go beyond keeping information passively by making attempts to organize it in order to promote its future retrieval. PIM is organic as we adapt it by repeatedly revisiting and restructuring our actions to the actual need and tasks, including the occasional deletion of old or irrelevant pieces of information (Whittaker 2011).

Among PIM tools, different reference management software, such as EndNote, RefWorks, or Zotero also have to be mentioned, while a different perspective opens by mind mapping to stimulate the creative and innovative use of information collected (Fourie 2011).

We can speak about personal knowledge management (PKM), as well. It is a way of coping with complex environmental changes and developments and is also deemed to be a form of sophisticated career and life management. It is an emerging concept that focuses not only on the importance of individual growth and learning, but on the technology and management processes, which have been traditionally associated with organizational knowledge management (Pauleen and Gorman 2011). PKM is an extension of Knowledge Management (KM), about the possibility of which there are well-founded doubts (Wilson 2002). Nonetheless, we can also accept the existence of PKM, if we accept the definition of knowledge management as "the process of creating and managing the conditions for the transfer and the use of knowledge" (Brophy 2001, p. 36).

PKM is not directly connected to information overload, at least not to the same extent as PIM does. The individual plays also a different role in it, first on account of PKM's close connection to the corporate world. Notwithstanding, in contrast to the traditional view of KM that is primarily concerned with managing organizational knowledge (including the knowledge that individuals possess), PKM is 'personal inquiry', i.e. it is the quest to find, connect, learn and explore (Clemente and Pollara 2005). Therefore, PKM's focus is on helping individuals to be more effective in personal, organizational and social environments (Pauleen 2009).

The closeness of PIM and PKM appears in a new hybrid concept that integrates PIM, PKM and IL and is called personal knowledge and information management

(PKIM). PKIM aims at improving the functioning of individuals in competitive environments. On the one hand, it is based on PKM. On the other hand, it focuses on individual assets of knowledge and information, mobilizing competences in building information and knowledge collections, along with their use. In other words, it is about learning and creating new information and knowledge (Świgoń 2013).

No wonder that in connection with PIM, the expression 'personal archiving literacies' also may make sense. Information professionals might impart this type of literacy because PIM is coupled to several challenges, including the difficulty of managing large groups of files and creating metadata. Desktop search may help finding information, but it is often difficult to find what someone is looking for, when the object is not known or is not remembered (Marshall et al. 2006). Personal archiving literacies includes appreciating the future value of someone's files and remembering where personal information is stored, identifying information that needs to be preserved, deleting unneeded items and maintaining important files (Zastrow 2014).

10.4   Discussion

This chapter investigated information overloads in its complexity by not only enumerating its sources, but emphasizing how it can be mitigated. The thrust of the argument was on utilizing information architecture, applying information literacy, data literacy and other literacies, as well as making use of personal information management. Since the time, when it was recognized that excessive information impairs performance, and this phenomenon has been labeled 'information overload', its definitions have not changed substantially. On the other hand, the causes of IO have expanded parallel to the development of technology (Benselin and Ragsdell 2016).

The amount of information, information-processing capacity, and available time are the intrinsic factors, while the characteristics of information, quality of information and personal factors (Jackson and Farzaneh 2012) can be regarded to be external. These factors mutually influence each other and it is difficult to disentangle which is dominant under a given circumstance. What is certain is that the influence of some extraneous factors can be mitigated. Therefore, this chapter addressed the majority of these, focusing mainly on the personal side of the extraneous factors in the light of the potential tools, also making use of a set of critical agendas as follows:

1. Social approaches that are meant to encourage better information consumption practices;
2. Technological approaches to foster designing for better information consumption practices;
3. Social approaches to helping people become good contributors to information sources (Forte et al. 2014).

Agenda 1 and agenda 3 are relatively clearly tied to literacies, outlined in this chapter. Agenda 1 reflects more traditional literacies, while Agenda 3 takes producing information into consideration. Agenda 2 is close to approaches that were mentioned in regard to information architecture.

The apparent loss of gatekeepers, like reviewers, editors, librarians and others lead to the consequence that readers themselves had to become the gatekeepers (Badke 2004). Notwithstanding, this chapter has been conceived in the belief that gatekeeping is not lost definitely, thus not only information users, but information architects, and information professionals should be well-prepared themselves to alleviate the symptoms of IO (Koltay 2011).

As information overload has many faces, our argument tried to be as diverse as possible. Nonetheless, in this chapter those approaches dominated that connected more or less directly to the idea, expressed by Forte et al in their Interdisciplinary Literacy Framework (Forte et al. 2014): Making people smarter instead of producing smarter computers.

10.5   Summary

Regardless of the various interpretations, information overload is perceived by many in different spheres. It hampers the flow of information and – to say the least – causes delays in decision making. Consequently, there is a need for mitigating information overload in academia, business environments and in everyday life information seeking.

Information technology both causes overload and offers tools for alleviating its symptoms. For the former role the capacity to store massive amounts of data can be blamed on account of the prevalence of social media and the abundance of data. The latter task falls within the competence of design and information architecture.

A broad and diverse sphere of activities in reducing information overload is related to the different ways of interacting with information by taking a critical stance that often materializes in making use of a number of different literacies. Adopting slow principles to information behavior and applying personal information management tools can also play a role in avoiding being overloaded.

Acknowledgements This research was supported by EFOP–3.6.1–16–2016–00001 'Complex Development of Research Capacities and Services at Eszterházy Károly University, Hungary'.

References

Alvarado R (2012) The digital humanities situation. In: Gold MK (ed) Debates in the digital humanities. University of Minnesota Press, Minneapolis. Available via http://dhdebates.gc. cuny.edu/debates/text/50A. Accessed 30 July 2016

Association of American Colleges and Universities (AACU) (2004) Greater expectations: a new vision for learning as a nation goes to college. AACU, Washington, DC. Available via https:// www.aacu.org/publications/greater-expectations. Accessed 26 July 2016

Association of College and Research Libraries (ACRL) (1989) Presidential committee on information literacy. Final report. ACRL, Chicago. Available via http://www.ala.org/acrl/publications/whitepapers/presidential. Accessed 26 July 2016

Association of College and Research Libraries (ACRL) (2000) Information literacy competency standards for higher education. ACRL, Chicago. Available via http://www.ala.org/acrl/standards/. Accessed 26 July 2016

Association of College and Research Libraries (ACRL) (2013) Intersections of scholarly communication and information literacy: creating strategic collaborations for a changing academic environment. ACRL, Chicago. Available via http://acrl.ala.org/intersections/. Accessed 26 July 2016

Association of College and Research Libraries (ACRL) (2015) Framework for information literacy for higher education. ACRL, Chicago. Available via http://www.ala.org/acrl/standards/ilframework. Accessed 26 July 2016

Badke W (2004) Research strategies: finding your way through the information fog, 2nd edn. iUniverse-Indigo, Lincoln

Badke W (2010) Information overload? Maybe not. Online 34(5):52–54

Bawden D (2001) Information and digital literacies: a review of concepts. J Doc 57(2):218–259

Bawden D (2008) Origins and concepts of digital literacy. In: Lankshear C, Knobel M (eds) Digital literacies: concepts, policies and practices. Peter Lang, New York, pp 17–32

Bawden D, Robinson L (2009) The dark side of information: overload, anxiety and other paradoxes and pathologies. J Inf Sci 35(2):180–191

Benselin JC, Ragsdell G (2016) Information overload: the differences that age makes. J Libr Inf Sci 45(3). Available via http://journals.sagepub.com/doi/abs/10.1177/0961000614566341?journalCode=lisb. Accessed 28 July 2016

Bergman O (2013) Variables for personal information management research. Aslib Proc New Inf Perspect 65(5):464–483

Blummer B, Kenton JM (2014) Reducing patron information overload in academic libraries. Coll Undergrad Lib 21(2):115–135

Boekhorst AK (2012) Becoming information literate in the Netherlands. Libr Rev 52(7):298–309

Borgman CL (2012) The conundrum of sharing research data. J Am Soc Inf Sci Technol 63(6):1059–1078

Boyd D, Crawford K (2012) Critical questions for big data: provocations for a cultural, technological, and scholarly phenomenon. Inf Commun Soc 15(5):662–679

Bradford P, Wurman RS (1996) Information architects. Graphis, Zurich

Brophy P (2001) The Library in the twenty-first century: new Services for the information age. Library Association Publishing, London

Brown D (2005) Eight principles of information architecture. Bull Am Soc Inf Sci Technol 36(6):30–34

Buckland M (2011) Information as thing. J Am Soc Inf Sci Technol 42(5):351–360

Buschman J (2009) Information literacy, new literacies and literacy. Libr Q 79(1):95–118

Butcher H (1998) Meeting managers' information needs. Managing information report. ASLIB, London

Calzada Prado J, Marzal MÁ (2013) Incorporating data literacy into information literacy programs: core competencies and contents. Libri 63(2):123–134

Campbell B (1990) What is literacy? Acquiring and using literacy skills. Aust Public Libr Inf Serv 3(3):149–152

Carlson JR, Fosmire M, Miller C, Sapp Nelson MR (2011) Determining data information literacy needs: a study of students and research faculty. Port Libr Acad 11(2) 629–657. Available via http://www.datainfolit.org/publications/. Accessed 26 July 2016

Clemente BE, Pollara VJ (2005) Mapping the course, marking the trail. IT Prof 7(5):10–15

Cushing AL (2016) "If it computes, patrons have brought it in": personal information management and personal technology assistance in public libraries. Libr Inf Sci Res 38(1):81–88

Dalbello M (2011) A genealogy of digital humanities. J Doc 67(3):480–506

D'Angelo BJ, Maid BM (2004) Moving beyond definitions: implementing information literacy across the curriculum. J Acad Librariansh 30(3):212–217

Davies A, Fidler D, Gorbis M (2011) Future work skills 2020. Institute for the Future, Palo Alto. Available via http://www.iftf.org/uploads/media/SR-1382A_UPRI_future_work_skills_sm.pdf. Accessed 26 July 2016

Davis N (2010) The business function of information architecture. DSIA Portal of Information Architecture. Available via http://www.methodbrain.com/dsia/the-basics-of-ia/The-Basic-Function-of-IA.cfm. Accessed 30 July 2016

Davis N (2011) Information overload, reloaded. Bull Am Soc Inf Sci Technol 37:45–49

Davis N (2012a) IA strategy: addressing the signatures of information overload. UXmatters. Available via http://www.uxmatters.com/mt/archives/2012/02/ia-strategy-addressing-the-signatures-of-information-overload.php. Accessed 26 July 2016

Davis N (2012b) Understanding information architecture differently. UXmatters. Available via http://www.uxmatters.com/mt/archives/2012/05/understanding-information-architecture-differently.php. Accessed 26 July 2016

Dillon A (2007) Library and information science as a research domain: problems and prospects. Inf Res 12(4). Available via http://InformationR.net/ir/12-4/colis/colis03.html. Accessed 30 July 2016

Eppler MJ, Mengis J (2004) The concept of information overload: a review of literature from organization science, accounting, marketing, MIS, and related disciplines. Inf Soc 20(5):325–344

Forte A, Andalibi N, Park T, Willever-Farr H (2014) Designing information savvy societies: an introduction to assessability. In: Proceedings of ACM SIGCHI Conference on Human Factors in Computing Systems (CHI'14). ACM, New York. Available via http://www.andreaforte.net/ForteCHI14Assessability.pdf. Accessed 26 July 2016

Frabetti F (2011) Rethinking the digital humanities in the context of originary technicity. Cult Mach 12:1–22

Franganillo J (2009) Gestión de información personal: elementos, actividades e integración. El Profesional de la Información 18(4):399–406. Available via http://franganillo.es/gip.pdf. Accessed 26 July 2016

Fourie I (2011) Personal information management (PIM), reference management and mind maps: the way to creative librarians? Libr Hi Tech 29(4):764–771

Giarlo MJ (2013) Academic libraries as quality hubs. J Librariansh Sch Commun 1(3):1–10

Gibbs F (2011) Critical discourse in digital humanities. J Digit Humanit 1(1). Available via http://journalofdigitalhumanities.org/1-1/critical-discourse-in-digital-humanities-by-fred-gibbs/. Accessed 26 July 2016

Hargittai E, Russell Neuman W, Curry O (2012) Taming the information tide: perceptions of information overload in the American home. Inf Soc 28(3):161–173

Hemp P (2009) Death by information overload. Harv Bus Rev 87(9):83–89

Himma KE (2007) The concept of information overload: a preliminary step in understanding the nature of a harmful information-related condition. Ethics Inf Tech 9(4):259–272

Hinton A (2009) The machineries of context: new architectures for a new dimension. J Inf Archit 1(1):37–47

Huang YM, Liu CH, Lee CY, Huang YM (2012) Designing a personalized guide recommendation system to mitigate information overload in museum learning. Educ Technol Soc 15(4):150–166

Huvila I (2011) The complete information literacy? Unforgetting creation and organization of information. J Librariansh Inf Sci 43:237–245

Ipri T (2010) Introducing transliteracy. What does it mean to academic libraries? Coll Res Libr News 71(10):532–567

Jackson TW, Farzaneh P (2012) Theory-based model of factors affecting information overload. Int J Inf Manag 32(6):523–532

Ji Q, Ha L, Sypher U (2014) The role of news media use and demographic characteristics in the possibility of information overload prediction. Int J Commun 8(16):699–714

Johnson CA (2012) The information diet: a case for conscious consumption. Oreilly & Associates Inc, Sebastopol

Jones D (1996) Critical thinking in an online world. University of California, Santa Barbara Library, Santa Barbara. Available via http://misc.library.ucsb.edu/untangle/jones.html. Accessed 30 July 2016

Jones W (2008) Keeping found things found: the study and practice of personal information management. Morgan Kaufmann Publishers, Boston

Kari J (2007) Conceptualizing the personal outcomes of information. Inf Res Int Electron J 12(2). Available via http://InformationR.net/ir/12-2/paper292.html. Accessed 30 July 2016

Katzer J, Fletcher PT (1992) The information environment of managers. Annu Rev Inf Sci Technol 27:227–263

Keen A (2007) The cult of the amateur. Nicholas Brealey Publishing, London

Koltay T (2011) Information overload, information architecture and digital literacy. Bull Am Soc Inf Sci Technol 38(1):33–35. Available via http://www.asis.org/Bulletin/Oct-11/OctNov11_Koltay.pdf. Accessed 26 July 2016

Koltay T (2015) Data literacy: in search of a name and identity. J Doc 71(2):401–415

Lankshear C, Knobel M (2004) "New literacies": research and social practice. In: Plenary Address, Annual Meeting of the National Reading Conference, San Antonio, 2004 December 02. Available via http://everydayliteracies.net/pubs.html. Accessed 26 July 2016

Leadbeater C, Miller P (2004) The Pro-Am revolution: how enthusiasts are changing our society and economy. Demos, London

Livingstone S (2004) Media literacy and the challenge of new information and communication technologies. Commun Rev 7(1):3–14

Livingstone S, Van Couvering E, Thumin N (2008) Converging traditions of research on media and information literacies: disciplinary and methodological issues. In: Coiro J, Knobel M, Lankshear C, Leu DJ (eds) Handbook of research on new literacies. Lawrence Erlbaum Associates, Hillsdale, pp 103–132

Mackey TP, Jacobson TE (2011) Reframing information literacy as a metaliteracy. Coll Res Libr 72(1):62–78

Marshall CC, Bly S, Brun-Cottan F (2006) The long term fate of our digital belongings: toward a service model for personal archives. In: Conference Proceedings of Archiving Conference 2016. Society for Imaging Science and Technology, Springfield, pp 25–30

Martin A (2006) Literacies for the digital age. In: Martin A, Madigan D (eds) Digital literacies for learning. Facet Publishing, London, pp 3–25

Mawby J, Foster A, Ellis D (2015) Everyday life information seeking behaviour in relation to the environment: disposable information. Libr Rev 64(6–7):468–479

Meyers EM, Erickson I, Small RV (2013) Digital literacy and informal learning environments: an introduction. Learn. Media Technol. 38(4):355–367

Morville P (2005) Ambient findability: what we find changes who we become. O'Reilly, Sebastopol

Murray MC, Jorge P (2010) Unraveling the digital literacy paradox: how higher education fails at the fourth literacy. Issues Inf Sci Inf Technol 11:85–100. Available via http://iisit.org/Vol11/IISITv11p085-100Murray0507.pdf. Accessed 26 July 2016

Nazari M, Webber S (2012) Loss of faith in the origins of information literacy in e-environments: proposal of a holistic approach. J Librariansh Inf Sci 44(2):97–107

Neylon C (2011) It's not filter failure, it's a discovery deficit. Serials 24(1):21–25

Pauleen DJ (2009) Personal knowledge management: putting the person back into the knowledge equation. Online Inf Rev 33(2):221–224

Pauleen DJ, Gorman G (2011) Personal knowledge management: individual, organizational and social perspectives. Gower, Farnham

Piez W (2008) Something called "Digital Humanities". DHQ Digit Humanit Q 2(1). Available via http://www.digitalhumanities.org/dhq/vol/2/1/000020/000020. Accessed 30 July 2016

Poirier L, Robinson L (2014) Informational balance: slow principles in the theory and practice of information behaviour. J Doc 70(4):687–707

Reid PH, Macafee C (2007) The philosophy of local studies in the interactive age. J Librariansh Inf Sci 39(3):126–141

Ridsdale C, Rothwell J, Smit M, Ali-Hassan H, Bliemel M, Irvine D, Kelley D, Matwin S, Wuetherick B (2015) Strategies and best practices for data literacy education. Knowledge synthesis report. Dalhousie University, Halifax. Available via https://dalspace.library.dal.ca/handle/10222/64578. Accessed 26 July 2016

Rowley J (2007) The wisdom hierarchy: representations of the DIKW hierarchy. J Inf Sci 33(2):163–180

Savolainen R (1995) Everyday life information seeking: approaching information seeking in the context of "way of life". Libr Inf Sci Res 17(3):259–294

Savolainen R (2007) Filtering and withdrawing: strategies for coping with information overload in everyday contexts. J Inf Sci 33(5):611–621

Schmidt BM (2011) Theory first. J Digit Humanit 1(1). Available via http://journalofdigitalhumanities.org/1-1/theory-first-by-ben-schmidt/. Accessed 30 July 2016

Schöch C (2013) Big? Smart? Clean? Messy? Data in the humanities. J Digit Humanit 2(3). Available via http://journalofdigitalhumanities.org/2-3/big-smart-clean-messy-data-in-the-humanities/. Accessed 30 July 2016

Schneider R (2013) Research data literacy. In: Kurbanoğlu S, Grassian E, Mizrachi D, Catts R, Špiranec S (eds) Worldwide commonalities and challenges in information literacy research and practice, communications in computer and information science series, vol 397. Springer International, Cham, pp 134–140

Schreibman S, Siemens R, Unsworth J (2004) The digital humanities and humanities computing: an introduction. In: Schreibman S, Siemens R, Unsworth J (eds) A companion to digital humanities. Blackwell, Oxford, pp XXIII–XXVII

SCONUL Working Group on Information Literacy. (2011) The SCONUL seven pillars of information literacy core model for higher education. SCONUL, London. Available via http://www.sconul.ac.uk/sites/default/files/documents/researchlens.pdf. Accessed 26 July 2016

Špiranec S, Banek Zorica M (2010) Information literacy 2.0: hype or discourse refinement? J Doc 66(1):140–153

Street BV (2008) New literacies, new times: developments in literacy studies. In: Hornberger NH (ed) Encyclopedia of language and education. Springer, New York, pp 418–431

Świgoń M (2013) Personal knowledge and information management – conception and exemplification. J Inf Sci 39(6):832–845

Tidline T (1999) The mythology of information overload. Libr Trends 47(3):485–506

Ulijn JM, Strother JB (2012) The influence of culture on information overload. In: Strother JB, Ulijn JM, Fazal Z (eds) Information overload: an international challenge for professional engineers and technical communicators. John Wiley & Sons, Inc., Hoboken, pp 79–98

Whittaker S (2011) Personal information management: from information consumption to curation. In: Cronin B (ed) Annual review of information science and technology, vol. 45. Information Today Inc., Medford, pp 1–62

Wilson TD (2002) The nonsense of knowledge management. Inf Res 8(1):144

Zastrow J (2014) PIM 101: personal information management. Comput Libr 34(2):22–24

Zikopoulos P, deRoos D, Bienko C, Andrews M, Buglio R (2015) Big data beyond the hype. A guide to conversations for today's data center. McGraw-Hill Education, New York

Chapter 11
Causal/Informational Theories of Mental Content

Fred Adams

Abstract This entry looks at information-based causal theories of mental content. Causal theories appeal to causal conditions that exist between a representation (such as a thought or belief) and the part of the world represented (the content of the thought or belief). According to informational theories, mental states acquire their content by standing in appropriate informational and causal relations to objects (and properties) in the world. Very crudely, thoughts of dogs are about dogs (and mean *dog*) because information about dogs causes the thoughts that our minds use to keep track of dogs. This article explains some of the leading informational and causal theories of mental content—their twists, turns, refinements, and some of their leading criticisms (This article is a very focused history starting with Grice, Stampe, Dretske, and Fodor. There are many other important thinkers not discussed only for lack of space, not import. However, this is the history that started for me with my first graduate course at Wisconsin with Dennis Stampe just prior to his landmark paper. I later worked closely with Fred Dretske during the writing of his 1981 book and even later met and studied briefly with Jerry Fodor. I am grateful to Dretske, Fodor, and Stampe for their help over the years. I also thank Alfons Schuster for his patience, and an unidentified referee for quite useful advice.).

11.1 Introduction

This essay is about theories of mental content. What is the goal of such theories? It is to explain how minds can come into existence in purely physical systems and be explained via purely physical events and laws. At this point in the twenty-first century this may not be a surprising goal, but it has not always been so. For centuries (and even most of the first half of the last century) it was believed that there was something mysterious about minds that could not be captured by the physical sciences. This essay and the theories it evaluates, abandons that perspective. The

F. Adams (✉)
Department of Linguistics and Cognitive Science, University of Delaware Newark, 19716, Newark, DE, USA
e-mail: fa@udel.edu

© Springer International Publishing AG 2017
A.J. Schuster (eds.), *Understanding Information*, Advanced Information and Knowledge Processing, DOI 10.1007/978-3-319-59090-5_11

expectations in the background here are that a mind is a purely physical mechanism and that meaning (one of those things earlier believed not to be the product of purely physical events) is the result of purely physical interactions between an organism and its environment. If one of these theories is true, we are purely physical and so are our minds. Understanding how we can think about the world with meaningful representations is the ultimate goal of the theories discussed below. We shall begin by asking how meaning comes into existence.

Once we can think, we can assign meaning, such as using the percent sign % as a symbol for percentages. But how are we able to think about percentages in order to assign symbols for them? How is the mind able to think about the world at all? Call the contents of our thoughts that are not assigned contents "unassigned meaning." What are the conditions of unassigned meaning, and how do purely physical systems acquire such meaning? The theories in this essay attempt to answer that question. They offer informational and causal conditions that a purely physical system could meet and in virtue of which acquire unassigned meaning. Thereby, thought and thought content is possible in purely physical, natural systems. In principle a computer would be able to think if it were to meet the causal conditions of the correct theory of mental content. These theories attempt to naturalize meaning—that is, not use the notion of meaning in the explanation of the acquisition of meaning, but use only natural causes and conditions.

I call these accounts "causal" and "informational." Of course, causation and information are not exactly the same notions, but they are related. They are not the same notions because there can be an informational relationship between events A and B, even when there is no direct causal relation between them (Dretske 1981). For example, when you and I are watching the same presidential debates on television in real time, I am receiving information on my television screen that tells me about what is on your television screen at the same time. However, there is no direct causal relation between your screen A and my screen B. There is a common cause C (the transmitters to each of our sets) that co-ordinates the events at A and B, even though there is not direct causal interaction between A and B.

What is more, causal interactions between events generate and convey information between the events. Fingerprints on the murder weapon carry information about who pulled the trigger. Rings in a tree carry information about seasons of growth. Rise and fall of barometric pressure carries information about high or low pressure fronts moving into the area.

In addition, these theories depend on a notion of information that is purely objective and part of the natural world. On this view, information is not mind-dependent. It is a feature of the natural world. Events happen against a background of what we may call a probability space. When it rains, there was a background probability of rain. When there is an earthquake it occurs against a background probability or likelihood of earthquakes in that area of the world. With the event's occurrence, there is a generation of information. There are various ways to measure that information (Shannon and Weaver 1949; Floridi 2016; Adams 2003b), but the import of information for the theories discussed below is the nomic relation between events and the world when information that a is F is carried by b's being G (information that there is fire in the forest carried by smoke in the forest, information that a storm is pending by drop in barometric pressure). Dretske (1981, 1988) and Fodor (1984, 1987, 1990a,b,c) called it *information* or *indication*. It is this kind of informational relationship between natural events that is the basis of the accounts of mind and meaning discussed below, beginning with Grice's notion of natural information that he calls "natural meaning."

11.2 Natural vs. Non-natural Meaning

Paul Grice (1989) certainly deserves mention here. In "Meaning," (originally appearing in 1948 and again in 1957) Grice distinguished *natural meaning* from *non-natural meaning*. Natural meaning is of a sort that would not generate falsity. Where x naturally means that p, x "entails p" (Grice 1989, p. 213). If Colleen's spots naturally mean measles, then Colleen has measles. If smoke in the unspoiled forest naturally means fire then, given the presence of smoke, there is (or was) fire. The effect indicates or naturally means the cause.

Grice gave the name *non-natural meaning* to things which have meaning but which can be false. Sentences can be false. I can say "Colleen currently has measles," where my utterance means but does "not entail" that Colleen currently has measles (Grice 1989, p. 214). Similarly, I can say "There is smoke in this forest" when there is no smoke or fire in this forest. Still, what I have said (though false) is perfectly meaningful. However, my utterances do not naturally mean or indicate measles or fire in the way that spots or smoke naturally mean or indicate them.

Grice did not attempt to fully *naturalize* meaning. For he explained how the non-natural meaning of an utterance depends upon the content of the speaker's intentions and the audience's recognition of speaker intention. "'A meant (non-naturally) something by x' is (roughly) equivalent to 'A intended the utterance of x to produce some effect in an audience by means of the recognition of this intention (Grice 1989, p. 220).'" Grice did not further offer fully naturalized conditions of the origin of mental content of speaker's intentions or audience recognition, but had a major influence on those who did.

11.3 Isomorphism Plus Causation and Conditions of Fidelity

Dennis Stampe (1975, 1977, 1990) was one of the pioneers of causal/informational theories of content and representation. Influenced by Wittgenstein's (1961) picture theory of meaning, Stampe realized that to the Tractarian requirement of structural isomorphism between representation and represented one needs to add a causal requirement. Isomorphisms are symmetrical, but representations are not. "My thought was just that what was missing was causation. And then if you make the thing represented not the state of affairs, the temperature is 70, but just the temperature, age of the tree, price of beans, etc., you can hold that the thing represented is the actual cause of the representation, and various determinate states of affairs causing various determinate representational states. And under ideal conditions or conditions of well-functioning, a certain identifiable state of affairs would cause a given representation, and that gives you the account of content and makes room for falsehood" [when things are not ideal$_{fa}$] (personal communication).

As for the classification of theories of content into causal accounts and teleological accounts, Stampe adds: "The idea that the specification of the relevant conditions ("fidelity" conditions, I called them) apparently requires bringing in reference to the function (teleology) of the representation-generating devices (not the representations themselves!) is put forward in Stampe (1977, 1990). So I take exception to some of the taxonomies of these theories that one sees" (personal correspondence).

For Stampe mental states (beliefs, desires, and intentions) both have representational objects (and contents) and are largely responsible for our success in the world. The harmony between representation and object represented cannot be accidental. "The idea that this determination is *causal* determination is, if not inevitable, only natural" (Stampe 1977, p. 82). Causal relations also explain *singularity* of representation. Consider two photographs of identical twins. What makes one a photo of *Judy* not of *Trudy* is not what is on the photographic film (there is no difference *in the photos*). It can only be that it was caused by *Judy* not *Trudy* that determines the singularity of representational content.

Still, what makes a representation of an object with property F *say that* the object is F? So the represented item and the representing item must co-exist and stand in some relation. "The hypothesis of my approach to the causal theory of content is that the theory of reference is a corollary of a causal theory of representation in general. This theory holds that it is by virtue of such a causal relation between representations generally and their objects that the latter are represented by the former. It may be that the thing represented is causally responsible for the representation [belief$_{fa}$] or vice versa [action$_{fa}$]. . . " (Stampe 1977, p. 84). All of this gives us the *representation of* relation, but we are stalking the *representation as* or *representation that* relation. How is that generated causally?

First, the appropriate causal relation for representation will hold between sets of properties F ($f_1 \ldots f_n$) of the thing represented (O), and a set of properties ($P_1 \ldots P_n$) of the thing doing the representing (R). The causal relation will establish an isomorphism between structures, between O's being F and R's being P. "The causal criterion requires that the relevant properties of the object represented cause the instantiation of the relevant properties in the. . . representation" (Stampe 1977, p. 85).

Second, if O's being F causes R to be P, then R is P only because O is F and wouldn't be P were it not for O's being F. That is, there is a nomic dependence of the sort that allows knowledge. Here, Stampe is influenced by Dretske's (1971) *conclusive reasons* theory of knowledge (where S knows that p on the basis of R when R wouldn't be the case unless p). When R wouldn't have P unless O was F,

R's being P tells one that O is F, on such an account of knowledge. So an example is, barring drought or other problems, one can tell from the rings in a tree how old it is.

Stampe calls the *represented as* properties the "expressed" properties of the representation. The expressed properties are the properties "the represented object would have if the representation of it were accurate," but he must "find a way to associate the concepts of accuracy and expression with natural processes and properties" (Stampe 1977, p. 87). Stampe appeals to "fidelity conditions." "If certain conditions do characterize those processes, the production of the representation would be caused by that state of affairs that the representation represents as being the case" (Stampe 1977, p. 89). The represented state does not have to be the actual cause of the representing state (or there would be no chance for falsity). In cases of natural representations (rings of a tree representing seasons of growth), fidelity conditions would include that there were no droughts, for instance. In cases of non-natural representations (linguistic utterances), fidelity conditions would include that the speaker does not intend to deceive, knows the language, and so on.

11.4   Information-Based Theories

Dretske's (1981) first attempt to explain mental content made use of the mathematical concept of information (Dretske 1981). For our purposes, it will suffice to say that a signal's carrying the *information* that *a* is *F*, like Grice's *natural meaning*, is a signal that cannot be false. If belief contents derive from information, as Dretske proposes, how can beliefs be false, when information cannot? This is one question Dretske set out to answer. Another was how a thought univocally could be that *a* is *F only*? For suppose that as a matter of scientific law, whatever is *F* is also *G*. Then no signal can carry the information that something is *F* without also carrying the information that something is *G*, just as nothing could naturally mean something is *F* without naturally meaning something is *G*. But Colleen's thought that Raven is a dog is only about being a *dog* (not about being a mammal, though Raven is both as a matter of natural law). Here we shall focus upon just these two matters.[1]

Take the second matter first. How can one develop a concept of dogs, when, upon receiving the information that something is a dog one is also receiving the information that something is a mammal? How can one's concept become specific to dogs alone (not mammals)? Dretske's answer is that it is due to what he calls *digitalization*. The basic idea is this. A signal that carries both the information that something is *F* and the information that something is *G*, carries the former piece of information in *digital* form if it carries the information that something is *G in virtue*

---

[1]For much more about information and its use in Dretske's philosophy, see Dretske (1983) and Adams (2003a,b, 2016).

of carrying the information that something is *F*. So if something is a dog, then it will be a mammal (and will be a mammal in virtue of being a dog, but not *vice versa*). Now one may be able to tell from the look and the bark that something is a dog, but not from that alone that it is a mammal (unless one already knows that dogs are mammals). So one may learn from the look and sound of dogs that they are dogs, but not (by look and sound alone) learn that the things seen and heard are mammals. Hence, one may acquire the concept *dog* without acquiring the concept *mammal*, even though one is getting both pieces of information.

Dretske goes on to say: "...we identify [a structure] *S*'s semantic content with its *outermost informational shell*, that piece of information *in which* all other information carried by *S* is nested.... This, of course, is merely another way of saying that *S*'s semantic content is...that piece of information *S* carries in digital form" (Dretske 1981, p. 178). Hence, a univocal concept is one that becomes selectively sensitive to a piece of information that something is *F* (carried in *digital form*). It is done when the content of a concept (of *Fs*) is caused by, informed by, a signal carrying a single piece of information (say that something is *F*) in completely digitalized form (Dretske 1981, p. 184).

We have reached a level where I can have a misrepresentation or false belief precisely because we have risen to a new level (a level beyond that of faithfully carrying information). This is Dretske's answer to Grice's challenge of going from *natural meaning* to *non-natural meaning* (at least for thought content, not utterances). Here is how Dretske puts it:

> But once we have meaning, once the subject has articulated a structure that is selectively sensitive to information about the F-ness of things, instances of this structure, tokens of the type, can be triggered by signals that *lack* the appropriate piece of information. When this occurs, the subject *believes* that *s* is *F* but, because this token of the structure type was not produced by the information that *s* is *F*, the subject falsely believes that *s* is *F*. We have a case of misrepresentation—at token of structure with false content. We have, in a word, meaning without truth (Dretske 1981, p. 195).

11.5   Attack on Wisconsin Semantics

Fodor's first foray into the world of naturalized semantics was to expose flaws in the accounts of Stampe and Dretske (both at Wisconsin at the time). He set *naturalistic* conditions on representation requiring, at a minimum, that "'*R* represents *S*' is *true iff C* where the vocabulary of *C* contains neither intentional nor semantic expressions" (Fodor 1990a, p. 32). While Fodor thinks the theories of Stampe and Dretske do not work, he emphasizes that "...something along the causal lines is the best hope we have for saving intentionalist theorizing, both in psychology and semantics" (Fodor 1990a, p. 34).

11.5.1 Contra Stampe

About *Wisconsin Semantics*, Fodor claims that there are "*two* Wisconsin theories about representation: one that's causal and one that's epistemic" (Fodor 1990a, p. 34). In support, Fodor gives this quote: "An object will represent or misrepresent the situation... only if it is such as to enable one to come to know the situation, i.e., what the situation is, should it be a faithful representation" (Stampe 1975, p. 223).

First, Fodor points out that what one can know from causal relations is non-symmetrical. Even though we can learn about the barometer (that it is low) from the weather (that it is storming), the weather doesn't represent the barometer. And second, Fodor approvingly agrees with Stampe (1977) that the epistemic account founders on the "singularity" of representation. Stampe at one point discusses a xerox machine making multiple copies. From each copy one can learn something about the other copies, but the copies do not represent one another. They only represent the one original—so only causal conditions will tease out the right representational object, according to Stampe.

Fodor believes Stampe's theory mishandles misrepresentation (because it is epistemic). Fodor gives this quote from Stampe (1975, p. 223):

> An object will represent or misrepresent the situation... only if it is such as to enable one to come to know the situation, i.e., what the situation is, should it be a faithful representation. If it is not faithful, it will misrepresent the situation. That is, one *may* not be able to tell from it what the situation is, despite the fact that it is a representation of the situation. In either case, it represents the same thing, just as a faithful and unrecognizable portrait may portray the same person.

Fodor maintains that this gets things the wrong way around. It is not that something is a faithful portrait, say of Mao, because one can learn something about Mao from it. Rather, one can learn something from it about Mao because it is a (faithful) portrait of Mao. Fodor also maintains that there is a "nasty scope ambiguity" (Fodor 1990a, p. 36) between:

(a) if R is faithful (you can tell what the case is); vs.
(b) you can tell (what the case is if R is faithful).

Despite this, Fodor admits it is clear "that it is (a) that Stampe intends. . . ." (Fodor 1990a, p. 36), and turns to the following example. Suppose that Tom is Swiss. Then suppose Denny says: "Tom is Armenian." Fodor says that Stampe maintains that the sentence represents (i.e, misrepresents) Tom's being Swiss because that is the fact to which, if faithful, the representation would provide epistemic access. Fodor maintains that there is no clear way to understand this claim. He claims that the only ways the sentence could be faithful would be to change the facts (make Tom Armenian) or change the sentence (say "Tom is Swiss"). There is further evidence that this is the general tenor of Fodor's complaint when he later discusses another of Stampe's examples (with much the same upshot over the disjunction problem). Consider the following longish quote from Stampe (1977, p. 49):

> The number of rings (in a tree stump) represents the age of the tree.... The causal
> conditions, determining the production of this representation, are most saliently the climatic
> conditions that prevailed during the growth of the tree. If these are normal... then one ring
> will be added each year. Now what *is* that reading.... It is not, for one thing, infallible. There
> may have been drought years.... It is a *conditional* hypothesis: that *if* certain conditions
> hold, then something's having such and such properties would cause the representation
> to have such and such properties.... Even under those normal conditions, there may be
> other things that would produce the rings—an army of some kind of borer, maybe, or an
> omnipotent evil tree demon.

As Fodor rightly points out, Stampe has to make a decision about what is "in"
and what is "out" of normalcy. Why, for instance, are droughts abnormal but not
borers? "And, of course, given Stampe's decision, it's going to follow from the
theory that the tree's rings represent the tree's age and that the tree-borer-caused
tree rings tokens are wild (i.e., that they *mis*represent the tree's age). The worrying
question is what, if anything, motivates this decision" (Fodor 1990a, p. 44–45).
Fodor accuses Stampe of not having a principled way of deciding the matter. Further,
he claims that Stampe does not give a principled reason for deciding what counts as
a *ring*. The borer marks look like rings, but that why do they count *as rings*? But
worst of all, Fodor's claims indicate that Stampe has not moved beyond natural
meaning. For there is no principled way to say when a "ring" is wild. Do the
"rings" produced by borers *mis*represent seasons, or veridically represent *seasons
or borers*? Without principled answers to the former, there is no principled answer
to the latter questions, and no solution to the disjunction problem (immediately
below).

Now Stampe does appeal to teleology and function in his account of representation. And Fodor admits (at least here, though he would deny it in other writings) that
if one could show there was a teleological mechanism that only produced genuine
rings in growth seasons, and wild tokens of *rings* when "Mother Nature is a little
tipsy", and things that look like but are not rings, when borers are at work, then we
could have misrepresentation (for the wild tokens). But this puts weight on teleology
that it will not bear.

11.5.2   Contra Dretske

Fodor's main complaint against Dretske's theory of 1981 is Dretske's use of the
learning period L to try to solve the "disjunction problem" (and explain how
misrepresentation occurs). He reminds us that Dretske's "... way out of the problem
about disjunction is to enforce a strict distinction between what happens in the
learning period and what happens after" (Fodor 1990a, p. 40). If we call a "wild"
tokening of a concept one caused by something that is not represented by the
concept, then wild tokenings are those that are uncorrected by the teacher and that
happen *after* the learning period... and thus, after concept formation. Hence, wild
tokenings are misrepresentations, on Dretske's view.

Fodor's reaction is classic. He says: "This move is ingenious but hopeless. . . . Just for starters, the distinction between what happens in the learning period and what happens thereafter surely isn't principled: there is no time after which one's use of a symbol stops being merely shaped and starts to be, as it were, in earnest" (Fodor 1990a, p. 41).

Even if we could draw a determinate line between what is inside and outside the learning period (a time line), Fodor claims that the account still "doesn't work" because "it ignores relevant counterfactuals" (Fodor 1990a, p. 41). Let's consider the fox example to explain. Dretske would say my concept "fox" has foxes as its content because during the learning period it was trained on foxes. The teacher conditioned my "fox" symbol to fire in the presence of foxes (on the information that something is a fox) and to extinguish on non-foxes (on the information that something is a non-fox). So my "fox" symbol became perfectly correlated with foxes in the learning period L. But Fodor asks what *would have* happened *in L*, had a sheltie with a trim been shown to me? Since we know by stipulation that *after L*, a sheltie with a trim would fire my "fox" symbol, we know shelties (the information that something is a sheltie) would activate my concept "fox." So we know that the information that something is fox would fire my "fox" concept. And we know that the information that something is a sheltie (with a trim) would fire my "fox" concept. So exactly what information was I sensitive to *during the learning period L*? Was it the information *that something is a fox*? Or was it the information *that something is a fox or sheltie*? Fodor claims that the appeal to the learning period L alone does not answer this question. The firing of my "fox" symbol is as well explained by either piece of information (indeed better explained by the latter), and if it is the latter disjunctive piece, then when I see a sheltie and say "fox" I do not misrepresent. For my thought content would be true. "Fox" for me would mean *fox or sheltie*, despite all diligence taken by the teacher during Dretske's learning period L. Thus, Fodor claims that Dretske has not solved the *disjunction problem* after all.

Later in this particular article (Fodor 1984), Fodor considers appealing to tokenings of symbols under *normal circumstances* (p. 42) as a way out, but later (Fodor 1990a,b) comes to reject this approach too as hopeless. Fodor also flirts briefly with the idea of tying an account of meaning to *teleology* (Fodor 1990a, p. 43; 1990c), but drops this idea entirely later (Fodor 1990a,b). The idea was that R's represents S's, when S's cause R's under normal conditions (or when S's are supposed to cause R's, i.e., when it is their function to do so). It is not clear whether he was considering these approaches on his own or just in thinking of the theories of Stampe and Dretske. In any case, he had thoroughly discarded these approaches in a very short time (Fodor 1987, 1990a,b), in part because "representations generated in teleologically normal circumstances must be true" (Fodor 1990a, p. 47). So he didn't foresee these considerations giving a happy account of misrepresentation.

11.6   Dretske's Response: Indicator Function Account

In 1988 Dretske revised his account of naturalized meaning.[2] He changed and
simplified the account. Dretske's new recipe for content involves three interlocking
pieces. (1) The content of a symbol "C" must be tied to its natural meaning
F (Fs—objects that are F). (2) Natural meaning (indication, information) must
be transformed to semantic content. The transformation of acquired information
content into cognitive (semantic) content—must be encoded in a form capable of
being harnessed to beliefs and desires in service of the production of behavior
M. (3) The causal explanation of the resultant behavior M must be in virtue of
the informational content of the input states. Thus, if a symbol "C" causes bodily
movements M because tokenings of "C" indicate (naturally mean) Fs, then "C"
is elevated from merely naturally meaning Fs to having the semantic content that
something is F.

$$F \leftarrow \text{indicates "C" and causes} \rightarrow M \text{ (because it indicates F)}$$

Dretske's account is essentially historical. In different environments, the same
physical natural signs may signify different things, and have different natural
meaning. On Earth, Al's fingerprints are natural signs or indicators of Al's presence.
On Twin-Earth, the same physical types of prints indicate Twin-Al's presence, not
Al's. For this to be true, there must be something like an *ecological boundary*[3] that
screens off what is possible in one environment from what is possible in another.

Dretske's solution to the disjunction problem has at least two components. The
symbol "C" must start out with the ability to naturally mean Fs. Even if "C"s
indicate Fs only, to acquire semantic content, a symbol must lose its guarantee of
possessing natural meaning. It needs to become locked to Fs and permit robust, and
even false, tokening, without infecting its semantic content. A "learning period"
doesn't quite work, unembellished. So Dretske now appeals to the explanatory
relevance of the natural meaning. For Dretske, it is not just what causes "C"s, but
what "C"s in turn cause, and why they cause this that is important in locking "C"s
to their content (F).

Let's suppose that a ground squirrel needs to detect Fs (predators) to stay alive.
If Fs cause "C"s in the ground squirrel, then the tokening of "C"s indicate Fs.
Dretske claims that "C"s come to have the content that something is an F, when
"C"s come to have the function of indicating the presence of Fs. When will that
be? For every predator is not just a predator, it is an animal (G), a physical object
(H), a living being (I), and so on for many properties. Hence, tokens of "C" will
indicate all of these, not just Fs. Dretske's answer is that when "C"s indication of Fs

---

[2]Many people (mistakenly) still think that Dretske's considered answer to the "disjunction
problem" and misrepresentation is his account in his 1986 paper (Dretske 1986). That is incorrect.
He abandoned that account in favor of the solution in his 1988 book (Dretske 1988, chapter 4).

[3]Let's think of an ecological boundary as akin to what Dretske (1981) calls a "channel condition."

(alone) *explains* the animal's behavior, then "C"s acquire the semantic content that something is a predator (F). Hence, it is the *intensionality* of explanatory role that locks "C"s to F, not to G or H or I.

For Dretske, behavior is a complex of a mental state's causing a bodily movement. So when "C" causes some bodily movement M (say, the animal's movement into its hole), the animal's movement consists of its trajectory into its hole. The animal's behavior is its causing that trajectory. The animal's behavior—running into its hole—consists of "C"s causing M ("C" → M). There is no specific behavior that is required to acquire an indicator function. Sometimes the animal slips into its hole (M1). Sometimes it freezes (M2). Sometimes it scurries away (M3). This account says that "C"s become *recruited* to cause such movements because of what "C"s indicate (naturally mean). The animal needs to keep track of Fs and it needs to behave appropriately in the presence of Fs (to avoid predation). Hence, the animal thinks there is a predator when its token "C" causes some appropriate movement M (and hence the animal behaves) because of "C"s indication (natural meaning). Not until "C"'s natural meaning *has an explanatory role* does "C" lock to its semantic content F. So "C"'s acquired function to indicate or detect predators elevates its content to the next, semantic level. Now "C" can be falsely or otherwise robustly tokened. The animal may run into its hole because it thinks there is a predator, even when spooked only by a sound or a shadow, as long as the presence of sounds or shadows doesn't explain why the "C"s cause relevant Ms (don't explain the animal's behavior).[4]

On this view, indicator functions are like other natural functions, such as the function of the heart or kidneys or perceptual mechanisms. The account of natural functions favored by Dretske is one on which the X acquires a function to do Y when doing Y contributes some positive effect or benefit to an organism and so doing helps explain why the organism survives. Then there is a type of selection for organisms with Xs that do Y. Consequently, part of the reason X's are still present, still doing Y, is that a type of selection for such organisms has taken place. Of course, this doesn't explain how X got there or began doing Y, in the beginning.

Naturally, the selection for indicator functions has to be within an organism's lifetime, not across generations. Dretske thinks of this kind of selection as a type of biological process of "recruitment" or "learning" that conforms with standard, etiological models of natural functions (Adams 1979; Adams and Enc 1988; Enc and Adams 1998).

Now the last piece of the puzzle is to show that the content of "C" at some level is relevant to the explanation of the organism's behavior. "C" may cause M, but not because of its natural meaning. "C"'s meaning may be idle. For this purpose, Dretske distinguishes *triggering* and *structuring* causes. A triggering cause may be the thing that causes "C" to cause M right now. Whereas a structuring cause is what

---

[4]Sticks and stones may break one's bones, but shadows and sounds cannot harm you. Every ground squirrel knows this. So no "C" is recruited to be an indicator of shadows or sounds. Predators. . . that is altogether different.

explains why "C" causes M, rather than some other movement N. Or, alternatively, structuring causes may explain why it is "C" rather than some other state of the brain D that causes M. So structuring causes highlight *contrastives*: (a) why "Cs" cause M, or alternatively, (b) why "C"s cause M. In either case if it is because of "C"s natural meaning, then we have a case of structuring causation, and content plays a role on this account of meaning mechanisms.

11.7 Fodor's Asymmetrical Causal Dependency Theory of Meaning

Fodor (1987, 1990a,b, 1994) offers conditions sufficient for a symbol "X" to mean something X.[5] Let's also be clear that Fodor is offering conditions for the meanings of primitive, non-logical thought symbols. This may well be part of the explanation of why he sees his conditions as only sufficient for meaning. The logical symbols and some other thought symbols may come by their meanings differently. Symbols with non-primitive (molecular) content may derive from primitive or atomic symbols by decomposing into atomic clusters. It is an empirical question when something is a primitive term, and Fodor is the first to recognize this.

Fodor's conditions have changed over time and are not listed by him anywhere in the exact form below, but I believe this to be the best representation of his current[6] considered theory. (This version is culled from Fodor (1987, 1990a,b, 1994).) The theory says that "X" means X if:

(1) 'Xs cause "X"s' is a law,
(2) For all Ys not = Xs, if Ys qua Ys actually cause "X"s, then Y's causing "X"s is asymmetrically dependent on Xs causing "X"s,
(3) There are some non–X–caused "X"s,
(4) The dependence in (2) is *synchronic* (not diachronic).

Condition (1) represents Fodor's version of natural meaning (information, indication). If it is a law that Xs cause "X"s, then a tokened "X" may indicate an X. Whether it does will depend on one's environment and its laws, but this condition affords[7] natural meaning a role to play in this meaning mechanism. For "X" to become a symbol for Xs requires more than being tokened by Xs. "X"s must be dedicated to, faithful to, locked to Xs *for their content*.

Condition (2) is designed to capture the jump from natural meaning to semantic content and solve the disjunction problem. It does the work of Dretske's learning

---

[5]Fodor's conditions for meaning are in flux and (subtly) change across these three works.

[6]Below we will consider another incarnation of the theory that adds a condition and discuss why he may have added and then dropped that condition. For more about this see Adams and Aizawa (1994).

[7]Fodor likes to refer to his view as an "informational" semantics (Fodor 1994).

period, giving us a new mechanism for locking "X"s to Xs. Fodor's fix is to make all non-X-tokenings of "X"s nomically dependent upon X-tokenings of "X"s from the very start. There is then no need[8] for a learning period. The condition says that not only will there be a law connecting a symbol "X" with its content X, but for any other items that are lawfully connected with the symbol "X", there is an asymmetrical dependency of laws or connections. The asymmetry is such that, while other things (Ys) are capable of causing the symbol to be tokened, the Y → "X" law depends upon the X → "X" law, but not *vice versa*. Hence, the asymmetrical dependence *of laws* locks the symbol to its content.

Condition (3) establishes "robust" tokening (Fodor 1990b). It acknowledges that there are non-X-caused "X"s. Some of these are due to false thought content, as when I mistake a horse on a dark night for a cow, and falsely token "cow" (believing that there is a cow present). Others are due to mere associations, as when one associates things found on a farm with cows and tokens "cow," (but not a case of false belief). These tokenings do not corrupt the meaning of "cow" because "cow" is dedicated to cows in virtue of condition (2).

Condition (4) is designed to circumvent potential problems due to kinds of asymmetrical dependence that are not meaning conferring (Fodor 1987, p. 109). Consider Pavlovian conditioning. Food causes salivation in the dog. Then a bell causes salivation in the dog. It is likely that the bell causes salivation only because the food causes it. Yet, salivation hardly means food. It may well naturally mean that food is present, but it is not a thought or thought content and it is not ripe for false semantic tokening. Condition (4) allows Fodor to block saying that salivation[9] itself has the semantic content that food is present, for its bell-caused dependency upon its food-caused dependency is diachronic, not synchronic. First there is the unconditioned response to the unconditioned stimulus, then, over time, there comes to be the conditioned response to the conditioning stimulus. Fodor's stipulation that the dependencies be synchronic not diachronic screens off Pavlovian conditioning and many other types of diachronic dependencies, as well.

11.8   Conclusion

There are many problems with Fodor's theory that I have detailed elsewhere and for which there is not space to include here (Adams 2003a; Adams and Aizawa 2010). I cannot help but believe that causal/informational theories of mental content have to be correct, in the end. If our ability to cognitively interact with our environments is not magic, or ultimately inexplicable, then the explanation of our cognitive abilities

---

[8]Nor is there a need for learning (period)—consistent with Fodor's penchant for nativism.

[9]One might think that it doesn't need blocking because salivation is not a vehicle in the language of thought (LOT). But Fodor does not restrict his theory to items in LOT. So in principle, even things outside the head can have meaning.

must rest with our causal and informational interactions with our environment. While it is true that there are alternative theories of mental content (causal role theories and teleological theories, for example), these theories too exploit causal and informational relations between organism and environment to explain the origin of mental content. The difference in these theories and the ones we have discussed ultimately are differences in the kinds of causal explanations required for mental content—not that some accept and some reject causal conditions as necessary for mental content. Further, as we have seen, some (such as Stampe) would even reject the taxonomic division of causal theories of mental content versus teleological theories, from the start (in sharp contrast with Fodor, of course). As discussion moves forward on the nature of the mind and cognition in philosophy of mind and cognitive science, generally, I predict that progress will be in the form of answering the worries and objections of the last section. I do not believe we will see progress made by moving away from causal and informational theories of mental content. That is why in Adams (2003b), I said there is no going back.

References

Adams F (1979) A goal-state theory of function attribution. Can J Philos 9(3):493–518

Adams F (2003a) Thoughts and their contents: naturalized semantics. In: Stich SP, Warfield TA (eds) The Blackwell guide to philosophy of mind. Basil Blackwell, Oxford, pp 143–171

Adams F (2003b) The informational turn in philosophy. Mind Mach 13(4):471–501

Adams F (2016) Information and cognition. In: Floridi L (ed) The Routledge handbook of philosophy of information. Routledge, New York, pp 345–356

Adams F, Aizawa K (1994) "X" means X: Fodor/Warfield semantics. Mind Mach 4(2):215–231

Adams F, Aizawa K (2010) Causal theories of mental content. Stanf Encycl Philos. Available via http://plato.stanford.edu/entries/content-causal/

Adams F, Enc B (1988) Not quite by accident. Dialogue 27(2):287–297

Dretske F (1971) Conclusive reasons. Australas J Philos 49(1):1–22

Dretske F (1981) Knowledge and the flow of information. MIT/Bradford Press, Cambridge

Dretske F (1983) Precis of knowledge and the flow of information. Behav Brain Sci 6(1):55–63

Dretske F (1986) Misrepresentation. In: Bogdan RJ (ed) Belief. Oxford University Press, Oxford, pp 17–36

Dretske F (1988) Explaining behavior: reasons in a world of causes. MIT/Bradford, Cambridge

Enc B, Adams F (1998) Functions and goal-directedness. In: Allen C, Bekoff M, Lauder G (eds) Nature's purposes. MIT/Bradford, Cambridge

Fodor JA (1984) Semantics, Wisconsin style. Synthese 59(3):231–250. (Reprinted in Fodor, 1990)

Fodor JA (1987) Psychosemantics: the problem of meaning in the philosophy of mind. MIT/Bradford, Cambridge

Fodor JA (1990a) A theory of content and other essays. MIT/Bradford Press, Cambridge

Fodor JA (1990b) Information and representation. In: Hanson PP (ed) Information, language, and cognition. University of British Columbia Press, Vancouver

Fodor JA (1990c) Psychosemantics or: where do truth conditions come from? In: Lycan WG (ed) Mind and cognition. Basil Blackwell, Oxford

Fodor JA (1994) The Elm and the expert. MIT/Bradford, Cambridge

Floridi L (2016) The Routledge handbook of philosophy of information. Routledge, New York/London

Grice P (1989) Studies in the way of words. Harvard University Press, Cambridge

Shannon CE, Weaver W (1949) The mathematical theory of communication. University of Illinois Press, Urbana/Chicago

Stampe DW (1975) Show and tell. In: Freed B, Marras A, Maynard P (eds) Forms of representation. North-Holland, Amsterdam, pp 221–245

Stampe DW (1977) Toward a causal theory of linguistic representation. Midwest Stud Philos 2(1):42–63

Stampe DW (1990) Content, context, and explanation. In: Villanueva E (ed) Information, semantics, and epistemology. Basil Blackwell, Oxford, pp 134–152

Wittgenstein L (1961) Tractatus Logico-Philosophicus. Routledge & Kegan Paul, London

Other Relevant Resources

(1)   Adams F, Aizawa K (1992) "X" means X: semantics Fodor-style. Mind Mach 2(2):175–183

(2)   Adams F, Aizawa K (1994) Fodorian semantics. In: Stich SP, Warfield TA (eds) Mental representation. Basil Blackwell, Oxford, pp 223–242

(3)   Adams F, Drebushenko D, Fuller G, Stecker R (1990) Narrow content: Fodor's folly. Mind Lang 5(3):213–229

(4)   Adams F, Dietrich LA (2004) What's in a(n empty) name? Pac Philos Q 85(2):125–148

(5)   Adams F, Stecker R (1994) Vacuous singular terms. Mind Lang 9(4):387–401

(6)   Antony LM, Levine J (1991) The nomic and the robust. In: Loewer BM, Rey G (eds) Meaning in mind: Fodor and his critics. Basil Blackwell, Oxford, pp 1–16

(7)   Baker LR (1989) On a causal theory of content. Philos Perspect 3:165–186

(8)   Baker LR (1991) Has content been naturalized? In: Loewer BM, Rey G (eds) Meaning in mind: Fodor and his critics. Basil Blackwell, Oxford, pp 17–32

(9)   Bar-On D (1995) "Meaning" reconstructed: Grice and the naturalizing of semantics. Pac Philos Q 76(2):83–116

(10) Boghossian PA (1991) Naturalizing content. In: Loewer BM, Rey G (eds) Meaning in mind: Fodor and his critics. Basil Blackwell, Oxford, pp 65–86

(11) Cummins R (1989) Meaning and mental representation. MIT/Bradford, Cambridge

(12) Dennett DC (1987) Review of J. Fodor's psychosemantics. J Philos 85:384–389

(13) Enc B (1982) Intentional states of mechanical devices. Mind 91:161–182

(14) Enc B (2002) Indeterminacy of function attributions. In: Ariew A, Cummins R, Perlman M (eds) Functions: new essays in the philosophy of psychology and biology. Oxford University Press, pp 291–313

(15) Fodor JA (1991) Replies. In: Loewer BM, Rey G (eds) Meaning in mind: Fodor and his critics. Basil Blackwell, Oxford, pp 255–319

(16) Fodor JA (1998) Concepts: where cognitive science went wrong. Oxford University Press, Oxford

(17) Fodor JA (1998) In critical condition: polemical essays on cognitive science and the philosophy of mind. MIT/Bradford Press, Cambridge

(18) Godfrey-Smith P (1989) Misinformation. Can J Philos 19(4):533–550

(19) Godfrey-Smith P (1992) Indication and adaptation. Synthese 92(2):283–312

(20) Jones T, Mulaire E, Stich S (1991) Staving off catastrophe: a critical notice of Jerry Fodor's psychosemantics. Mind Lang 6(1):58–82

(21) Loar B (1991) Can we explain intentionality? In: Loewer BM, Rey G (eds) Meaning in mind: Fodor and his critics. Basil Blackwell, Oxford, pp 119–135

(22) Maloney CJ (1990) Mental misrepresentation. Philos Sci 57(3):445–458

(23) Manfredi PA, Summerfield DM (1992) Robustness without asymmetry: a flaw in Fodor's theory of content. Philos Stud 66(3):261–283

(24) Possin K (1988) Sticky problems with Stampe on representations. Australas J Philos 66(1):75–82

(25) Stampe DW (1986) Verification and a causal account of meaning. Synthese 69(1):107–137
(26) Sterelny K (1990) The representational theory of mind. John Wiley & Sons
(27) Wallis C (1994) Representation and the imperfect ideal. Philos Sci 61(3):407–428
(28) Wallis C (1995) Asymmetrical dependence, representation, and cognitive science. South
       J Philos 33(3):373–401
(29) Warfield TA (1994) Fodorian semantics: a reply to Adams and Aizawa. Mind Mach 4(2):
       205–214
(30) Wright L (1973) Functions. Philos Rev 82(2):139–168

- Field Guide to the Philosophy of Mind Entry on Fodor's Asymmetrical Causal Dependency
  Theory of Meaning (and related entries on thought and language). Available via
  http://host.uniroma3.it/progetti/kant/field/asd.htm.
- Teleological Theories of Mental Content (Ruth Millikan). Available via
  http://www.ucc.uconn.edu/~wwwphil/Teleocnt.pdf.
- Externalism about mental content, Intentionality, Language of thought hypothesis, Narrow
  mental content, Non-conceptual mental content, Representational theories of consciousness,
  Teleological theories of mental content.

Index

© Springer International Publishing AG 2017
A.J. Schuster (eds.), *Understanding Information*, Advanced Information
and Knowledge Processing, DOI 10.1007/978-3-319-59090-5

CPSIA information can be obtained
at www.ICGtesting.com
Printed in the USA
LVHW021600150419
614225LV00014B/359/P